To Joan,
with much
gratitude and
admiration,
Molly

FEMINISM, MARRIAGE, AND THE LAW
IN VICTORIAN ENGLAND,
1850–1895

Feminism, Marriage, and the Law in Victorian England, 1850–1895

···

MARY LYNDON SHANLEY

Princeton University Press
Princeton, New Jersey

LIBRARY OF CONGRESS CATALOGING-IN-PUBLICATION DATA
Shanley, Mary Lyndon, 1944–
Feminism, marriage, and the law in Victorian England, 1850–1895 /
Mary Lyndon Shanley.
p.   cm.
Bibliography: p.
Includes index.
ISBN 0-691-07819-X (alk. paper)
1. Married women—Great Britain—History. 2. Marriage law—Great
Britain—History. 3. Marital property—Great Britain—History.
4. Feminism—Great Britain—History.   I. Title.
KD758.S47   1989
346.4201'6—dc19
[344.20616]   89-3758

Publication of this book has been aided by the
Whitney Darrow Fund of Princeton University Press

This book has been composed in Linotron Sabon

Clothbound editions of Princeton University Press books are
printed on acid-free paper, and binding materials are chosen for
strength and durability. Paperbacks, although
satisfactory for personal collections,
are not usually suitable for library rebinding.

Printed in the United States of America by
Princeton University Press,
Princeton, New Jersey

To my father,
J. Lyndon Shanley,

and to the memory of my mother,
Barbara Smith Shanley

CONTENTS

ACKNOWLEDGMENTS

It is a pleasure to acknowledge the very considerable help I have received from many individuals and institutions. Without their assistance, I could not have completed this study.

Sanford Thatcher, my editor at Princeton University Press, encouraged me to undertake this book many years ago. That early support and his advice throughout have been invaluable.

Librarians at the British Library of Political and Economic Science, the British Library, and the Fawcett Library in London, the Newnham College Library in Cambridge, the Manchester Central Library, the Langdell Library at Harvard University Law School, the Columbia University Libraries, the New York Public Library, and the Vassar College Library were extremely helpful. David Doughan of the Fawcett Library shared his vast knowledge of sources in women's history both at the Fawcett and elsewhere. Lee Holcombe and Martha Vicinus also suggested valuable materials to me. The reference and interlibrary loan librarians at Vassar College, particularly Rebecca Mitchell and Shirley Maul, worked expertly and tirelessly on my behalf. John Conliffe, editor of the *Congleton Chronicle*, shared with me his index to that newspaper and introduced me to Frank Stockton, whose remembrances of Ben Elmy and Elizabeth Wolstenholme Elmy helped bring them to life. The members of the Senior Common Room of Newnham College, Cambridge, extended their hospitality to me during the summer of 1984; I am particularly grateful for the intellectual exchanges I enjoyed with Gillian Sutherland and Jane Humphries.

Norma Basch, Joanne Long, and Judith Walkowitz read a preliminary version of this manuscript and helped me to sort out (and in some instances to discover) what I most wanted to say. Their generosity in talking with me about the themes of this book when the manuscript was still in very rough form made it possible for me to continue and complete the book. Mona Harrington, Susan Kent, Nannerl Keohane, and Susan Okin read a later version of the manuscript and offered detailed and invaluable suggestions for its revision. Elizabeth Adams Daniels read the completed manuscript and caught many mistakes and oversights. The care and intelligence with which all these readers critiqued these pages saved me from many errors, aided my understanding of both feminist theory and British history, and improved my writing considerably. Despite their generous and painstaking efforts, I must take full responsiblity for any defects or errors that remain.

ix

ACKNOWLEDGMENTS

Vassar College has been a most congenial community in which to work. The library, computer center, and copy bureau all provided essential services. Carolyn Priest-Dorman solved innumerable practical problems involved in converting my rough draft into a finished manuscript. My colleagues in the Department of Political Science were unfailingly supportive, and Peter Stillman made useful comments on various parts of the manuscript. Anthony Wohl of the Department of History shared his expertise concerning Victorian Britain with me. Anne Constantinople of the Department of Psychology offered timely practical advice as well as encouragement. A small grant from the Mellon Foundation funded an interdisciplinary summer seminar on feminist theory in which Miriam Cohen, Judith Goldstein, Eileen Leonard, Deborah Dash Moore, and Patricia Wallace read and commented upon part of this manuscript. To all of them and to the many other colleagues from Vassar and elsewhere who nourished the intellectual exchange essential to sustain scholarly work—particularly Vivian Berger, Ann Congleton, Jean Elshtain, Nancy Erickson, Francis G. Hutchins, Carole Pateman, Arlene Saxonhouse, and Elizabeth V. Spelman—I am deeply grateful.

Grants from the Vassar Committee on Faculty Research enabled me to visit the British Library and the Fawcett Library during 1982, and helped defray expenses incurred in preparing the manuscript for publication. A National Endowment for the Humanities Fellowship for College Teachers provided me with a year free of normal academic responsibilities. Vassar College, and in particular Dean H. Patrick Sullivan and President Virginia B. Smith facilitated the scheduling of that leave and a maternity leave. Without such time to write, I could not have completed this book.

The contributions of my family to this book are many and various. My great debt to my parents is reflected in the Dedication. One of my treasured memories of my mother is of a week we spent together in London while I was engaged in research there. My brother, F. Sheppard Shanley, read and commented very helpfully on several chapters of the manuscript. Concetta and Fred C. Chromey provided innumerable forms of support and encouragement, as did Doris and Stanley Osgood. My husband, Fred Chromey, made many suggestions on the manuscript that clarified my thoughts and improved my writing. His confidence and love sustained me throughout the years it took to complete this work. Our children, Kate and Anthony, were too young to provide any practical assistance, but they made us profoundly happy, which was perhaps the greatest help of all.

FEMINISM, MARRIAGE, AND THE LAW
IN VICTORIAN ENGLAND,
1850–1895

INTRODUCTION

When John Stuart Mill and Harriet Taylor married in 1851, Mill wrote out a formal protest against the laws that would govern their marriage. He objected to

> the whole character of the marriage relation as constituted by law
> . . . for this amongst other reasons, that it confers upon one of the
> parties to the contract, legal power & control over the person,
> property, and freedom of action of the other party, independent
> of her own wishes and will. . . . [H]aving no means of legally di-
> vesting myself of these odious powers . . . [I] feel it my duty to put
> on record a formal protest against the existing law of marriage, in
> so far as conferring such powers; and a solemn promise never in
> any case or under any circumstances to use them.[1]

While such a formal declaration on the eve of marriage was unusual, Mill was by no means alone among Victorians in finding the laws of marriage unjust and an affront to his understanding of what marriage should be. A considerable number of nineteenth-century Victorian feminists made the reform of marriage laws one of their main concerns during the latter half of the century.[2] This book examines the ideas that inspired and informed their activities, the actual changes in the laws that their agitation produced, and the implications for political thought and feminist theory of their ideas and activities.

The feminists' task was to persuade Parliament to pass a series of statutes recasting the laws governing divorce, married women's property, child custody, wife abuse, and the action for "restitution of conjugal rights" (which in effect gave a husband custody of his wife's body by ordering an errant spouse to return home). Their efforts collided head-on both with popular depictions of marriage and with the teachings of liberal political theory concerning the proper relationship between husband and wife and between the family and the state. Victorians tended to view the family as a peaceful and love-filled refuge from the impersonal and competitive world of work and politics. Women presided over the home, while men sallied forth into the public realm.

---

[1] F. A. Hayek, *John Stuart Mill and Harriet Taylor: Their Friendship and Subsequent Marriage* (London: Routledge & Kegan Paul, 1951), 168.

[2] Although the term *feminist* was not used until the late nineteenth century, it makes sense to apply it to the mid-century activists studied here, who urged the liberation of women from restrictive social custom and law alike.

Liberal theory reinforced this division of labor and power, for although feminists were able to appropriate the liberal values of individual autonomy and equal rights for their own purposes, liberal theorists since the seventeenth century had assumed that there was a natural division of labor between men and women. The presumed distinction between the "public" world of politics and law and the "private" world of the family had been invoked by thinkers from John Locke onward to exempt family relationships from the rules of justice that were to govern human relations in the public realm.

The Victorian feminists studied here took it as their task to expose the falsity of the idealization of marriage and to show how repressive marriage and family life could be for women. This was no small undertaking; in order to modify popular views of marriage and liberal theory's distinction between the private world of family life and the public world of politics, feminists had to gain acceptance for their contention that the family was a locus of male power sustained by the judicial authority of the state. Their efforts were partially—but only partially—successful. Although they procured many of the changes they sought in marriage law, no piece of legislation ever fully reflected the principle that the only proper basis for marriage law was full legal equality between husband and wife. This book examines both the theory that motivated these remarkable feminists and the practical successes and failures of their efforts to translate the ideal of spousal equality into law.

THE FEMINIST ATTACK ON COVERTURE

Certainly when most Victorians spoke or wrote about themselves they testified to the importance of home and hearth in their constellation of values. As Anthony Wohl has pointed out, Victorians regarded the home as both a refuge from the tensions and turmoil of the larger society and the nursery of civic virtues: "[T]he Victorians regarded it as axiomatic that the home was the foundation and the family the cornerstone of their civilization and that within the family were first learned the moral, religious, ethical and social precepts of good citizenship."[3] John Ruskin wrote, "This is the true nature of home—it is the place of Peace; the shelter, not only from all injury, but from all terror, doubt, and division."[4] "Home Sweet Home," the enormously popular song first heard in the 1870s, and mottoes such as "East, west, home's

[3] Anthony Wohl, ed., *The Victorian Family* (New York: St. Martin's Press, 1978), 10.
[4] John Ruskin, "Of Queen's Gardens" (1864) in *Works*, ed. E. T. Cook and A.D.C. Wedderburn, 39 vols. (London: G. Allen, 1902–1912), 18:122.

best," "Bless our home," and "Home is the nest where all is best," which adorned the walls of many working-class houses, reflected the firm hold of the ideal of the home on the Victorian imagination.[5]

Emphasizing the role of the family in shaping the British citizen, Lord Shaftesbury insisted that "the strength of the people rests upon the purity and firmness of the domestic system. . . . At home the principles of subordination are first implanted and the man [*sic*] is trained to be a good citizen." For Shaftesbury, the "authority" of the husband and father, and the "genial influence" of the wife and mother, were complementary pillars of both domestic and civil society.[6] An Edwardian observed that

> it is customary to point to the ideal of a united and home-loving family as the deepest tradition of English life. The English dinner, with its complete circle—the father at the head, the mother at the foot of the table, and the youngest saying grace—it is a picture frequently compared with the restaurant life of the Continent, or the greater independence of boys and girls in the United States. So strong is the belief in this family life as the key to true English happiness, so intense the desire to retain it throughout the land, that it has become usual to test each social or economic reform that is advanced by calculating its effect upon this national characteristic.[7]

The family life symbolized by the family dinner table distinguished England in the eyes of contemporary Britons from less orderly and less moral societies.

As the image of the family seated around the dinner table suggests, everyone in the Victorian family was thought to have his or her special place in the family circle as well as in the larger society. Husband and wife occupied "separate spheres," and each had distinct, but complementary, functions to perform. In addition to bearing children, middle-class women directed, and working-class women performed, the work involved in maintaining the household—care of children, sewing, cooking, and cleaning. Men earned the money to purchase the goods needed by their households and debated and decided matters of public concern. Women sustained the families, which produced healthy and

[5] Robert Roberts, *The Classic Slum* (Manchester: Manchester University Press, 1971), 35, quoted in Edward Shorter, *The Making of the Modern Family* (New York: Basic Books, 1975), 234.

[6] Lord Shaftesbury, quoted in Wohl, *Victorian Family*, 9–10.

[7] Sir Alexander Patterson, quoted in Wohl, *Victorian Family*, 10.

loyal citizens; men took care of the business of the state (including fighting its wars), which protected the families within its borders.

These distinct roles were thought by many to be not simply the result of social practice, but a necessary consequence of male and female biology. In 1874 Henry Maudsley, M.D., an eminent psychologist, wrote in the *Fortnightly Review* that "the male organization is one, and the female organization is another. . . . [I]t will not be possible to transform a woman into a man . . . she will retain her special sphere of development and activity determined by the performance of those [reproductive] functions." Nature had endowed women with a finite amount of energy. Since reproductive processes needed most of that energy, Maudsley concluded, women could not and should not pursue higher education or the work of the professions.[8] Exercise of the vote would be even worse. Frederic Harrison cautioned that women's suffrage would "disintegrate families" and "plant anarchy in the Home."

> No thoughtful man or woman denies that the cry of "Votes for Women" cannot be separated from the entire consensus of the domestic, social, and spiritual existence of Woman as a sex distinct from Man. Education, manners, social philosophy, religion, are all essentially involved in the change. It is no mere affair of Constituencies and House of Commons. It affects life on a thousand sides.[9]

Women's proper functions were assigned by nature, and it was folly and hubris to try to alter them. As Patrick Geddes and J. Arthur Thomson asserted in *The Evolution of Sex*, "What was decided among the prehistoric *Protozoa*, can not [sic] be annulled by act of Parliament."[10] Many Members of Parliament agreed, and bowed to the protozoa on matters of marriage law as well as the franchise.

The material conditions of life created by the spread of industrial capitalism also reinforced the distinction between male and female roles in Victorian society. The movement of labor and resources away from primary production (agriculture, fishing, forestry) toward manufacturing, commercial, and service activities caused the family economy based on shared productive activity to give way to individual waged labor. Patterns of women's paid employment varied consider-

---

[8] Henry Maudsley, "Sex in Mind and Education," *Fortnightly Review* 15 (1874): 466, quoted in Susan Kent, *Sex and Suffrage in Britain, 1860–1914* (Princeton: Princeton University Press, 1987), 43.

[9] Frederic Harrison, *Votes for Women* (London, 1909), 1, quoted in Kent, *Sex and Suffrage*, 56.

[10] Quoted in Kent, *Sex and Suffrage*, 35.

ably by region, but the vast majority of urban women workers—mill girls, domestic servants, and garment workers—were young and single. Increasingly, married women worked in isolation from men, who now earned money outside the home. Women's responsibility for managing the household did not decrease once the family became a wage-earning rather than a productive unit. For middle-class families the separation of spheres was sharply drawn; leisure was the ideal for "ladies," who did not work for wages. Married working-class women tended not to work outside the home continuously, but only before their children were born, in times of financial crisis, and after their children were grown. Men's and women's spheres might be less sharply delineated in working-class than in middle-class families, but the separation of home and workplace influenced these families as well, eliminating married women from participation in most of the better-paying jobs and increasing their importance as household managers and careful consumers.[11] The ideology of the home encouraged women of all classes to tend to domestic duties and to make the household a haven from the turmoil and competition of the marketplace.

When Victorian feminists began their crusade to change the laws regulating marriage, they explicitly and forcefully challenged what they regarded as society's sentimentalization of family life. They would have looked askance at the interpretations of many modern historians that "companionate marriage"—characterized by "affective individualism," "romantic love," and "a conscious ideological egalitarianism"—was the norm in both England and the United States by the mid-nineteenth century.[12] While acknowledging the existence of many

[11] Louise Tilly and Joan Scott, *Women, Work and Family* (New York: Holt, Rinehart & Winston, 1978), 63, 144.

[12] Several historians have traced the development from the late seventeenth to the mid-nineteenth century of what they see as "companionate" marriage in which husband and wife were bound by strong ties of affection. Lawrence Stone argues that during the eighteenth century the "restricted patriarchal family," characterized by clear paternal authority and constant reminders of the authority of a husband over his wife and parents over their children, gave way to the "closed restricted nuclear family," characterized by "affective individualism" (Lawrence Stone, *The Family, Sex and Marriage in England 1500–1800* [New York: Harper & Row, 1977]). Randolph Trumbach believes that aristocratic family members responded to "a conscious ideological egalitarianism," and internalized in their domestic relations "at the earliest possible moment the morality of the revolutions of the modern age" (Randolph Trumbach, *The Rise of the Egalitarian Family: Aristocratic Relations in Eighteenth-Century England* [New York: Academic Press, 1978], 11). Edward Shorter also chronicles the emergence of what he regards as the "modern family," characterized by a new form of "romantic love" between husband and wife (Shorter, *Making of the Modern Family*, 17). Historians have argued that the "sentimental family" had also become the norm in the United States by the nineteenth

happy families in England, the feminists insisted that such happiness was fragile and vulnerable, existing as it did *despite* the legal rules that gave any husband who cared to invoke them virtually despotic powers over his wife. Feminists pointed out that marriage law was based on the premise that a wife owed obedience to her husband, and where she did not voluntarily follow his will the law would leave her no other option. Against Ruskin's idealization of the home as a place of light and love, "a sacred place, a vestal temple, a temple of the hearth watched over by Household Gods," feminists insisted with John Stuart Mill that despite all the supposed advances of Christian civilization "the wife is the actual bond-servant of her husband: no less so, as far as legal obligation goes, than slaves commonly so-called."[13]

For feminists, one of the most striking manifestations of this marital "slavery" was the fact that under the common law a wife was in many ways regarded as the property of her husband. The common law doctrine of coverture dictated that when a woman married, her legal personality was subsumed in that of her husband. William Blackstone, in his *Commentaries on the Laws of England*, stated the rationale of the law succinctly: if husband and wife were "one body" before God, they were "one person" in the law, and that person was represented by the husband.[14] From the legal "unity" of the husband and wife it followed that a married woman could not sue or be sued unless her husband was also party to the suit, could not sign contracts unless her husband joined her, and could not make a valid will unless he consented to its provisions (a consent which he could withdraw at any time before probate). Further, a man assumed legal rights over his wife's property at marriage, and any property that came to her during marriage was legally his. While a husband could not alienate his wife's real property entirely, any rents or other income from it belonged to him. On the

---

century. See Carl Degler, *At Odds: Women and the Family in America from the Revolution to the Present* (New York: Oxford University Press, 1980); Christopher Lasch, *Haven in a Hartless World: The Family Besieged* (New York: Basic Books, 1977); Robert Griswold, *Family and Divorce in California, 1850-1890: Victorian Illusions and Everyday Realities* (Albany: State University of New York Press, 1982). For critiques of these views, see Susan M. Okin, "Women and the Making of the Sentimental Family," *Philosophy and Public Affairs* 11 (1982): 65–88 and her "Patriarchy and Married Women's Property in England: Questions on Some Current Views," *Eighteenth-Century Studies* 17 (1984): 121–38.

[13] Ruskin, "Of Queen's Gardens," in *Works*, 18:122; John Stuart Mill, *The Subjection of Women*, reprinted in *Essays on Sex Equality*, ed. Alice Rossi (Chicago: University of Chicago Press, 1970), chap. 2, 158.

[14] William Blackstone, *Commentaries on the Laws of England*, 4 vols. (Oxford: Clarendon Press, 1765–1769), vol. 1, chap. 11, 430.

other hand, a woman's personal property, including the money she might have saved before her marriage or earned while married, passed entirely to her husband for him to use and dispose of as he saw fit. Other laws consonant with coverture reinforced a husband's authority: he decided the family domicile, he had the right to correct his wife physically, and he determined how and where their children would be raised.[15] Legally the wife had no veto over or means of opposing her husband's decisions. Thus, according to an irate pamphleteer, the common law with respect to married women, combined with the ecclesiastical doctrine that marriage was indissoluble, amounted to a "nefarious custom" by which women when they married were "despoiled of their money, goods and chattels . . . and condemned to prison for life."[16]

Aggravating a married woman's plight was the fact that it was extremely difficult for her to extricate herself from the bonds of matrimony. Prior to the Divorce Act of 1857 the only way to end a marriage other than by ecclesiastical annulment was by private Act of Parliament, an extraordinarily complex and expensive procedure. Even under the Divorce Act, only if a husband was physically cruel, incestuous, or bestial in addition to being adulterous could his wife procure a divorce. If she left him without first obtaining a divorce, she was guilty of desertion and forfeited all claim to a share of his property (even that which she might have brought to the marriage) and to custody of their children.

Social and economic pressures as well as the law made it very difficult for Victorian women to leave their husbands or to choose a single life in the first place. The pressures on women to marry were enormous in nineteenth-century England, and in 1871 nearly 90 percent of English women between the ages of forty-five and forty-nine were or had been married.[17] The plight of a woman who did not marry, who in the

[15] For the persistence of aspects of coverture in England, see Carol Smart, *The Ties that Bind: Law, Marriage and the Reproduction of Patriarchal Relations* (London: Routledge & Kegan Paul, 1984). For the United States, see Leo Kanowitz, *Women and the Law: The Unfinished Revolution* (Albuquerque: University of New Mexico Press, 1969); Lenore Weitzman, *The Marriage Contract: Spouses, Lovers and the Law* (New York: The Free Press, 1981); and Lenore Weitzman, *The Divorce Revolution: Unexpected Social and Economic Consequences for Women and Children in America* (New York: The Free Press, 1985).

[16] *Remarks on the Law of Marriage and Divorce; suggested by the Honourable Mrs. Norton's Letter to the Queen* (London: James Ridgway, 1855), 4.

[17] Jane Lewis, *Women in England 1870–1950* (Bloomington, Ind.: Wheatsheaf, 1984), 3. John Gillis describes the rise in church and civil weddings in the late nineteenth century in working-class neighborhoods where informal or common-law marriages had

parlance of the age was "left on the shelf," could be economically as well as socially disastrous. The average wage that working-class women could command was below subsistence level. Occupations for middle-class women, primarily those of governess, teacher, shop assistant, nurse, office clerk, and civil servant, were few and poorly paid.[18] A few fortunate middle-class women might be supported by a father, brother, or other relative, but for most middle-class as well as working-class women marriage was an economic necessity. Legal rules, social practices, and economic structures all worked together to induce a woman to marry, and then insured that once married she would be dependent upon and obedient to her husband.

In mounting their challenge to popular, sentimental notions of married life, Victorian feminists attempted to show that the rules of coverture and divorce violated some of the most fundamental principles of English legal and political thought. Liberal political theory became in their hands a tool with which to dismantle the ideological, and especially the legal, underpinnings of the subordination of married women and their exclusion from public life. As the feminists proceeded, they exposed not only the injustices of English marriage law, but also the false nature of the traditional distinction in liberal theory between that which is "public," and therefore the proper object of politics and legislation, and that which is "private," and therefore removed from political scrutiny.

Liberal political theorists from Thomas Hobbes and John Locke in the seventeenth century to Jeremy Bentham and John Stuart Mill in the nineteenth had contended that people were by nature free and equal beings. They could enter into relationships of super- and subordination only by their own consent, and they could not permanently relinquish their personal autonomy. Feminists argued that marriage law grossly violated a married woman's rights to freedom and equality by taking away her independent legal personality when she married, subordinating her to her husband's will, and subjecting her to restrictions that did not apply to unmarried women or to any men. The only other persons who suffered anything like the "civil death" of married women were children, whose legal dependency ended when they reached their majority, idiots, who were incapable of fully rational activity, and criminals, who forfeited their rights through their own actions. Was matri-

---

been accepted practice early in the century; see Gillis, *For Better, For Worse: British Marriages, 1600 to the Present* (New York: Oxford University Press, 1985), chap. 8.

[18] Lewis, *Women in England*, 3; see also Lee Holcombe, *Victorian Ladies at Work: Middle-class Working Women in England and Wales 1850–1914* (New York: Archon Books, 1973).

mony such a crime for a woman that she deserved to lose her rights for taking such a step, or was a woman who married so irrational that she should be treated as an insane person? If marriage was neither a crime nor an act of madness, then the principle that adults should receive equal treatment under the law was a standing condemnation of coverture.

That liberal theory in the nineteenth century was blind to this point was due to its assumption, as old as liberalism itself, that family relationships lay outside the general principle that all legitimate authority must be based upon consent. The authority of parent over child was dictated by the facts of birth and by the child's inability to live without the care and nurture of an adult.[19] The "natural" subordination of a wife to her husband seemed no more problematic to most liberal theorists than that of offspring to parents.[20] John Locke's writings gave expression to some of the inconsistencies and contradictions concerning marital authority found in much liberal theory. On the one hand, Locke said, marriage did not require absolute sovereignty of husband over wife, because "the ends of Matrimony requiring no such Power in the Husband, the Condition of *Conjugal* Society put it not in him, it being not at all necessary to that State." On the other hand, marriage could not be an egalitarian relationship, because if husband and wife disagreed, their dispute could not be settled by majority rule. But "the last Determination, i.e., the Rule," must be placed somewhere, or disputes will be endless, and such rule "naturally falls to the Man's share, as the abler and the stronger." Natural strength, rather than rational agreement, allocated domestic authority.[21]

[19] Parental authority was, however, only temporary. John Locke insisted that children cast off their subordination to their parents as inevitably as they cast off their swaddling clothes: "Age and Reason as [children] grow up, loosen [the bonds of subjection to parents] till at length they drop quite off, and leave Man at his own free Disposal" (John Locke, *Two Treatises of Government*, ed. Peter Laslett, rev. ed. [New York: Mentor Books, 1963], second treatise, para. 55, 347).

[20] A notable exception was Thomas Hobbes, who argued that women must have agreed to their subordination. See Carole Pateman and Teresa Brennan, " 'Mere Auxiliaries to the Commonwealth': Women and the Origins of Liberalism," *Political Studies* 27 (1979): 183–200; and Carole Pateman, *The Sexual Contract* (Stanford: Stanford University Press, 1988), chap. 3.

[21] Locke, *Two Treatises of Government*, second treatise, para. 78, 362; para. 83, 365; para. 82, 364. On the tensions concerning marital authority in Locke's political thought, see Mary Lyndon Shanley, "Marriage Contract and Social Contract in Seventeenth-Century English Political Thought," *Western Political Quarterly* 32 (March 1979): 79–91; and Pateman and Brennan, " 'Mere Auxiliaries,' " 183–200. On patriarchal theory, see Gordon Schochet, *Patriarchalism in Political Thought* (New York: Basic Books, 1975). Rousseau, like Locke, believed that "the oldest of all societies, and the only natural

Liberal theorists could assume the "natural" authority of husband over wife because they depicted the family as an entity that preceded the formation of civil society and existed independently of state authority. Most liberal theorists assumed without discussion that it was male heads-of-household, not women, who were parties to the social contract. The virtue of the state, brought into existence by this social contract, was justice. The virtue of the family, brought into existence "naturally" by human sexual attraction, was love. Thus from its inception liberal political thought embraced and reinforced the notion of the family as the locus of virtues and values distinguishing it from the political world. And it was this distinction that muted the principles of equality and consent by making them seem applicable to the public realm, but not to the private realm, populated by women.[22]

Victorian feminists used the liberal principles of freedom and equality to pose a radical challenge to the assumption that family and state, private and public spheres, were of different conceptual and moral orders. Only by assuming that the principles of justice which should govern the public realm did not apply to family relations, feminists argued, could one rationalize the legal subordination of wives to their husbands in marriage. And only by assuming that being members of a family excluded women, but not men, from the public sphere could one justify women's disfranchisement. Women's domestic and political subjection were interlocking and mutually reinforcing; only when married women had equal rights with their husbands in both the family and the state could either institution be based upon principles of justice.

The feminists' application of liberal principles to notions of women's status did not expose all the sources of married women's subordination. The activists' struggle against coverture kept their attention focused on the *legal* preconditions for spousal equality, rather than on the economic structures that created class as well as gender divisions and injustices. As Barbara Taylor observed of the politics of Barbara Leigh Smith, an early proponent of marriage law reform, she was "of

---

one, is that of the family." The sexes were equal only when isolated from one another, but this was an asocial and unnatural condition. As Carole Pateman says, Rousseau believed that "in social life women are 'naturally' made to be 'at the mercy of man's judgement' and 'to endure even injustice at his hands' " (Carole Pateman, " 'The Disorder of Women': Women, Love, and the Sense of Justice," *Ethics* 91 [October 1980]: 26).

[22] Pateman, " 'The Disorder of Women,' " 20–34. On the public/private distinction more generally, see Jean Bethke Elshtain, *Public Man, Private Woman: Women in Social and Political Thought* (Princeton: Princeton University Press, 1981).

12

liberal but far from levelling convictions."[23] Liberal individualism did
not readily suggest a critique of the role that industrial capitalism
played in women's subjection, and Leigh Smith and many of her contemporaries gave little attention to ways of restructuring the organization of work under capitalism in order to achieve gender equality for
all economic classes. The next generation of feminists, those becoming
active around the turn of the century, embraced socialist ideas along
with their feminism, but most of those active in the struggle to reform
marriage laws directed their ire against legal inequalities.[24]

Most of the Victorian feminists also did not challenge the way in
which sex-based division of labor in the home created barriers to
spousal equality. Their attack on separate spheres was meant to provide opportunities for women to participate in largely male-defined
structures; they did not ask that women be relieved of some of their
domestic responsibilities in order to move freely into the male world,
nor that men participate more actively in the home. Mrs. Emmeline
Pankhurst spoke for many when she declared that "not one woman
who enters this agitation [for women's suffrage] need feel that she has
got to give up a single one of women's duties in the home. She learns
to feel that she is attaching a larger meaning to those duties which have
been women's duties since the race began, and will be till the race has
ceased to be."[25] What this meant, in effect, was that a woman with
children would either not be able to work outside the home, or would
double her workload if she did find outside employment.

Despite these shortcomings, the marriage law reforms that were
achieved through the efforts of the Victorian feminists did significantly
alter the relationship between husband and wife. For although a married woman's right to hold property did not equalize men's and wom-
en's vastly different economic resources, a woman had to be able to
possess her own property before she could effectively counterpoise her
will to that of her husband. Similarly, laws allowing mothers to apply
for custody of their children were essential before many women could
contemplate leaving abusive husbands. The principle of equality con-

[23] Barbara Taylor, *Eve and the New Jerusalem: Socialism and Feminism in the Nineteenth Century* (New York: Pantheon, 1983), 279.

[24] On the socialist ideals of some turn-of-the-century feminists, see Olive Banks, *Becoming a Feminist: The Social Origins of 'First Wave' Feminism* (Athens: University of
Georgia Press, 1986); Jill Liddington and Jill Norris, *One Hand Tied Behind Us* (London: Virago, 1978); and Jill Liddington, *The Life and Times of a Respectable Rebel:
Selina Cooper 1864–1946* (London: Virago, 1984).

[25] Mrs. Emmeline Pankhurst, "The Importance of the Vote" (London, 1913), quoted
in Sandra Stanley Holton, *Feminism and Democracy: Women's Suffrage and Reform
Politics in Britain, 1900–1918* (Cambridge: Cambridge University Press, 1986), 14.

sistently applied to marriage law did not altogether do away with the imbalance of power between husband and wife, but it did alter the terms of what mid-twentieth-century feminists would call "sexual politics." The legal reforms won by nineteenth-century feminists were crucial preconditions for women's emancipation, and the feminists' analysis of the interlocking character of women's subjection in marriage and in the state was a major contribution to feminist theory.

PARLIAMENT AND MARRIAGE LAW

The feminists studied in this book undertook a variety of campaigns to get Parliament to alter the laws governing marriage. Their efforts and successes with respect to statutory reforms can be briefly summarized.[26] In the 1850s Barbara Leigh Smith and members of what came to be known as the Langham Place Circle petitioned Parliament to treat married women's property in the same manner as men's property. When that request appeared doomed, they pressed for insertion of provisions favorable to women in the Divorce Act of 1857. Although the Divorce Act did contain provisions to protect the property of deserted wives, these fell short of feminists' hopes. In the outburst of political activity that followed John Stuart Mill's election to the House of Commons in 1865, a group of feminists centered in the Manchester area organized campaigns for a married women's property law and the expansion of mothers' rights to custody of their children. Enacted partly in response to these efforts, the Married Women's Property Acts of 1870 and 1882 made it possible for every married woman to hold property in her own name and to make a will without her husband's agreement. Similarly, the Infant Custody Acts of 1873 and 1886 gave mothers certain rights to appeal for custody of their minor children. In the 1870s Frances Power Cobbe took up the cause of winning legal protection for abused wives. Her efforts resulted in the passage of the Matrimonial Causes Act of 1878, which, along with the Summary Jurisdiction (Married Women) Act of 1895, significantly extended the Divorce Act's provisions for separation by establishing various grounds on which an abused or mistreated wife might obtain a legal separation from her husband at a local magistrates' court.

[26] In studying the statutory changes in marriage law, I have had to leave it for others to analyze the case law that developed as judges interpreted these statutes, as well as the actual effects, measured by demographic and economic statistics, of the legal changes enacted by Parliament. That additional work will be necessary to construct a more complete picture of the law's ability to shape women's understanding and experience of marriage.

The parliamentary debates surrounding each legislative initiative to reform marriage law reveal both the practical and the ideological difficulties feminists faced as they tried to translate their convictions into law. Most of the activists were women who on account of their sex could not vote, much less sit in Parliament. The parliamentary debates make it clear that feminists were correct in asserting that men were reluctant to relinquish domestic as well as political authority: any marriage law reform bill that proposed to "introduce into every house in England the principle of separate rights, separate interests, and a separate legal existence between man and wife" threatened, in Mr. Chambers's words, "to nullify and destroy the law of marriage altogether."[27] Although reformers did not envision the wholesale destruction of marriage law, they did intend to do away with the legal support that the rules of coverture gave to patriarchal authority in the home. In many respects the feminists and their strongest opponents understood one another better than the feminists and their parliamentary allies did, for feminists and their opponents debated the issue of domestic authority head-on, while many of the feminists' friends in Parliament avoided that issue. The task confronting the Members of Parliament who championed the cause of women's rights was not easy. They had to represent the positions of feminist leaders to their colleagues, and to procure legislation that would alleviate the hardships women faced. These ends were not always compatible. In order to pass marriage reform bills, Members of Parliament occasionally downplayed their feminist goals and emphasized other, more generally acceptable aspects of the legislation.

Several broad social and economic trends in English society that developed independently of feminist agitation aided the legislators who sought reforms in marriage law. The rise of a middle class whose wealth lay in movable rather than real property led many men who had no interest in women's rights per se to advocate laws allowing married women to handle their own property. In order to provide a daughter with some economic security independent of her husband's fortunes, wealthy fathers were accustomed to establishing trusts or "separate estates" in equity for their daughters at marriage. But drawing up a trust was an expensive process, and some middle-class men began to advocate legislation that would make the exceptional procedures of equity applicable to the property of all married women.[28]

[27] *Hansard Parliamentary Debates*, 3d ser., vol. 142 [10 June 1856], col. 1283 (hereafter cited as 3 Hansard 142 [10 June 1856], 1283).

[28] Dorothy Stetson, *A Woman's Issue: The Politics of Family Law Reform in England* (Westport, Conn.: Greenwood Press, 1982), 58–59.

Tradesmen and creditors had a strong interest in ridding the law of the confusion caused by the common law rule that a wife was not responsible for her prenuptial debts, and might pledge her husband's credit without herself incurring any obligation.[29] Some men were even willing to forego automatic entitlement to their wives' property when they realized that such property would remain free from their own creditors and provide a cushion for the family should the husband suffer bankruptcy.[30] Part of the impetus for creating the capacity for independent action by married women lay not in feminist ideas but in the shift of wealth from land to movable property and the uncertainties of nineteenth-century economic life.

Another spur to parliamentary action benefiting women was the growth of social science and an increasing sensitivity to the needs of the poor, particularly the urban poor. Feminists found many of their staunchest allies among members of the Social Science Association, whose practice of promoting social reform through parliamentary action made them receptive to the feminists' legal strategy. Beyond that, some reform measures such as the married women's property law and provisions to facilitate separation from brutal husbands could be presented as measures to help the "deserving poor" to be self-sustaining. Parliament was ready to help a working-class wife retain her own earnings and leave a good-for-nothing husband both out of sympathy for her plight and to keep her and her children off the public assistance rolls. Several bills originally advanced by feminists outside Parliament as women's rights issues were accepted within the halls of Westminster because they were regarded as measures to help women in poverty.

The conjunction of these various interests helped convince Parliament to pass many of the measures sought by feminists. The reforms dealing with marriage law, however, invariably fell short of the principle of spousal equality, which lay at the heart of the feminists' proposals. The parliamentary compromises were not simply due to the inevitable hammering out of statutory language to make it acceptable to people with a variety of interests and motives, but they reflected as well the reluctance of legislators to abandon the patriarchal model of

[29] Lee Holcombe, *Wives and Property: Reform of the Married Women's Property Law in Nineteenth-Century England* (Toronto: University of Toronto Press, 1983), 186–91.

[30] Suzanne Lebsock and Norma Basch both make this point in their studies of married women's property laws in the United States: Suzanne Lebsock, *The Free Women of Petersburg: Status and Culture in a Southern Town* (New York: W. W. Norton, 1984), 54–86; and Norma Basch, *In the Eyes of the Law: Women, Marriage and Property in Nineteenth-Century New York* (Ithaca, N.Y.: Cornell University Press, 1982).

the family contained in the common law for the egalitarian model feminists put forward. As the feminists clearly saw, making husband and wife equal before the law could profoundly alter the structure and conduct of familial and political life alike. Parliament had no interest in encouraging such a revolution. Parliament did *enlarge* the rights of married women significantly in the course of the nineteenth century, but it repeatedly rejected the invitation held out by feminists to *equalize* the rights and obligations of husbands and wives. Parliament's persistent rejection of the feminists' most fundamental tenet lent substance to the latter group's charge that men constituted a "sex class," as jealous of their power and privilege as any economic class.

IDEOLOGY AND ACTIVITY

The campaigns for marriage law reform studied here took place over more than half a century, starting with Caroline Norton's attack in the 1830s on the law governing child custody. Between 1855 and 1895, a concentrated and coordinated series of efforts to change the laws regulating the relationship between husband and wife replaced such individual efforts. This book focuses primarily on the ideas and activities of the generation of Victorian feminists born between the early 1820s and the mid-1830s, who orchestrated those campaigns and helped British feminism become an organized political movement. As Barbara Taylor has said, these activists espoused "a mode of feminist thought and organization which was both narrower and wider than the Socialist feminism of the preceding decades." Mid-century feminism was narrower in being largely middle and upper-middle class, and wider in involving far more women than Owenite socialism ever did.[31] It was also broad in the range of issues it addressed: the opening of higher education to women, the admission of women to the medical profession, moral reform and the repeal of the Contagious Diseases Acts, women's suffrage, and reform of marriage laws. Marriage law reform itself encompassed efforts to equalize the grounds of divorce for men and women, enact a married women's property law, expand mothers' custody rights, allow battered wives to separate from their husbands, and give magistrates the authority to issue support and maintenance orders to deserted and abused women.

Those drawn to work on such a wide range of reforms inevitably held very different views of the proper roles for women in both the family and public life. Some, like Caroline Norton and Eliza Lynn Lin-

[31] Taylor, *Eve and the New Jerusalem*, 279.

17

ton, regarded women as naturally inferior to men and found the suffrage agitation anathema, yet supported divorce, married women's property, and custody reform on the grounds that when husbands neglected their "natural" duty to protect their wives the state had an obligation to do so. Others, like Frances Power Cobbe and Frances Hoggan, were strong supporters of suffrage, more public work for women, and marriage law reform, yet believed that women and men had different natures and that women's most fundamental duties were maternal and domestic. Still others, like Elizabeth Wolstenholme Elmy and Ursula Mellor Bright, advocated eliminating all distinctions in the treatment of men and women under the law; profoundly egalitarian thinkers, Wolstenholme Elmy and Bright were agnostics concerning the question of whether women and men had different natural talents and obligations. All of the parties working for marriage law reform did agree, however, that the common law doctrine of coverture worked great harm on all women (particularly those married to tyrannical husbands), their children, and even on men, and that traditional marriage law was incompatible with liberal ideas of justice.

Several of these activists tried to realize in their own marriages the goal of equal partnership that they promoted through their campaigns for marriage law reform. Harriet Taylor and John Stuart Mill married only after he had renounced the rights accruing to him through marriage. Both before and after their marriage they engaged in intense intellectual exchanges and collaborative writing. After Barbara Leigh Smith married Eugène Bodichon, a French physician who had settled in Algiers, she regularly spent part of each year in Algeria with her husband, and part by herself in England pursuing her work on women's education and women's rights. She was also a serious artist, and her husband encouraged her in all of these pursuits. Elizabeth Wolstenholme and Ben Elmy felt so strongly about the inequities of marriage law that they refused to marry until Ursula Bright convinced them that their illicit union was hurting the women's causes about which they cared so deeply. Little is known about the marriage of Ursula Mellor and John Bright, but it was one that clearly gave Ursula great latitude for political activity of her own, and that involved the Brights in extensive political collaboration on a variety of women's rights issues.

Given the number of legal reforms feminists demanded as part of their attack on traditional marriage law and the many years it took even partially to accomplish their agenda, I have found the most manageable way of presenting this analysis of the movement for marriage law reform to be a series of chapters devoted to specific legislative issues. Each chapter discusses the development of feminist ideas about a specific aspect of marriage law, explicates the traditional law and the statutory changes proposed by feminists, and analyzes Parliament's responses to these proposals. The order of the chapters is roughly chronological, although some overlap occurs, since activity on various measures often took place simultaneously. Chapter 1 concerns the Divorce Act of 1857 and the married women's property bill of 1856; chapters 2 and 4 trace the development of the Married Women's Property Acts of 1870 and 1882, respectively; chapter 3 analyzes three issues of the 1870s—protective labor legislation, the regulation of prostitution, and the punishment of infanticide—which involved many feminists working on marriage law reform; chapter 5 describes the struggles to expand mothers' rights to custody, which culminated in passage of the Infant Custody Act of 1886; and chapter 6 studies the efforts to free women's bodies from their husbands' abuse and control through the Matrimonial Causes Act of 1878 and the Summary Jurisdiction (Married Women) Act of 1895.

It is a significant aspect of the account that follows that in no instance, even when their efforts resulted in Parliament's passing a new law, did feminist reformers realize their most fundamental goal, statutory recognition of full legal equality between husband and wife. The resistance in the British Parliament to ending the male monopoly of domestic authority, as well as of the franchise, was strong and deep. The confrontation between the notion of marriage based on hierarchy and male dominance and the vision of marriage based on spousal equality and marital friendship did not, therefore, end at the close of the nineteenth century. It is a struggle that continues in philosophical and public policy debates in our own day.

THE chapters that follow recount one of a long tradition of human efforts to translate the ideal of equality into social practice. The nineteenth-century feminists studied here, like democratic revolutionaries of the eighteenth century, abolitionists of the nineteenth century, and Marxist and socialist reformers of the twentieth century, felt themselves to be heralding an age of greater justice than had previously been known. Although the transformation of the relations between men and women that Victorian feminists saw as essential to a just society was not achieved in their lifetime, the legal reforms they procured were crucial prerequisites for the reconstruction of gender relations in both the family and the state.

Victorian feminists saw legal reform as the key to women's emancipation. They believed that the enactment of gender-neutral laws that made no distinction between the rights and obligations of men and

19

women, husbands and wives, was the way to achieve spousal equality. Experience has shown, however, that "equality in form" does not always produce "equality in fact." Unless women and men have access to similar economic, social, and political resources, gender-neutral laws do not result in equal opportunity in the public world or genuine reciprocity at home.[32] Victorian feminists on occasion recognized this, for example in discussions concerning whether a wife and mother should be required to contribute a portion of any income she might have to the maintenance of her children, regardless of her husband's income. But for the most part the saliency of the injustices of coverture and women's exclusion from the vote made the achievement of formal legal equality the clear focus of these feminists' concern and activity.

In their campaigns, feminists relied heavily on the liberal principles of individual autonomy and equality to persuade Parliament to end the legal subordination of married women. In the process they used liberal theory itself to demolish the traditional distinction between the "public" world of politics and the "private" world of the family. The history of the struggle to reform marriage law shows the radical potential of liberal theory in the hands of dedicated feminists.[33] The fact that their successes were only partial and that legal reform based on the concept of individual rights could not by itself procure the spousal equality that Victorian feminists desired in no way diminishes their substantial practical and theoretical achievements.

Victorian feminists' condemnation of their society's sentimentalization of patriarchal power in the family, and their commitment to the ideal of spousal friendship, were both rooted in their belief in the necessity and possiblity of male-female equality in both the family and the larger society. Their hope for a new egalitarian marriage animated American feminists as well, who engaged in many similar legal struggles during the latter nineteenth century.[34] The shared vision of these

---

[32] Some scholars have argued that gender-neutral laws, which do not recognize, for example, the different impact of childbearing on women and men, actually foster inequality by depriving women of resources they need if they are to combine having children with a full life as workers and citizens. See Deborah Rhode, "Feminist Perspectives on Legal Ideology," in *What Is Feminism?* ed. Juliet Mitchell and Ann Oakley (New York: Pantheon, 1986), 151–60; Lucinda M. Finley, "Transcending Equality Theory: A Way Out of the Maternity and the Workplace Debate," *Columbia University Law Review* 86 (1986): 1118–82; and Christine Littleton, "Equality and Feminist Legal Theory," *University of Pittsburgh Law Review* 48 (Summer 1987): 1043–59.

[33] For an extended discussion of the radical potential as well as the limitations of liberal feminism, see Zillah Eisenstein, *The Radical Future of Liberal Feminism* (New York: Longman, 1981).

[34] See Basch, *In the Eyes of the Law*; Lebsock, *Free Women of Petersburg*; and Eliza-

feminists has not yet been realized. The transformation of marriage requires the creation of economic and social, as well as legal, conditions that actively promote male-female equality in political life, the workplace, and the home. The political and legal struggles of the Victorian feminists therefore set an agenda for the present day. The spirit of coverture still haunts the law of both Britain and the United States, our understanding of how to achieve justice within the family and the state is still incomplete, and the goal of spousal equality remains to be realized by all who seek human liberation.

beth Pleck, *Domestic Tyranny: The Making of Social Policy against Family Violence from Colonial Times to the Present* (New York: Oxford University Press, 1987).

· 1 ·

WHAT KIND OF A CONTRACT IS MARRIAGE? MARRIED WOMEN'S PROPERTY, THE SEXUAL DOUBLE STANDARD, AND THE DIVORCE ACT OF 1857

> Why is England the only country obliged to confess
> she cannot contrive to administer justice to women?
> ... Simply because our legists and legislators [will
> never] succeed in acting on the legal fiction that mar-
> ried women are "non-existent", and man and wife are
> still "one", in cases of alienation, separation, and en-
> mity, when they are about as much "one" as those
> ingenious twisted groups of animal death we some-
> times see in sculpture; one creature wild to resist, and
> the other fierce to destroy.
>
> —Caroline Norton, *A Letter to the Queen*
> *on Lord Chancellor Cranworth's Marriage*
> *and Divorce Bill* (1855), 28

In 1855, when Caroline Norton painted this picture of husband and wife as wild beasts locked in deadly struggle, she had endured more than twenty years of an extremely painful and rancorous marriage. In the 1830s her husband, George Norton, had publicly accused the prime minister, Lord Melbourne, of adultery with his wife, and Caroline had gone to Court to try to get custody of their children. In 1854 creditors suing the Nortons for payment of debts exposed the bitter financial disputes that plagued their marriage. The prominent trials involving the Nortons' rights as husband and wife exposed the violence and personal unhappiness of their relationship to public scrutiny and prompted Caroline to publish biting pamphlets condemning the English marriage laws, which she regarded as partly responsible for her troubles. In particular, she denounced the obliteration under the common law of a woman's legal personality upon marriage, which made it impossible for a wife to hold property in her own name. She also condemned a proposed divorce law that would have lent statutory sanction to the sexual double standard by making it possible for husbands to divorce their wives, but not wives their husbands. These stipulations were, of course, related, for both implied that a wife was herself the "property" of her husband, since he could claim her earnings and her body when she could not make similar claims upon him. Newspaper accounts of the Nortons' trial as well as Caroline Norton's pamphlets provided dramatic lessons in the laws governing marriage to the English reading public. They also gave impetus to the first organized feminist effort to challenge the laws governing marriage. A brief recital of the Nortons' history may instruct readers in the twentieth century as much as it did the people of their own day.

THE MULTIPLE INJUSTICES OF MARRIAGE LAW: THE CASE OF CAROLINE NORTON

Caroline Sheridan Norton, born in 1808, was the granddaughter of Richard Brinsley Sheridan, the renowned playwright, and the daughter of Henrietta Callander and Thomas Sheridan.[1] When Caroline was five, her father, who was in poor health, was offered a post as colonial secretary at the Cape of Good Hope. His wife and eldest daughter accompanied him, while Caroline and her younger sister stayed with aunts in Scotland. Three years later Thomas Sheridan died. His widow returned to England and was given a "grace and favor" apartment at Hampton Court, where Caroline, her sisters and her brother grew up. At age fifteen Caroline was sent to a small school in Surrey. While there she visited Wonersh Park, the home of Lord Grantly, and met his younger brother and heir, George Norton. George was infatuated with Caroline, and in 1827, when she was nineteen and he twenty-six, they married.

By all accounts Caroline and George were profoundly mismatched. He was not very bright and had few social graces; she was quick-witted, a dazzling beauty, and loved to be in society. He had a fearsome temper, which was exacerbated by Caroline's lack of subservience and her biting wit. He was not wealthy, and resented his need for the money that Caroline's growing career as a poet and novelist brought them. George's temper led on occasion to outbursts of brutal violence, especially when he was drunk, and he and his wife separated several times. In large part their mutual love of their three sons kept them together.

In 1836 the fragile truce in the Norton household was shattered. While Caroline was on a visit to her sister, George had the children taken off to an undisclosed location, and barred the house to Caroline.

[1] Much of the biographical information on Caroline Norton is drawn from Margaret Forster, *Significant Sisters: The Grassroots of Active Feminism 1839–1939* (London: Secker & Warburg, 1984); and Joan Huddleston, ed., *Caroline Norton's Defense* (Chicago: Academy Chicago, 1982), i–xiii.

He then announced that, unless she agreed to a separation, he was going to sue her for divorce on the grounds of alienation of affection by Lord Melbourne. The terms George proposed were that the children would live with him, Caroline would receive no allowance from him, and she would live with her brother. Not surprisingly, Caroline found these terms unacceptable.

George then began his divorce action. His first step was to sue Lord Melbourne for "criminal conversation" with Caroline. In a case of criminal conversation, a husband charged another man with adultery with his wife, and, if the defendant was found guilty, the husband recovered "damages." The action for criminal conversation could only be initiated by men, not women. It reflected the notion that a husband in some manner owned his wife's affection and sexual services, that she was his property, but a wife did not have a similar legal claim on her husband. In addition to providing a monetary reward, a successful action for criminal conversation was a prerequisite for entering a suit for a parliamentary divorce, the only way to end a marriage other than by ecclesiastical annulment.[2] The jury dismissed George Norton's case against Lord Melbourne without ever leaving the jury box. Several commentators have speculated that George entered the suit not as a preliminary to divorcing his wife but in order to extract money from Lord Melbourne. Whatever George's intentions, once the suit for criminal conversation was defeated, he could proceed no further in any divorce action against Caroline. The two could not live together, and were indeed bitter enemies, but they could not legally end their marriage.

The case infuriated Caroline. Despite the jury's dismissal of the charges, her reputation was badly damaged. More than that, she was incensed by the legal rule that wives were prohibited from testifying in their own defense in such actions. A suit for criminal conversation was a civil action by the husband against his wife's alleged lover, and the burden of proof was on the husband to prove the defendant's guilt. The rule barring a wife from giving evidence in court increased the sense that this was an action between men for alleged damage to a husband's "property." All kinds of things fatal to a woman's reputation could be alleged with no possibility of rebuttal on her part. Even if a defendant was legally declared "not guilty," no wife was considered "innocent" after such a proceeding.

[2] On the action for criminal conversation, see Judith Schneid Lewis, "The Price of a Woman's Chastity: The Criminal Conversation Procedure in England" (Paper presented at the Annual Meeting of the Southern Historical Association, November 1984).

The trial for criminal conversation was quickly followed by Caroline's discovery that the law could not help her to be reunited with her children. Under the common law fathers had absolute right to custody of their children. Repeated efforts to gain access to her children availed Caroline nothing. So great was her distress, and so clear was the legal rule that kept her children from her, that Caroline set out to change the law. She induced Thomas Talfourd, a serjeant-at-law and Member of Parliament, to introduce a bill to give mothers the right to appeal to the Court of Chancery for the custody of their children under seven years of age. She then drafted *A Plain Letter to the Lord Chancellor on the Infant Custody Bill*, a plea for the bill's passage. Parliament passed the Infant Custody Act of 1839 [2 & 3 Vict., c. 54], which allowed the Court of Chancery to award mothers custody of their children under the age of seven and access to their children under sixteen.[3] This was an important first step towards obtaining maternal custody rights (it and later efforts are examined in chapter 5). But it took a tragedy as well as the threat of a suit in Chancery to win Caroline access to her own children; her youngest son was fatally injured in a riding accident and died before she could reach him. After that George allowed her regular access to the boys.

Some twelve years elapsed before George Norton's greed and the state of English marriage law again brought the Nortons into court. In 1848 George Norton was short of funds, and Caroline agreed to allow him to raise money by a mortgage on trust property that had been settled on her and her children. In exchange he signed a separation deed (a financial document, not a decree of separation from an ecclesiastical court) giving her an income of £500 and limiting his responsibility for her debts.[4] That year, Lord Melbourne died, stipulating in his will that Caroline was to continue to receive some financial support from his estate. In 1851 Mrs. Sheridan died and left Caroline £480 yearly, secured to her alone. Such trusts and bequests, explicitly secured to a married woman alone and known as her "separate estate," were the means of avoiding the common law rule that a married woman's property belonged to her husband. The courts of equity, not of common law, dealt with married women's separate estates. A wife with a separate estate could deal with *that* property as if she were un-

[3] Acts of Parliament are identified by title, date of the regnal year, the monarch's name (abbreviated), and chapter number. Thus the Infant Custody Act of 1839 [2 & 3 Vict., c. 54] was passed in the parliamentary session that spanned the second and third years of Victoria's reign, and can be found at chapter 54 of *Statutes at Large* for that session.

[4] Lee Holcombe, *Wives and Property: Reform of the Married Women's Property Law in Nineteenth-Century England* (Toronto: University of Toronto Press, 1983), 55.

married, or what the law called a *feme sole*.[5] George, who inherited from Mrs. Sheridan's estate the life-interest on Caroline's portion from her father, declared that since Caroline now had additional income he would reduce the allowance agreed to in the separation deed. Caroline retaliated by referring all her creditors to her husband. George refused to pay these debts, and a carriage repairman whom Caroline had not paid sued him in 1853.

The case turned on the question of the validity of the deed of separation. Caroline had received poor legal advice when she signed the deed, because well-established common law rules based on the doctrine of coverture stipulated that a married woman was incapable of signing any contract without being joined by her husband as co-signer. Although she was living apart from George, Caroline Norton was still a married woman, and was thus under the strictures of coverture. Deprived of any legal remedy for his chicanery over their separation deed in 1853, Caroline Norton privately circulated her *English Laws for Women in the Nineteenth Century* (1854), an impassioned defense of her own activities and an indictment of the laws governing married women's property rights. If she could not win her case in the English courts of law, she would appeal directly to public opinion and the verdict of history.

> I propose to take a lease; and am told, that being 'non-existent' in law, *my* signature is worthless. . . . I am informed, that, being 'non-existent' in law, it would be a mere farce my attempting to make a will. . . . I accept Mr. Norton's terms [for separation] after demanding others . . . and I am informed, that being 'non-existent' in law, I have signed that which binds him to nothing.

Norton had no complaint, she said, against the law's treatment of married persons as "one" when they lived "under a common roof," but when such rules were applied to a husband and wife who were living apart, the results were "unjust, unfit, and unnatural, and . . . productive only of social disorder and scandalous struggle." What was needed, according to Norton, was that "failing her natural protector, the law should be able to protect; that some direct court of appeal should exist, in which . . . the circumstances of each case should guide its result, and the LAW exercise remedial control."[6]

[5] Erna Reiss, *The Rights and Duties of Englishwomen* (Manchester: Sheratt & Hughes, 1934) is an excellent source on property laws as they affected women.

[6] Caroline Norton, *English Laws for Women in the Nineteenth Century* (printed for private circulation, 1854), 160–61, 167–68.

Caroline Norton repeatedly spoke of women as being in need of "protection": "What I write is written in no spirit of rebellion; it puts forward no absurd claim of equality; it is simply an appeal for protection." She found the language of "women's rights" and sexual "equality" anathema: "I, for one (I, with millions more), believe in the natural superiority of men, as I do in the existence of God. . . . Masculine superiority is incontestable; and with superiority should come protection."[7] Such passages have led some critics to denigrate Norton's contribution to the women's rights movement, saying she would simply have exchanged dependence on a husband for dependence on the state. But as Mary Poovey has argued, the very act of making a public appeal was a radical challenge to the laws that held that a married woman could claim no legal personality independent of her husband's. Norton transformed herself "from the silent sufferer of private wrongs into an articulate spokesperson in the public sphere." Moreover, even though Norton couched her appeal in terms of "protection" for married women, she exposed the multiple injustices of coverture and insisted that private wrongs were proper topics for legislative (and therefore political) scrutiny. In transforming her personal misfortunes into a critique of existing laws, "she collapse[d] the boundary between the private sphere, where injustice goes unchecked, and the public domain, where laws are made and enforced by men."[8] Finally, the specific measures Norton advocated would have involved a substantial increase in legal rights for married women with regard to custody of their children, ability to testify at legal proceedings, and control of their property and contracts.

The following year Norton published another biting condemnation of a proposed bill to provide England for the first time with procedures and grounds for civil divorce. *A Letter to the Queen on Lord Chancellor Cranworth's Marriage and Divorce Bill* (1855) was aimed at provisions of the proposed statute that would have allowed men to divorce adulterous wives but provided women with no recourse against adulterous husbands except to separate from them. All that the law would offer such a woman, said Norton, was " 'the Woman's Divorce';—leave to remain ALONE. Alone—married to your name. Never to know the protection of this nominal husband—nor the joys of fam-

---

[7] Ibid., 2, 165.

[8] Mary Poovey, *Uneven Developments: The Ideological Work of Gender in Mid-Victorian England* (Chicago: University of Chicago Press, 1988), chap. 3.

ily—nor the every-day companionship of a real home." English lawyers believed with Scripture that

> "it is not good for MAN to be alone,"—but extremely good for
> woman. Hard that a husband should not divorce an adulterous
> wife! Hard that he should not form a "purer connection!" Hard
> (though *he* has a career and occupations out of his own home),
> that a second chance of domestic happiness should not again greet
> him! But not the less hard that . . . she, who if she has not a home
> has nothing—should be left stranded and wrecked on the barren
> sands, at the foot of the world's impassive and impassable rocks.

Such a woman might well reflect that she would have been better off
"a sinner and divorced" than a wife in name only. Any law that produced such thoughts, as Cranworth's proposed measure must, was not
only unfair but a "bad, wicked law." "Either let men renounce the
privilege of divorce, and the assertion that marriage is a dissoluble contract,—or allow the weaker party that refuge from intolerable wrong,
which they claim as a matter of necessity for themselves."⁹
  Why did men balk so at the suggestion that Parliament should enact
a uniform divorce law holding men and women to the same standards
of conduct? In part because "men fear to curb the license of their own
pleasures," Norton asserted. They had come to regard sexual indulgence outside of marriage as their right. Further, the sexual double
standard did not simply dictate what kinds of sexual behavior would
be tolerated in men and women, but also reflected and reinforced
power relationships between the sexes. Even while thoughtful men admitted that the laws were "a disgrace to England," each individual
man "seems to dread that he is surrendering some portion of his own
rights over women, in allowing these laws to be revised."¹⁰ In 1851
Harriet Taylor Mill had asked why women were kept legally subordinate to men, and concluded that "the only reason which can be given
is, that men like it. It is agreeable to them that men should live for their
own sake, women for the sake of men."¹¹ Norton, who was far more
conservative than Taylor on women's rights, in this concurred, and she
denounced such brute sexual subjection.
  In 1856, a year after the appearance of *A Letter to the Queen on*

⁹ Caroline Norton, *A Letter to the Queen on Lord Chancellor Cranworth's Marriage
and Divorce Bill* (London: Longman, Brown, Green, & Longmans, 1855), 57–59.
  ¹⁰ Norton, *Letter to the Queen*, 150–51.
  ¹¹ Harriet Taylor Mill, "Enfranchisement of Women," *Westminster Review* (July
1851), reprinted in *Essays on Sex Equality*, ed. Alice Rossi (Chicago: University of Chicago Press, 1970), 91–121.

Lord Chancellor Cranworth's Marriage and Divorce Bill, the issues of married women's right to control their own property and of the sexual double standard and divorce became inextricably intertwined as Parliament debated and amended the bill that would become the Divorce Act of 1857. For several years preceding these debates, however, the issues of married women's property reform and divorce law reform were regarded not only as quite separate issues, but as having very little to do with women's rights. The rest of this chapter will trace the emergence of specifically feminist demands for married women's property and divorce law reform in the mid-1850s, and Parliament's responses to those demands.

THE MOVEMENT TO REFORM MARRIED WOMEN'S PROPERTY LAW

In 1854, the same year in which Caroline Norton circulated *English Laws for Women in the Nineteenth Century*, Eliza Lynn (later Mrs. Linton) wrote "One of Our Legal Fictions" for Charles Dickens's *Household Words*. Without mentioning the Nortons by name, Lynn rehearsed the details of their case and urged reform of married women's property law. Lynn was no friend of the organized women's movement, and regarded women's entry into male employments and the political world with abhorrence.[12] But like Norton, Lynn felt that the law governing a married woman's property left wives unprotected and vulnerable. Her pleas for married women's property rights implied

> no preposterous escape from womanly duty . . . ; no mingling of women with the broils of political life, nor opening to them of careers which nature herself has pronounced them incapable of following; no high-flown assertion of equality in kind; but simple justice. The recognition of their individuality as wives, the recognition of their natural rights as mothers, the permission to them to live by their own honourable industry.[13]

Even as Lynn clung tenaciously to her view that men and women had different natures and must inhabit different spheres, her writings, like Norton's, instructed and inspired others who were seeking reform of marriage law. Chief among them was Barbara Leigh Smith, whose

---

[12] Eliza Lynn Linton's famous essay, "The Girl of the Period," published in 1868, was a biting condemnation of the vacuity and frivolity of most middle-class women's lives. It called for women not to find a larger scope for their talents but to rededicate themselves to domestic responsibilities.

[13] Eliza Lynn, "One of Our Legal Fictions," *Household Words* 9 (April 1854): 260.

short book, *A Brief Summary in Plain English of the Most Important Laws of England Concerning Women*, also appeared in 1854, but based its brief for married women's rights on each individual's claim to equality under the law.[14]

Barbara Leigh Smith was the daughter of the radical M.P. for Norwich, Benjamin Leigh Smith. Her parents had five children together, but never married. Although Leigh Smith was only seven when her mother died, the status of being a child born out of wedlock haunted her youth (Benjamin's family was referred to by some relatives as the "forbidden family").[15] Benjamin undertook to raise the children himself after their mother's death, much to the disapproval of the rest of his family. Undaunted, he was involved with and encouraging to his children, and gave each child, girls as well as boys, a legacy of £300 a year for life when they turned twenty-one. Such an income, rare for a woman, gave Barbara Leigh Smith independence and security unusual for women of her day.

Leigh Smith was inspired both by Caroline Norton's case and by the troubles of Anna Murphy Jameson. Born in 1794, Anna Murphy became a governess at age sixteen, and in 1825, when she was thirty-one, married Robert Jameson, who later became attorney-general of Upper Canada. The marriage was unhappy, and in 1838 the couple separated. The yearly allowance that Robert Jameson provided his wife was inadequate, and when he died in 1854 he left her nothing. From 1838 until her death, therefore, Anna Jameson supported herself, her mother, and her sisters by writing.[16]

Jameson was a generation older than Barbara Leigh Smith and a close friend of Leigh Smith's aunt, Julia Smith; indeed, she referred to Leigh Smith and her friends Bessie Parkes, Adelaide Proctor, Anna Mary Howitt, and Eliza Fox as her "adopted nieces."[17] Jameson's ideas, as well as the example of her personal hardships, shaped the early reform efforts of these younger women. Although she believed that men and women had quite different capabilities and natures, and that women were more domestic, gentle, self-sacrificing, and moral than men, Jameson held that "Work in some form or other is the ap-

[14] Barbara Leigh Smith, *A Brief Summary in Plain English of the Most Important Laws of England Concerning Women* (London, 1854).

[15] Diana Mary Chase Worzala, "The Langham Place Circle: The Beginnings of the Organized Women's Movement in England, 1854–1870" (Ph.D. diss., University of Wisconsin, 1982), 60.

[16] Ibid., 74–78.

[17] Sheila R. Herstein, *A Mid-Victorian Feminist, Barbara Leigh Smith Bodichon* (New Haven: Yale University Press, 1985), 71.

pointed lot of all." Precisely because men's and women's natures were different, only by working together in a "communion of labour" would men's rationality join with women's tenderness to produce proper institutions and social policies. This incorporated a conservative notion of women's nature, but the conclusions Jameson drew were startling. She advocated that women be hired by schools, workhouses, hospitals, reformatories, and prisons. Gone was the notion that women needed to be sheltered and protected from life's harsher realities. Jameson converted the belief that women's special nature suited them only for the hearth and home into a moral imperative for women's public work.[18]

Women's work was not to be understood simply as another form of charitable activity, however. To work, to earn money, and to possess the fruits of her labor were a woman's right.

> Morally, a woman has a right to the free and entire development of every faculty which God has given her to be improved and used in His honour. Socially, she has the right to the protection of equal laws; the right to labour with her hands the thing that is good; to select the kind of labour that is in harmony with her powers, . . . to exist, if need be, by her labour or to profit others by it if she chooses. These are her rights, no more nor less than the rights of man.[19]

The right to possess the fruits of one's labor seemed as self-evident to Jameson as it had to Eliza Lynn.

Barbara Leigh Smith began the campaign for systematic legal reform aimed at insuring that the difficulties and injustices experienced by Jameson and Norton did not continue to befall married women. The notion of approaching Parliament to change the law came more readily to Leigh Smith than it would have to most Victorian women. Among the many colleagues her father had brought home frequently was serjeant-at-law Thomas Talfourd, who had guided the Infant Custody Bill of 1839 through Parliament. Another was Matthew Davenport Hill, who had been Recorder of Birmingham, and who was commissioner of bankrupts for the Bristol district. Leigh Smith turned to her friend Hill for instruction on the finer points of law when she drafted *A Brief Summary . . . of the Laws . . . Concerning Women*. The rhetorical strategy of Leigh Smith's pamphlet was quite different from that of

---

[18] The idea of a "moral imperative" comes from Worzala, "The Langham Place Circle," 107.

[19] Anna Murphy Jameson, *Sisters of Charity and the Communion of Labour* (London, 1859), 78.

Norton's highly personal and impassioned recital of the wrongs she had suffered. Using the traditional headings of legal treatises on the laws affecting women—single women, married women, women as mothers, widows, women and crime—Leigh Smith set forth in concise and plain language the laws bearing on women's estate. The cumulative effect of this simple listing of married women's disabilities was devastating. The pamphlet sold for a few pence and was widely read; a second edition was issued in 1856 and a third in 1869. In an article written near the end of the century, Bessie Parkes looked back at Leigh Smith's *A Brief Summary . . . of the Laws . . . Concerning Women* and judged that it had been "the small end of the wedge which was to change the whole fabric of the law."[20]

In addition to writing her pamphlet, Leigh Smith organized a small committee, whose members included Bessie Parkes and Mary Howitt, to draw up and circulate a petition to Parliament asking that it amend the laws of property affecting married women. This committee was the core of what would become known as the Langham Place Circle, a group of friends and acquaintances interested primarily in advancing women's opportunities for education and employment. The wording of the petition indicates the kinds of arguments that the Married Women's Property Committee found important and persuasive with respect to women's rights.

Asking the House of Commons to consider women's economic plight "and apply such remedy as to its wisdom shall seem fit," the petitioners listed grievances which they said affected women of the upper, middle, and working classes. For upper- and middle-class women the issue of property might seem "comparatively theoretical," but it really was not so, "since married women of education are entering on every side the fields of literature and art, in order to increase the family income by such exertions." Marriage settlements and appeals to the Courts of Equity helped such women, but the courts occasionally failed to do justice, and moreover "legal devices, patched upon a law which is radically unjust, can only work clumsily." For women of the lower classes, marriage settlements and actions in equity were out of the question. In manufacturing districts the employment of married women was widespread, and the current law worked hardship not only on them but on their children, who might be driven to the "temptations of the street, so fruitful in juvenile crime." Moreover, remarked the petitioners (playing on stereotypes of working-class men), "the ed-

[20] Bessie Rayner Parkes, "Barbara Leigh Smith Bodichon," *Englishwomen's Review* 210 (July 1891): 146.

ucation of the husband and the habits of his associates offer no moral guarantee for tender consideration of a wife." Perhaps as an after-thought calculated to appeal to their parliamentary allies, they added that husbands, too, suffered under the law in being held responsible for their wives' debts, a holdover from an age when "the man was the only money-getting agent." In conclusion the petitioners pointed out that other countries had recognized the changed nature of the modern world and had adjusted their laws accordingly, and they prayed that Parliament would do the same for England.[21] By the early months of 1856 the petition had gathered more than three thousand signatures in London, and some twenty-six thousand throughout the country.[22] In March the petition was submitted to both houses of Parliament.

There were significant differences between the demands of the Married Women's Property Committee and those of Caroline Norton. Norton's rhetoric accepted, indeed played upon, the notion that men and women occupied "separate spheres." It was George Norton's duty to protect her, as it was the duty of all husbands to protect their wives. She demanded recognition of her independent legal personality not as a right, but as a remedy against a husband who had violated his obligation of support. The Married Women's Property Committee, by contrast, insisted that married women, like all other adults, had an inalienable right to their own property and the fruits of their own labor. Coverture did not simply cause hardship in exceptional cases where husband and wife lived apart, it was itself "radically unjust." Whereas Norton appealed to the differences between men and women to justify her appeal, the Married Women's Property Committee insisted that the state recognize the fundamental and equal rights of men and women to possess property, regardless of marital status.

Leigh Smith's pamphlet and the married women's property petition

---

[21] The text of the "Petition for Reform of the Married Women's Property Law Presented to Parliament 14 March 1856," is reprinted in Holcombe, *Wives and Property*, 237–38.

[22] Mary Howitt, head of the petition campaign in London, was careful to place the names of prominent and respected women at the head of the list of twenty-four signatories that circulated with each petition. Most of these were authors: Elizabeth Barrett Browning, Elizabeth Gaskell, Anna Jameson, Harriet Martineau, Mary Cowden Clarke, Jane Webb Louden, Jane Carlyle, and Geraldine Jewsbury. (Marian Evans, better known as George Eliot, also signed the petition, but not prominently, for she had begun living with George Henry Lewes in 1854.) Only the Hon. Julia Maynard, the daughter of Henry, Viscount Maynard, was of a noble family, and she took no active part in other feminist causes. The preponderance of literary women on the list was a reflection of the fact that literature was one of the few professions open to women in the mid-nineteenth century. See Holcombe, *Wives and Property*, 85, 70.

made a considerable impact, which was due in part to the existence of a parallel movement outside of feminist circles to alter the common law as it affected married women's property. In 1851 the Law Amendment Society (LAS), an organization founded in 1844 by Lord Brougham to promote a wide variety of reforms, formally recommended the fusion of the courts of law and equity, in order to eliminate the confusion and legal complications that arose from the existence of two courts administering two distinct and often contradictory bodies of legal rules. (The LAS was one of the main contributors to the agitation which, twenty-five years later, would restructure English law through the Judicature Act of 1873. The Judicature Act decreed that in administering the law, in cases of conflict between the rules of law and equity, those of equity would prevail.) In 1854, in a review of Caroline Norton's *English Laws for Women in the Nineteenth Century* and other books on women and the law, the journal of the LAS used married women's property law as an example of the confusion and injustice caused by the conflict between the common law and equity.[23] The LAS objected to married women being forbidden under the common law to possess property, while under equity they could hold property if it was designated as their separate estate.

Richard Monckton Milnes, a liberal M.P., member of the LAS, and friend of the Leigh Smith family, submitted Barbara Leigh Smith's pamphlet to the LAS's Personal Laws Committee to help buttress its case for abolishing the common law rules governing married women's property.[24] In the spring of 1856 the Law Amendment Society issued the *Report of the Personal Laws Committee . . . on the Laws Relating to the Property of Married Women*, and embarked on a campaign to enact a law giving every married woman the status of feme sole with respect to her property and contracts.[25] On May 31, 1856, the society

[23] "The Laws Relating to Women," *The Law Review* 20 (1854): 18–21.

[24] Richard Monckton Milnes was to prove one of the feminists' most loyal parliamentary allies, first in the Commons and after 1863 in the House of Lords as Baron Houghton. Milnes never held a high governmental office, but he worked hard in Parliament on the Factory Acts and the establishment of reformatories for youthful offenders. He had proposed marriage to Leigh Smith's cousin, Florence Nightingale, in 1849 (before she became famous through her work in the Crimea). Although Nightingale acknowledged that he was "the man I adore," she would not marry him for fear that it would lock her into a continuation of domestic duties when she sought a larger sphere of moral action. See Forster, *Significant Sisters*, 104–5.

[25] Law Amendment Society, *Report of the Personal Laws Committee . . . on the Laws Relating to the Property of Married Women* (London, 1856). On the Law Amendment Society's report, see Caroline Cornwallis, "The Property of Married Women," *Westminster Review* 66 (1856): 331–60.

held an open meeting on the status of women under the law. Consistent with its earlier efforts to eliminate the conflict between law and equity, the assembly unanimously adopted a resolution condemning the common law rule of married women's property, and endorsed the equitable concept of separate estates.

In the meantime, the married women's property petition had been presented to the House of Lords by Lord Brougham and to the Commons by Sir Thomas Erskine Perry.[26] Perry also presented to the House of Commons the LAS's resolution condemning the common law rules of property respecting married women. On the assurance of the government that it would take up the matter the following year, Perry agreed to withdraw his resolution.[27]

At virtually the same moment that Lord Brougham and Perry were bringing the issue of married women's property before Parliament, the House of Lords was debating a bill to create a civil Divorce Court. Up to this point the two measures had been conceived of and dealt with quite independently, but from the spring of 1856 through 1857 the issues of married women's property and divorce law reform were inseparably linked. In order to understand the significance of what Parliament did—and of what it refused to do—one must trace the history of the divorce bill.

PARLIAMENT, DIVORCE LAW REFORM, AND MARRIED WOMEN'S PROPERTY

The Traditional Law of Divorce and Cranworth's Divorce Bill

The proposal for divorce law reform originated quite independently of women's rights advocates and initially manifested a striking indifference to women's needs and concerns. In 1850 the government ap-

[26] 3 Hansard 141 (14 March 1856), 120. Lord Brougham, lord chancellor from 1830 to 1834, had a long and distinguished career as a jurist and legal reformer. He piloted the Reform Act of 1832 through the House of Lords and was in the forefront of the fight to abolish slavery. He founded the Law Amendment Society in 1844 and was president of the National Association for the Promotion of Social Science from its founding in 1858 until his death. Lord Brougham's advocacy of women's rights during the debates on married women's property and divorce law was consonant with his life-long commitment to the principle of legal equality. Sir Thomas Erskine Perry, a fervent supporter of the Reform Act of 1832, had been a law reporter for many years before being appointed to the Supreme Court of Bombay, where he served from 1840 to 1852. He served in Parliament from 1854 to 1859, when he resigned his seat to serve as a member of the Council for India (*Dictionary of National Biography*).

[27] 3 Hansard 142 (10 June 1856), 1284.

pointed a Royal Commission on Divorce. This followed a long series of efforts dating back to the 1830s to alter England's traditional divorce law, which essentially followed the canon law inherited from Rome.[28] Under that system, jurisdiction over divorce cases rested with the ecclesiastical courts, which issued two kinds of decrees. A divorce *a mensa et thoro* (divorce from bed and board) was granted only for adultery, extreme cruelty, or desertion, and it allowed neither partner to remarry. A divorce *a vinculo matrimonii* (divorce from the bonds of marriage), or an absolute dissolution of the marriage bond with permission to remarry, was granted only when the marriage was found to have been invalid due to age, mental incompetence, sexual impotence, or fraud.

Except for a brief period under the Commonwealth (1649–1660), England had no provision for civil divorce other than the extraordinary procedure of a private act of Parliament. By the nineteenth century some ten private acts for divorce passed Parliament each year. Until 1804 all of the successful plaintiffs were men protesting their wives' adultery, and only four women—each of whom complained of adultery aggravated by another enormity such as incest or bigamy—ever received a parliamentary divorce.[29] Divorce was seen essentially as a punitive measure against an adulterous wife, and a way for a man to assure himself of legitimate offspring.

Obtaining a parliamentary divorce was legally complex and extraordinarily expensive. A plaintiff first had to obtain a decree of divorce a mensa et thoro from the ecclesiastical courts. The husband then had to win damages against his wife's alleged paramour in a civil action for "criminal conversation" by proving his wife's adultery with the accused. Only after success in these two proceedings could a plaintiff

---

[28] In 1552 Archbishop Cranmer had supported the adoption of a more liberal divorce law in the *Reformatio Legum Ecclesiasticarum,* a treatise which recommended that both adultery and desertion be grounds for divorce. But Henry VIII died before he could force the reforms through Parliament, and the House of Commons defeated them under Edward VI. English law therefore recognized only actions for separation. On early divorce law in England, see L. Chilton Powell, *English Domestic Relations 1487–1653* (New York: Columbia University Press, 1917), 61–65.

[29] For information on early parliamentary divorces, see *Parliamentary Papers,* 1852–1853, (1604), vol. XL, *First Report of the Commissioners Appointed by her Majesty to Enquire into the Law of Divorce,* p. 12, n. 6. (Hereafter references to *Parliamentary Papers* will be cited as *PP.*) Two histories of divorce in England are O. R. MacGregor, *Divorce in England: A Centenary Study* (London: Heinemann, 1957); and Allen Horstman, *Victorian Divorce* (New York: St. Martin's, 1985). On the technicalities of obtaining a parliamentary divorce, see J.J.S. Wharton, *An Exposition of the Laws Relating to the Women of England* (London: Longman, Brown, Green & Longmans, 1853), 450–90.

present a bill for parliamentary divorce. These stipulations meant that divorce with permission to remarry was available for all practical purposes only to wealthy men. Delivering a decision in a bigamy case, Mr. Justice Maule derided the state of the law. The judge asked the working-class defendant, who had been convicted of bigamy, why he should not be sentenced. The man replied, " 'My wife was unfaithful; she robbed me and ran away with another man, and I thought I might take another wife.' " To this Maule replied,

"You are quite wrong in assuming that. You ought to have brought an action for criminal conversation; that action would have been tried by one of Her Majesty's judges at the Assizes; you would probably have recovered damages; and then you should have instituted a suit in the ecclesiastical court for a divorce *a mensa et thoro*. Having got that divorce, you should have petitioned the House of Lords for a divorce *a vinculo*, and should have appeared by counsel at the bar of their Lordships' House. Then . . . you might have married again. The whole proceeding would not have cost you more than £1,000."

The prisoner: "Ah, my Lord, I never was worth a thousand pence in all my life."

Mr. Justice Maule: "That is the law, and you must submit to it."[30]

The exchange, which occurred in 1845, was widely reported, as Maule had surely intended it should be, and generated pressure for some means by which such marriages might be ended.

The Royal Commissioners of 1850 found both the jurisdiction of the ecclesiastical courts over what they regarded as secular matters and the use of parliamentary action for what was essentially a judicial proceeding, to be inappropriate.[31] They recommended that Parliament create instead a civil court empowered to grant divorce a vinculo and to hear the matrimonial cases then heard by the ecclesiastical courts. The commissioners also recommended that the *only* ground for divorce a vinculo should be a *wife's* adultery, while a divorce a mensa et thoro should be granted to men and women alike for adultery, gross

[30] R. H. Graveson and F. R. Crane, *A Century of Family Law* (London: Sweet & Maxwell, 1957), 8.

[31] On earlier efforts to reform divorce procedure which influenced the Royal Commission, see "Report of the Society for Promoting the Amendment of the Law. Ecclesiastical Committee," *Law Review* 13 (1848): 347–52; "Divorce," *Law Review* 1 (1844–1845): 353–81; and 3 Hansard 73 (8 March 1844), 691–700.

cruelty, and perhaps willful desertion for an extended period.[32] In rejecting the parliamentary practice of granting a divorce a vinculo to at least some women, the Royal Commissioners made an absolute distinction between male and female adultery. This distinction, as Keith Thomas has argued, was based on "the desire of men for absolute property in women." A wife should forgive a guilty husband, no matter how extreme or repeated his behavior, but a husband could not forgive a guilty wife, no matter how short-lived her error.[33]

The government adopted the proposals of the Royal Commissioners, and in June 1854, Cranworth, the lord chancellor, submitted to the House of Lords a divorce bill which would have created a new Divorce Court to hear cases for divorce a vinculo and given the Court of Chancery jurisdiction over judicial separations.[34] Due to the lateness of the session and the opposition of some powerful Lords to any provision whatsoever for divorce, the bill died after a second reading in the House of Lords.[35]

No parliamentary consideration of the divorce bill took place during 1855, because Lord Aberdeen's government collapsed that year over charges of mismanagement of the Crimean War. Cranworth continued as lord chancellor in Palmerston's government, however, and in 1856 he again submitted his divorce bill. The debate that year took a very different turn from that of 1854, due in large part to the public controversy surrounding Caroline Norton's recently published *A Letter to the Queen on Lord Chancellor Cranworth's Marriage and Divorce Bill* and the married women's property agitation. The submission of the property petition and bill to Parliament had called attention to the

[32] There was no dissenting opinion in favor of a more liberal view; only one commissioner, Lord Redesdale, who could not accept divorce a vinculo on any grounds, filed a separate opinion (*PP*, 1852–1853, (1604), XL, 16 and 22).

[33] Keith Thomas, "The Double Standard," *Journal of the History of Ideas* 20 (April 1959): 195–216.

[34] In a slight deviation from the recommendations of the Royal Commission, a clause was included permitting a wife to sue for divorce a vinculo if her husband was guilty of adultery aggravated by incest, bigamy, or gross cruelty, making the bill consonant with past parliamentary practice. To those who thought the grounds of divorce too narrow, Cranworth argued that adultery was the only ground mentioned in Scripture. To those who wanted equal grounds for divorce for men and women, he said that if women were allowed to divorce their husbands for a single act of adultery, husbands could force their wives into divorce by a simple infidelity. As for adultery by men, it was reprehensible but certainly not unbearable. Opposition to Cranworth's bill at this stage came primarily from conservative opponents of *any* provision for civil divorce. Lord Redesdale and the Bishop of Oxford opposed the bill and argued that at least it should be amended to prohibit adulterers from remarrying.

[35] On Lord Chancellor Cranworth's bill of 1854, see 3 Hansard 134 (13 June 1854), 1–28.

plight of wives separated from their husbands who still could not hold property in their own names. Many of those who had supported married women's property reform now joined Norton in denouncing the clauses in the divorce bill specifying different grounds for divorce for men and women. If Parliament was to create a procedure for civil divorce, then whatever grounds were specified should apply equally to women and men, argued those who protested the sexual double standard.

During the spring of 1856 Lord Lyndhurst chaired a Select Committee of the House of Lords on the proposed divorce bill. The Select Committee recommended that a wife who was legally separated but not divorced from her husband should be treated as a feme sole with respect to her own property and contracts. It also stipulated that cruelty, bigamy, willful desertion for four years, and incest were aggravations which, when combined with adultery, would allow a woman to divorce her husband.[36] Compared to the proposal in the married women's property bill that would have given *every* married woman the rights of a feme sole, the proposal to give a *separated* wife the status of a feme sole was a minor concession. Similarly, compared to the suggestion that the grounds for divorce be the same for men and women, allowing wives to divorce their husbands for adultery only when it was aggravated by a severe additional offense offered minimal relief and sanctioned very different moral standards for husbands and wives. Although the adjustments in the bill were simply tinkerings with patriarchal authority in marriage, without feminist intervention the debates on the Divorce Act would have been confined exclusively to questions about the relationship of ecclesiastical to civil law and the justifiability of civil divorce. As it was, feminists altered the nature of Parliament's consideration of the bill, so that from being regarded as a measure concerned with curtailing the jurisdiction of the ecclesiastical courts and abolishing parliamentary divorce, it came to be seen as one affecting the rights and legal status of married women with respect to both sexual relations and property.

Parliament Accepts the Sexual Double Standard in Divorce Law

Unlike the debates on the divorce bill of 1854, which dealt primarily with jurisprudential issues such as the composition of the court, the frequency of its sittings, and the expenses of its proceedings, the more

[36] Parliament, *Sessional Papers* (Lords), 1856 (H.L. 181), vol. xxiv, *Report from the Select Committee of the House of Lords on the Divorce and Matrimonial Causes Bill . . . together with the Proceedings of the Committee.*

extensive discussions of 1856 and 1857 found the Lords grappling with issues concerning the marital relationship itself. Lord Lyndhurst was the staunchest supporter in either house of equalizing the grounds of divorce for men and women, arguing that "in principle, there ought to be no distinction made between the adultery of the husband and that of the wife."[37] In the Commons, Henry Drummond accused his colleagues who treated women's infidelity more severely than men's of being like "Turks legislating for the inhabitants of the seraglio," or slave traders voting against abolition.[38] But most Members of Parliament were very far from thinking that a husband's adultery was as serious as a wife's. Indeed, William Gladstone, who led the opposition to the divorce bill itself, hoped to defeat the entire measure by insisting that if divorce were to be allowed, it should be granted equally to men and women. Gladstone typically referred to Scripture in defending his opinion: "It is the special and peculiar doctrine of the Gospel respecting the personal relation in which every Christian, whether man or woman, is placed to the person of our Lord that forms the firm, the broad, the indestructible basis of the equality of the sexes under Christian law."[39] Gladstone knew that such an interpretation would be quite unacceptable to the majority of his colleagues. Neither the Lords nor the Commons accepted Lord Lyndhurst's proposal to equalize the grounds for divorce. In a society in which women were thought of as celibate spinsters, married women, or prostitutes, a wife who experienced sex outside of marriage removed herself from the category of wife and placed herself, in the bishop's eyes, in the position of a whore.

Parliament's greater tolerance of male than female philandering was clear in Cranworth's statement in 1854 that it would be too harsh to bring the law to bear against a husband who was "a little profligate."[40] Cranworth's offhand remark provoked some outraged comment when it was reported in the press; the anonymous author of *Remarks upon the Law of Marriage and Divorce* (1855) observed that to describe a husband's adultery as "a little profligate" while making a wife's adultery the grounds for divorce was like refusing to prosecute a murder because it was not parricide.[41] The *Times* also rebuked Cranworth for

---

[37] 3 Hansard 142 (20 May 1856), 416.

[38] 3 Hansard 147 (13 August 1857), 1587.

[39] 3 Hansard 147 (7 August 1857), 1272. Gladstone was a master at using egalitarian arguments *against* legal reforms to aid women. Thirty years later he helped defeat women's suffrage by arguing against granting women the vote on the same terms as men because it would enfranchise only women of property, not all women.

[40] 3 Hansard 134 (13 June 1854), 7.

[41] *Remarks on the Law of Marriage and Divorce; suggested by the Honourable Mrs. Norton's Letter to the Queen* (London: James Ridgway, 1855), 35.

his "unfortunate phrase," but it was offended by Cranworth's language, not his ideas, and did not endorse equal grounds for divorce.[42]

While Members of Parliament seemed reluctant to curtail the sexual adventures of men of their own class, their debates revealed an undercurrent of fear of unrestrained sexuality on the part of the poor and women. Gladstone warned his colleagues: "Take care, then, how you damage the character of your country men. You know how apt the English nature is to escape from restraint and control; you know what passion dwells in the Englishman."[43] Viscount Dungannon feared that the divorce bill "would supply additional encouragement to the indulgence of illicit desires."[44] The Earl of Desart expressed his fear that if the poor were allowed to divorce, they would come to regard marriage as no more than "connubial concubinage."[45] The Bishop of Oxford was sure that "facilities [for divorce] could not be given to the lowest classes without endangering the moral purity of married life."[46] In 1856 Parliament also debated and defeated (as it did more than nineteen times between 1849 and 1907), a bill to remove the ban on marriage with a deceased wife's sister. Proponents and opponents of the bill agreed that the greatest temptation to illicit sex with a wife's sister would occur in poorer households where a spinster aunt joined the family to keep a roof over her head and to help with the housework and child care.[47] Fear of the disturbing power of sexual passion also helped to pass the Obscene Publications Act of 1857. Members of Parliament were not as offended by the contents of pornography (which some of them contended was no more explicit than poems and plays by classical authors) as they were by the fact that sexually provocative tracts could now be purchased for a few shillings and thus were widely available.[48] Perhaps as a result of concern about lower-class immorality the Divorce Act effectively barred the lower classes from divorce by

[42] "The Law of Divorce," *Times* (London), 27 January 1857, p. 4b.

[43] 3 Hansard 147 (31 July 1857), 854. On the parliamentary debates, see Mary Lyndon Shanley, " 'One Must Ride Behind': Married Women's Rights and the Divorce Act of 1857" *Victorian Studies* 25 (Spring 1982): 255–76.

[44] 3 Hansard 145 (19 May 1857), 514.

[45] 3 Hansard 143 (3 July 1856), 244.

[46] 3 Hansard 142 (26 June 1856), 1980.

[47] For example, 3 Hansard 141 (25 April 1856), 1475–1528.

[48] 3 Hansard 146 (25 June 1857), 327–38; 3 Hansard 147 (12 August 1857), 1475–81. The fears that the Divorce Act would increase lower-class immorality were like those described by Edward Bristow as being discernible in the years after the French Revolution—that "irreligion, immorality, and sexual licence were the harbingers of social dissolution," and that sexual order and restraint were essential preconditions of social order. See Edward Bristow, *Vice and Vigilance: Purity Movements in Britain since 1700* (Totowa, N.J.: Rowman & Littlefield, 1977), 3.

establishing only one court, situated in London, to grant divorces, despite the reformers' insistence that one of their aims in abolishing divorce by private act of Parliament was to get rid of "one law for the rich, one for the poor."

Fear of the disruptive potential of female sexuality was clearest in the Bishop of Oxford's proposal to prohibit the remarriage of adulterers. Because the provisions for divorcing a husband were so narrow, this prohibition would have applied overwhelmingly to women. That was what the bishop intended: he could not believe that "the woman who had committed adultery [should] be entitled, by reason of her sin, to greater privileges than those extended to other women."[49] Had the amendment passed, a husband would have been able to commit adultery repeatedly with total legal impunity, while a single transgression by a wife would have subjected her to divorce without the possibility of remarriage. The bishop's amendment was finally defeated not because it was judged to be unfair, but because opponents conjured up the image of an adulterous wife denied remarriage being driven by unbridled passion into a life of repeated sin, even prostitution, rather than accepting one of celibacy.[50]

Despite the fact that parliamentary opinion regarded a wife's adultery as a far more fundamental offense against marriage than a husband's, members were unwilling to close the possibility of divorce to women altogether. Debates over what should be the grounds of divorce for men and women were, in essence, disputes over what constituted a violation of the marriage contract, and therefore over the fundamental purpose of marriage. The House of Lords argued heatedly about the possible aggravations that would, when combined with adultery, justify a woman in seeking release from her marriage vows. From a list that included rape, sodomy, desertion, transportation, penal servitude, incest, bigamy, and cruelty, they accepted only the last three, indicating that they did not regard crimes of sexual violence or prolonged absence by the husband as fatal to the marriage bond.[51] Sexual violence within marriage was not even considered by the Lords. A husband had the right of access to his wife's body, and by definition could not be charged with marital rape.

In 1857 the Commons debated the question of aggravating offenses in long and grueling sessions. At one point Lord John Manners pro-

[49] 3 Hansard 145 (19 May 1857), 524.

[50] See Lord Brougham's denunciation of the suggested prohibition on the remarriage of adulterers, 3 Hansard 145 (4 June 1857), 1098.

[51] *Sessional Papers* (Lords), 1856 (H.L. 181), vol. xxiv, pp. 6–7; and 3 Hansard 145 (25 May 1857), 812–19.

posed that "adultery committed in the conjugal residence" should entitle a wife to divorce. The obstructionists took hold of the amendment and "worked themselves and many other members into a hypnotic frenzy over the possibility of sin."[52] In addition to exercising prurient imaginations, the members were also trying to convey their varying understandings of the conditions that disrupted marital companionship. To support their view that a wife's adultery was a unique and fatal offense against marriage, Members of Parliament repeatedly quoted Jesus' admonition, "but I say to you, that whosoever shall put away his wife, saving for the cause of fornication, causes her to commit adultery," to show that he intended only wives, and not husbands, to be "put away."[53]

Secular considerations were also important. The most frequently mentioned evil result of female adultery was, as Lord Cranworth put it, that it might be "the means of palming spurious offspring upon the husband."[54] In the House of Commons, Spencer Walpole, who had sat on the Royal Commission on the Divorce Law in 1850, appealed to the same patrilineal concern about property and family inheritance to defeat a proposal for equal grounds of divorce for men and women.[55] The notion that only a wife's adultery justified severing the marriage bond assumed that a man's sexual authority and the legitimacy of his offspring were the basic considerations of the marriage contract. Parliament's disregard of the threat to a family line posed by a husband's adultery reflected the assumption that men committed adultery with women who did not belong to the "respectable classes" and whose family life was consequently considered unimportant. If a man did seduce the wife of a gentleman, her husband could divorce her to protect himself against illegitimate heirs.[56]

Despite the misogynistic and patriarchal tenor of many of these parliamentary debates, the discussions of the grounds for a wife's divorce contained the seeds of the idea that marriage could not properly be understood solely as an institution for sexual or reproductive bonding, but must also be regarded as a locus for companionship and mutual support. In rejecting the ecclesiastical doctrine of the indissolubility of

[52] Margaret K. Woodhouse, "The Marriage and Divorce Bill of 1857," *American Journal of Legal History* 3 (1959): 273.

[53] Matt. 5:32; see also Matt. 19:9.

[54] 3 Hansard 145 (25 May 1857), 813.

[55] 3 Hansard 147 (7 August 1857), 1282.

[56] Constance Rover, *Love, Morals and the Feminists* (London: Routledge & Kegan Paul, 1970), 42–43. Other threats to family life that might follow from a husband's adultery, such as venereal disease, were not even considered during the debates.

marriage and by debating aggravating grounds for divorcing an adulterous husband, Parliament had opened the door a crack to further debate about the purpose and nature of marriage itself. The majority in the Parliaments of 1856 and 1857, however, would go no further than to allow women to divorce their husbands for such egregious offenses as incest, bigamy, or gross physical cruelty—a reflection of their ardent desire to change the traditional law of marriage, and the traditional status of married women, as little as possible.

Parliament Rejects Married Women's Property Reform

Lord Lyndhurst's motion to establish a Select Committee to amend the Divorce Bill in 1856 brought together the related issues of the grounds for divorce and married women's property. Married women's property law, he noted, "is closely connected with the law of divorce, but is not touched by the present bill." A married woman who had separated from her husband by a decree from the ecclesiastical courts continued to be governed by the common law rules concerning the property of married women. Any legacy left to her became her husband's, income from any real property was at his disposal, and "if a wife tries to eke out a scanty subsistence for herself and her children by the exercise of any art . . . the husband can seize upon the proceeds of her industry and bestow them upon his mistress." As Lord Lyndhurst summed up the situation, from the moment of separation "the wife is almost in a state of outlawry. She may not enter into a contract, or, if she do, she has no means of enforcing it. The law, so far from protecting, oppresses her. She is homeless, helpless, hopeless, and almost wholly destitute of civil rights."[57] The following year Lord St. Leonards pointed out that wives who had been deserted by their husbands were in a similar bind, being officially married but unable to act for themselves and without a male to act for them.

To deal with the first of these hardships Lyndhurst successfully moved an amendment providing that any woman who obtained a decree of judicial separation (which under the Divorce Act replaced the ecclesiastical divorce a mensa et thoro) should thenceforth be treated as a feme sole with respect to her property and contracts.[58] Lord St. Leonards was similarly successful in convincing his colleagues to accept an amendment stipulating that a woman who was deserted by her hus-

[57] 3 Hansard 142 (20 May 1856), 408–10.
[58] 20 & 21 Vict., c. 85, secs. xxv–xxvi.

band could go before a local magistrate and receive an order allowing her thenceforth to control her earnings as a feme sole. It is worth noting that Lord St. Leonards's proposal was the *only* provision in the Divorce Act that could possibly be of use to women of the poorer classes, since it required only an appeal to a local magistrate, not to the expensive Divorce Court in London.[59] Although the amendments by Lords Lyndhurst and St. Leonards made inroads in the common law doctrine of spousal unity as it affected married women's property rights, neither measure recognized the principle that a wife in an *ongoing* marriage had a right to control her own property. The amendments simply suspended the common law rules in cases where cohabitation had ceased and the marriage was for all practical purposes at an end.

The limitations of these amendments with respect to married women's rights are clear when one compares them with the provisions of the married women's property bill. Early in the short session of 1857, Lord Brougham took up the cause that Sir Erskine Perry had advocated in the Commons, and introduced a married women's property bill which would have abolished altogether the common law doctrine of spousal unity with respect to married women's property.[60] When Parliament reconvened after the March general election, Sir Erskine Perry and Richard Monckton Milnes presented a similar bill to the House of Commons.[61] Milnes explained that the "object of the Bill ... was to make that the law for all classes, which by custom it had become for the wealthy classes," that is, to substitute the rules of equity for those of the common law.[62] Perry contended that the common law was "unjust in principle and grievous in operation, and ought to be altered," and reminded his colleagues that the bill rested on principles that the Law Amendment Society had adopted almost unanimously. But even as he debated the married women's property bill, Perry confessed that he entertained not "the slightest expectation" of passing the bill that session.[63] If the Divorce Act passed, as appeared likely, its

[59] 20 & 21 Vict., c. 85, sec. xxi.

[60] The speech introducing the bill was one of the most eloquent of Brougham's later years. Brougham reminded the Lords of previous reform measures that had seemed visionary at first but later triumphed, and revealed his perception of the issue of married women's property as simply the logical extension of Whig principles of individual freedom and responsibility. See 3 Hansard 144 (13 February 1856), 605–19.

[61] 3 Hansard 145 (14 May 1857), 266.

[62] 3 Hansard 146 (15 July 1857), 1516.

[63] Ibid., 1520; 3 Hansard 145 (14 May 1857), 267; and 3 Hansard 146 (15 July 1857), 1523.

provisions to protect the property of separated and deserted wives would lessen the pressure to pass a comprehensive property act.

Perry was an astute judge of parliamentary politics and his colleagues' attitudes about marriage. Although one cannot know for certain what the fate of the married women's property bill might have been had it not been introduced in the midst of debates on divorce, the conjunction of the measures doomed the comprehensive married women's property law. The notion that a married woman might act in her own name with respect to her property and contracts deeply threatened many members' sense of the stability and unity of the home.

Indeed, the idea of married women's property rights posed a much greater threat to the notion of family unity than did the provisions for divorce itself. Divorce simply gave legal recognition to de facto marital breakdown. A married woman's property law, on the other hand, would have recognized the existence of two separate wills within an *ongoing* marriage. As Caroline Cornwallis said in an article commenting on the *Report* of the LAS, "Marriage makes no mental change in the individual; the will remains as strong, the reason as clear as before; individual needs are as separate as ever."[64] That married women should remain *individuals* with independent wills and justiciable rights was exactly the principle that feminists wished to establish. In contrast, very few Members of Parliament believed that two independent wills could exist in one household without inviting disaster. Lord Campbell advised that Lord Brougham's married women's property bill "would lead to perpetual discord . . . [I]t was a proposal shocking to all the habits of the people of the country."[65] A. J. Beresford Hope feared that the feminists' efforts, if not stoutly resisted, would lead to the "breakdown of . . . the distinguishing characteristic of Englishmen—the love of home, the purity of husband and wife, and the union of one family."[66] J. D. Fitzgerald asserted that Perry's bill would "effect a complete revolution in the law, which would disturb all the relations of husband and wife."[67] To listen to Members of Parliament one would have thought that never again would parents and children sit around the dining table or the family gather about the hearth, if wives were to possess the right to control their own property.

A few Members of Parliament perceived a link between the demand for legal rights for married women and the even less acceptable notion that women take part in public life. If wives were not to be subordinate

[64] Cornwallis, "Property of Married Women," 339.
[65] 3 Hansard 144 (13 February 1857), 619.
[66] 3 Hansard 145 (14 May 1857), 280.
[67] 3 Hansard 146 (15 July 1857), 1521.

to their husbands in domestic matters, what was to keep them from demanding a larger role in affairs outside the home? Beresford Hope chided his colleagues that in considering giving married women independent legal status, they were responding to the "rather extravagant demands of the large and manly body of 'strong-minded women,' " who in meetings and pamphlets were beginning to press for a larger scope for female activities and for greater equality before the law.[68] In proposing his amendment to protect the property of deserted wives, Lord St. Leonards appealed to the widespread fear that a comprehensive married women's property law would upset more than domestic order. He urged his colleagues to adopt his amendment precisely because it "did not go anything like the length of the bill which had been introduced in the other House" (that is, Perry's married women's property bill), the effect of which would be "to place the whole marriage law of this country on a different footing, and would in fact give a wife all the distinct rights of citizenship." Lord St. Leonards knew that his colleagues in both houses would wish to avoid this "greater evil" by adopting the mild measure he proposed.[69]

The link Beresford Hope and Lord St. Leonards drew between a married women's property statute and women's suffrage was a telling point in the debates of 1857. No organized group was advocating women's suffrage, although occasional articles like Harriet Taylor Mill's "Enfranchisement of Women" argued the injustice of an exclusively male franchise. As the movement for improving the legal status of married women gained in intensity in the 1860s and 1870s, however, reformers and their opponents alike increasingly emphasized the connection between women's legal subordination to their husbands in marriage and their lack of the vote. Women could not be full citizens as long as they were subordinate to their husbands, and they could not be their husbands' true companions and partners in marriage while they were their political inferiors. The understanding of marriage reflected in the Divorce Act of 1857 shows how threatening the demand for married women's rights was to male dominance in both the home and civil society.

WHAT Parliament accomplished in the Divorce Act must in the final analysis be judged in the light of what it failed to do. Usually hailed in histories of English jurisprudence as a watershed statute that created both the action for civil divorce and the new Court of Divorce, the

[68] 3 Hansard 145 (14 May 1857), 278.
[69] 3 Hansard 145 (25 May 1857), 800.

Divorce Act also sanctioned and perpetuated a patriarchal understanding of the marriage bond. Parliament was so deeply wedded to notions of marital hierarchy that the contractarian arguments of Caroline Norton, Barbara Leigh Smith, and others for equal grounds for divorce made very little impression, even when they were advanced in Parliament by such eminent figures as Lords Lyndhurst and Brougham. When presented with proposals to allow married women to control their own property and to equalize the grounds for divorce for men and women, Parliament rejected both almost out-of-hand. Only in providing that a deserted or separated wife could be treated as a feme sole did Parliament grant nominally married women any legal autonomy.

The debates over the Divorce Act of 1857 reflect the inability of the majority of Victorian gentlemen to envision a form of marriage in which husband and wife met as political and economic equals. As a writer in the *Law Review* put it, "in the words of the proverb, 'If two ride on a horse, one must ride behind.' "[70] (Why marriage was best represented as a single horse with two riders rather than, say, a team pulling together—or why horseback riding was relevant to marriage—no one ventured to say, but the proverb was reiterated throughout the century by opponents of marriage law reform.)

Images of hierarchy and of male domination, of the man holding the reins of the horse, were so central to the rules of coverture and the new divorce law that feminists perforce defined their task as getting Parliament and the courts to adopt notions concerning individual rights and equality within marriage. Yet underlying their individualistic critique of marriage law was a belief, or a yearning to believe, that equality of rights before the law would lead to greater reciprocity, understanding, and intimacy—intellectual, emotional, and sexual—between husband and wife. These ideas, which emerged in a handful of brilliant pamphlets during the 1850s, became staples of feminist ideology in the upsurge of organized political feminism that followed the submission of the women's suffrage petition to Parliament in 1867.

[70] "Women's Law: Mrs. Norton's Letter to the Queen," *Law Review* 23 (1855–1856): 340.

· 2 ·

EQUAL RIGHTS AND SPOUSAL FRIENDSHIP:
THE MARRIED WOMEN'S
PROPERTY ACT OF 1870

> When the theory of the "Divine Right of Husbands"
> has followed to limbo that of the "Divine Right of
> Kings," . . . then will become possible a conjugal love
> and union nobler and more tender by far than can
> ever exist while such claims are even tacitly supposed.
>
> —Frances Power Cobbe,
> "Celibacy v. Marriage" (1862)

After the defeat of the married women's property bill of 1856, feminists concentrated most of their energies on increasing women's opportunities for education and employment. They judged that they would make greater headway in gaining a foothold for women in the public realm by focusing on women's education and employment (which were far from universally accepted) than by suggesting that all was not well with women's position in the home.[1] During the next decade there was a rapid proliferation of organizations promoting the expansion of women's opportunities outside the home, including the Society for Promoting the Employment of Women, the Female Middle-Class Emigration Society, the Workhouse Visiting Society, and the Ladies' Sanitary Association. In addition, publications such as the *English Woman's Journal* (1858–1864), the *Englishwoman's Review of Social and Industrial Questions* (1866–1906), and the *Victoria Magazine* (1863–1880) were essential to the development of feminist ideas and their communication to readers throughout Britain. These organizations and publications were sustained by a small but energetic network of friends and fellow-workers, which included letter writers, circulators of petitions, essayists, financial donors, and persons who had access to Members of Parliament. Frequently scholars chronicle the activities of the Victorian feminists as individual triumphs: Sophia Jex-Blake storming the medical schools, Emily Davies founding Girton College, Emily Faithfull creating the Victoria Press, and so forth. But

---

[1] Diane Mary Chase Worzala, "The Langham Place Circle: The Beginnings of the Organized Women's Movement in England, 1854–1870" (Ph.D. diss., University of Wisconsin, 1982), 124.

49

far from acting in isolation, these and other women were part of a multifaceted movement for women's emancipation.

This chapter examines the ideas and activities of the network of feminists active in the cause of procuring a married women's property law. They saw such a measure as necessary for the recognition of equal rights for men and women, whether married or single, protection of working-class wives, and the transformation of marriage from a relationship of hierarchy and domination to one of reciprocity and friendship. The drafting of and lobbying for the married women's property statute was carried out primarily by members of the North of England circle of feminists centered in the Manchester area. During the course of Parliament's consideration of their bill, they saw their comprehensive measure to protect all forms of property reduced to a bill to protect women's earnings, particularly those of working-class women. The struggle to pass the Married Women's Property Act of 1870 clearly demonstrated the mutually reinforcing nature of women's subordination in the household and the polity, and revealed Parliament's determination to alter married women's legal status as little as possible.

THE IDEAS AND ACTIVITIES OF MARRIED WOMEN'S PROPERTY REFORMERS

The married women's property campaign had roots in other women's rights organizations of the late 1860s. One of these was the Kensington Society, formed by Emily Davies in the winter of 1865–1866 and named after the London neighborhood in which it met. Davies's intention was to draw together "persons above the average of thoughtfulness and intelligence who are interested in common subjects, but who have not many opportunities of mutual intercourse."[2] The Kensington Society brought together several groups of women interested in women's social, educational, and economic advancement: those from the Langham Place Circle (which had drawn up the married women's property petition of 1856, published the *English Woman's Journal*, and formed the Society for Promoting the Employment of Women), including Barbara Leigh Smith Bodichon, Jessie Boucherett, and Frances Power Cobbe; those involved in women's education like Elizabeth Wolstenholme; and those from the circle around John Stuart Mill, including Helen Taylor, his stepdaughter.[3]

[2] "Family Chronicle," 423, Davies Papers, quoted in Worzala, "The Langham Place Circle," 283.
[3] Worzala, "The Langham Place Circle," 283–84.

In November 1865 the Society discussed the question, "Is the extension of the parliamentary franchise to women desirable, and if so, under what conditions?" After a heated discussion, a vote showed that the majority of those present favored some sort of women's franchise. Barbara Leigh Smith Bodichon (she had married Eugène Bodichon, a physician residing in Algeria, in 1859) immediately wanted to organize a campaign for the vote, but was deterred by Emily Davies's warning that it would hurt the efforts of those working for women's education.[4] In the spring of 1866, when Parliament began debating the bill that would eventually become the great Reform Act of 1867, extending the franchise to borough householders (that is, to virtually all English men except agricultural day-laborers), however, Bodichon could not be contained. John Stuart Mill had been elected to Parliament in 1865, where he served until 1868; his election gave feminists a highly respected (although not politically powerful) spokesperson in the House of Commons. During the month of May 1866, Bodichon and several friends collected 1,499 signatures on a petition for women's suffrage.[5] Mill presented the petition to the Commons on June 7, 1866. During the following winter, women's suffrage committees were formed in Manchester, London, and Edinburgh.[6]

The year 1867 was one of extraordinary activity among feminists, and nowhere more so than in the Manchester circle, which not only took up suffrage, but was to provide the driving force for a married women's property bill. A short-lived Manchester society for women's suffrage had been formed in 1865, and its members collected signatures for the suffrage petition presented by John Stuart Mill. On January 11, 1867, the Manchester Women's Suffrage Society was reconstituted by Jacob Bright, Rev. S. A. Steinthal, Mrs. Elizabeth Gloyne, Max Kyllman, Elizabeth Wolstenholme, and Dr. Louis Borchardt.[7]

[4] Ibid., 284–86.

[5] On May 9, 1866, Bodichon wrote to Helen Taylor expressing her desire to start a petition compaign, and asking Taylor what she and Mill thought might be expedient and appropriate language. Taylor responded that Mill would present a petition to Parliament if it contained at least one hundred signatures, as fewer names would look foolish and do more harm than good. See Barbara L. S. Bodichon to Helen Taylor, 9 May 1866, John Stuart Mill-Harriet Taylor Mill Collection, British Library of Political and Economic Science (BLPES).

[6] Helen Blackburn, *Women's Suffrage: A Record of the Women's Suffrage Movement in the British Isles with Biographical Sketches of Miss Becker* (London: Williams & Norgate, 1902), 58–59, 63–65.

[7] Blackburn, *Women's Suffrage*, 59. The Manchester suffrage society's claim to have existed since 1865 (and therefore to be the oldest British suffrage society, a claim disputed by the London society), is discussed in Constance Rover, *Women's Suffrage and*

The Manchester suffrage society expanded in February, when Lydia Becker and Richard Pankhurst became active members.[8]

The married women's property campaign originated in this Manchester (or more precisely North of England) circle of feminists, drawn from both the Manchester Women's Suffrage Society and those who had worked for women's higher education.[9] The groundwork for a parliamentary campaign to pass a married women's property bill was laid by Elizabeth Wolstenholme, Elizabeth Gloyne, Jessie Boucherett of London, and Josephine Butler of Liverpool. Wolstenholme was headmistress of a girls' boarding school near Manchester, and Gloyne was president of the Manchester Board of Schoolmistresses. Boucherett was a member of the Langham Place Circle and had founded the Society for Promoting the Employment of Women in 1859. Butler, the wife of the Rev. George Butler, principal of Liverpool College, was deeply involved in rescue work for prostitutes as well as in the women's education movement. In the autumn of 1867, Wolstenholme, Gloyne, Butler, and others had founded the North of England Council

---

Party Politics in Britain 1866–1914 (London: Routledge & Kegan Paul, 1962), 6 n. 1.

Jacob Bright was the Radical M.P. for Manchester, and the brother of John Bright, M.P. for Birmingham. A firm advocate of a wide array of women's rights measures, he was one of women's strongest parliamentary supporters. His wife, Ursula Mellor Bright, acted as Treasurer of the Married Women's Property Committee from 1876 to 1882. Rev. S. A. Steinthal served on the Council of the Social Science Association and was involved in many social issues in the Manchester area, including promoting Mechanics' Institutes for working people. Mrs. Elizabeth Gloyne was president of the Manchester Board of Schoolmistresses and a founding member of the North of England Council for Promoting the Higher Education of Women. Both Max Kyllman and his wife were involved in early suffrage activity. Elizabeth Wolstenholme, headmistress of a small girls' boarding school in Congleton, had been one of nine women to testify before the Schools Inquiry Commission in 1865. About Dr. Louis Borchardt I have been unable to find more information.

[8] Lydia Becker, whose interest in women's rights was sparked by hearing Barbara Bodichon's paper on women's suffrage at the Social Science Association meeting in October 1866, devoted the rest of her life to the suffrage movement. In 1870 Becker began publication of the *Women's Suffrage Journal*, which she edited until her death in 1890. She was elected to the Manchester school board in 1870, one of four women elected that year (the first year that women were eligible to vote and hold office), and she served on the board until her death. Richard Marsden Pankhurst drafted the 1868 married women's property bill, the amendment to the Municipal Franchise Act of 1869 giving women householders the right to vote in municipal elections, and the 1870 women's disabilities removal bill (women's suffrage bill).

[9] A collection of seventeen letters written between 3 January and 30 March 1867, from Emily Davies of London to Lydia Becker of Manchester, gives some indication of the intense level of discussion and activity that accompanied the formation of the women's suffrage committee in Manchester (Manchester Society for Women's Suffrage Collection, Manchester Central Library).

for Promoting the Higher Education of Women.[10] They asked Richard Pankhurst, a radical Manchester attorney, to draft the married women's property legislation in 1868.[11]

Letters written by Lydia Becker between March 21 and November 29, 1868, reveal both the constant exchange of letters and visits among Becker, Wolstenholme, Butler, and Pankhurst, and the extent to which they intermingled their work on suffrage, married women's property, and education. On June 8 Becker advised Wolstenholme to change the language that the latter had proposed for the constitution of the Married Women's Property Committee as it too closely paralleled that of the suffrage society's constitution: new language was especially desirable since "you hope to enlist the sympathies of many opponents of the franchise movement." On July 10 another letter from Becker to Wolstenholme cautioned her not to combine suffrage and married women's property meetings, but to hold the sessions on property either before or after those on suffrage, so that those who found suffrage too radical could be enlisted in the married women's property campaign.[12]

A long and heartfelt letter from Becker to Josephine Butler, urging her to give up her philanthropic work with prostitutes for political work, provides a fascinating glimpse of the personalities and priorities of the North of England women involved in the resurgence of political feminism:

> I grudge your effort being so much turned towards things that noble, and praiseworthy in themselves, and arising out of your deep sympathy with suffering, are yet but *palliatives*. You are

[10] The North of England Council aimed to improve the condition of women by popularizing the Oxford and Cambridge local examinations (which had been opened to girls through the efforts of Emily Davies and Barbara Bodichon), promoting series of local lectures for women delivered by university teachers, and persuading Cambridge University to establish special higher examinations for women (this last was anathema to Davies, who feared it would draw support away from the notion of equal education for men and women). Members of the North of England Council also spurred the establishment of a residence in Cambridge for women preparing to take the higher examinations; it became Newnham College.

[11] The final *Report* of the Married Women's Property Committee (MWPC) says that the MWPC acted "in ignorance of the labour of their predecessors" of the 1850s, and this was probably true of Butler, Gloyne, and Wolstenholme. But Boucherett would certainly have known of the earlier effort. It is very likely that Elizabeth Wolstenholme Elmy wrote the *Report*, and that it reflected her remembrance of the formation of the Married Women's Property Committee. See Married Women's Property Committee, *Final Report*, 18 November 1882 (Manchester: A. Ireland, 1882), 12.

[12] Lydia Becker to Elizabeth Wolstenholme, 8 June 1868 and 10 July 1868, Manchester Society for Women's Suffrage, Manchester Central Library.

spending your means and your strength in rescuing a few brands from the burning—and I want you rather to turn your effort to putting out the fire!!!

Why are so many women starving? asked Becker rhetorically. "Because women are trained to be dependent on men, and then men leave them without means of subsistence. . . . Why are men able to treat women in this way? Because women have no political power." Since Butler knew that women's suffering was related to their lack of political power, she would have done better to work for women's franchise in Liverpool than for an Industrial Home. "You can never make any impression on the mass of human misery, by mere charitable efforts to save a few individuals," was Becker's trenchant observation.[13]

Becker's attribution of prostitution to women's lack of economic and particularly political power, not to moral weakness (which many contemporary social reformers cited as its cause), shows the link feminists drew among all of their reform activities and women's disfranchisement. In part to mask that radical critique and to dissociate other activities from the suffrage campaign, in part to conserve and channel their energies, the feminists soon divided the responsibilities they had shared so extensively in 1867 and 1868. Before long Butler devoted her energies to the movement to repeal the Contagious Diseases Acts (Anne Jemima Clough succeeded her as head of the North of England Council for Promoting the Higher Education of Women), Wolstenholme became sole secretary of the Married Women's Property Committee, and Becker headed the Manchester National Society for Women's Suffrage and published the *Women's Suffrage Journal.* Jessie Boucherett lived in London, where she was deeply involved in work for women's employment; she appears not to have played an active part in the later work of the Married Women's Property Committee.

As Barbara Leigh Smith had turned to the Law Amendment Society to make her views of married women's property known in parliamentary circles in the 1850s, so Wolstenholme, Butler, Gloyne, and Boucherett used the podium, the prestige, and the expertise of the National Association for the Promotion of Social Science to advance their cause. Several men who were deeply committed to women's causes were members of the Social Science Association, as it was commonly called, and the Association became an active partner in pressuring Parliament to enact a married women's property law. The Social Science Associa-

[13] Lydia Becker to Josephine Butler, 19 October 1868, Manchester Society for Women's Suffrage Collection, Manchester Central Library.

tion had been founded in 1856 by Lord Brougham and others to bring together the large number of groups working for social reform, and it soon incorporated the Law Amendment Society. Members of the association held yearly conferences from 1857 to 1884 to discuss the issues they deemed to be important to the moral, social, and political reform of England. Although its influence declined during its later years, until the mid-1870s the Social Science Association drew together social reformers of diverse professions—doctors, ministers, lawyers, Members of Parliament, civil servants, businessmen, educators, and trade unionists—to discuss proposals for reform from juvenile reformatories to proportional representation to sanitary conditions in the colonies.[14]

The Social Science Association had, from its inception, opened its doors to women. This was due to the combined influence of Lord Brougham and George Hastings, general secretary of the association, who was an early supporter of women's rights and a good friend of Barbara Bodichon.[15] In 1859 Hastings appointed Isa Craig, a member of the Langham Place circle, to be the assistant secretary of the Social Science Association, thereby assuring the feminists another ready ear at the association. In a time when women rarely spoke in public, at least one and often several women presented papers on some aspect of the women's movement at almost every meeting between 1858 and 1870.[16] Meetings of the Social Science Association drew some women, such as Becker and Isabella Tod, into the women's rights movement. Becker had been inspired by Bodichon's paper on suffrage at the 1866 meeting in Manchester; Tod, backbone of the women's movement in

[14] Lawrence Ritt, "The Victorian Conscience in Action: The National Association for the Promotion of Social Science 1857–1886" (Ph.D. diss., Columbia University, 1959).
[15] Lee Holcombe, *Wives and Property: Reform of the Married Women's Property Law in Nineteenth-Century England* (Toronto: University of Toronto Press, 1983), 125.
[16] Worzala, "The Langham Place Circle," 181. For example, in Dublin in 1861 Jane Crow gave a paper on the Society for Promoting the Employment of Women (SPEW), Emily Faithfull on female compositors, Jessie Boucherett on local SPEWs, Mrs. Overend on remunerative employment, Maria Rye on the emigration of educated women, Mrs. Bayley on the employment of women, Frances Power Cobbe on the sick in workhouses, and Mary Carpenter on pauper children. In 1859 in Bradford both Bessie Parkes and Jessie Boucherett read papers on women's employment, as did many others in subsequent years. In 1865 in Sheffield, Dorothea Beale and Elizabeth Wolstenholme addressed sessions on girls' education. At the 1866 meeting in Manchester, Barbara Bodichon advocated giving the vote to women freeholders and householders, and in 1868 in Birmingham Emily Davies outlined her plan for a women's college. See National Association for the Promotion of Social Science (NAPSS), *Transactions*.

Ireland, was moved by papers at the Belfast meeting in 1867 to devote herself thereafter to a wide range of women's causes.[17]

Given the decade-long connection between women reformers and the Social Science Association, it was natural for those interested in married women's property reform to turn to the Social Science Association to publicize their cause and to develop a proposal which could be brought before Parliament. At the October 1867 annual meeting, George Hastings read a paper advocating passage of a law that would leave a married woman in the position of a feme sole.[18] In December, Wolstenholme, Butler, Boucherett, and Gloyne presented the Executive Council of the Social Science Association with a memorial with three hundred signatures, and asked the association to take up the cause of married women's property law reform. The Committee on Jurisprudence and Amendment of the Law (chaired by Frederic Hill, younger brother of the Matthew Davenport Hill who had helped Barbara Leigh Smith draft *A Brief Summary of the . . . Laws* in 1854) produced a bill, drafted by Richard Pankhurst, which was essentially the same as that which Sir Erskine Perry had introduced in Parliament in 1857.[19] After the Social Science Association's annual congress in Birmingham in the fall of 1868, at which the jurisprudence section adopted a resolution calling on the Council to "continue its exertions to obtain from Parliament a remedial measure," advocates of the property law persuaded Mr. George Shaw Lefevre, M.P., to sponsor the measure in the House of Commons.[20]

In the meantime, women's rights activists had set about forming a Married Women's Property Committee to pressure Parliament from without. The *Final Report* of the Married Women's Property Committee reports simply that "a general committee with a small executive was immediately formed to promote action in support of the Bill, which . . . was finally constituted in April, 1868, as the Married Women's Property Committee, with Miss Becker as Treasurer, and Miss Wolstenholme as Secretary of the Executive."[21] The formation of the

[17] "Miss Isabella Tod: Social Reformer," *Women's Penny Paper* (October 1889), 1–2.

[18] NAPSS, *Transactions* (1867), 292; *Englishwoman's Review* 1 (October 1867): 320–21.

[19] Holcombe, *Wives and Property*, 166, 125; *Englishwoman's Review* 2 (April 1868): 418.

[20] NAPSS, *Transactions* (1868), 39, 275–81, see also 238–49.

[21] MWPC, *Final Report* (1882), 13. Early *Reports* and letterhead stationery list Josephine Butler and Elizabeth Wolstenholme as joint secretaries; Butler soon devoted herself almost exclusively, at least in public, to the agitation to repeal the Contagious Dis-

Committee was more arduous than the *Final Report* indicates. Elizabeth Wolstenholme had made married women's property her particular concern, and on May 3 she wrote to Helen Taylor asking her to lend her name to the Married Women's Property Committee.[22] But Wolstenholme apparently did not feel she could be permanent secretary (probably due to ill health, to which Lydia Becker's letters frequently refer), and on June 8 Lydia Becker wrote to ask her whether Jessie Boucherett might undertake the job. The same letter cautioned Wolstenholme that the government of the organization was not yet clearly spelled out: "Who appoints the committees? Are they to be *self-appointed?*" Becker was also concerned that it would be difficult to conduct the property campaign from Manchester: "Whom have you to depend upon in London—that you think it safe to trust the *life* of the Society in the South?"[23] Nonetheless, Wolstenholme continued at her post, rounding up witnesses to appear before the Select Committee on Married Women's Property, which was formed to hold hearings on Shaw Lefevre's bill during the summer.[24] Other married women's property committees were soon formed in Belfast, Dublin, and Birmingham, and one of the great women's rights campaigns of the Victorian period, which would have repercussions in other areas of the law as well, was launched.

Coming as they did from work for women's employment, higher education, and suffrage rights, it is not surprising that those who advocated reform of property law relied extensively on arguments about the equal right of men and women to control their own property regardless of marital status. Their program for legal reform involved substituting laws based on a strict gender neutrality for the different rights and obligations of men and women under existing marriage laws. The reformers argued that the automatic expropriation of an adult woman's property upon marriage violated the individual right to own property, particularly the fruits of one's own labor. The only distinction they would have maintained was a husband's obligation to support his wife, an obligation which they saw as resting on his vastly greater ability to earn money and her involvement in childbearing and child-rearing.

eases Acts (MWPC, 3rd and 4th annual *Reports* [1869 and 1870], and the Mill-Taylor Collection, BLPES).

[22] Elizabeth Wolstenholme to Helen Taylor, 3 May 1868, Mill-Taylor Collection, BLPES.

[23] Lydia Becker to Elizabeth Wolstenholme, 8 June 1868 (two letters), Manchester Society for Women's Suffrage Collection, Manchester Central Library.

[24] Ibid., and 21 June 1868.

In addition to their "equal rights" argument, however, these feminists advanced two other important grounds for seeking reform of the laws governing married women's property. First, existing law sanctioned the existence of two sets of legal rules, those of law and equity, and subjected working-class wives to legal constraints that did not apply to well-to-do women. Second, the transformation of the marriage relationship itself was important, and could not take place without first establishing the legal equality of husband and wife. Only if there were no legally enforced hierarchy or precedence between spouses could love flourish, for there could be no true intimacy between superior and subordinate, "master" and "slave." These feminists emphasized equal rights because they desired both greater personal autonomy *and* greater spousal unity. As Butler wrote, "[T]he opening out of a freer life for women would ultimately . . . tend to the increase of marriage, for the worth and therefore the attractiveness of women would be increased, and undoubtedly it would tend to the preservation of all that we wish to preserve in existing homes."[25] Autonomy and unity were not only compatible, but the latter was impossible without the former.

The argument that the common law rules amounted to the unjustifiable expropriation of a married woman's property was set forth wittily and memorably in Frances Power Cobbe's "Criminals, Idiots, Women and Minors: Is the Classification Sound?" published in *Fraser's Magazine* in 1868. Single women held property, contracted, and sued and were sued, and it was unjust that upon marriage these rights were taken from them. The only other persons who forfeited such capacity through their own actions were felons, those convicted of the most serious criminal acts. Because of their inherent incapacity, idiots and minors were not allowed to hold property in their own names or to bind themselves by contract. In an engaging flight of fancy, Cobbe imagined a visitor from another planet coming to earth and in the course of his stay asking to have England's marriage customs explained: " 'Pardon me; I must seem to you so stupid! Why is the property of the woman who commits Murder, and the property of the woman who commits Matrimony, dealt with alike by your law?' " At another point in the essay Cobbe brushed aside the vexing and divisive question of whether women were men's equals in intellect or strength as irrelevant to the question of whether it was just that they be deprived of property rights when they married. " '[L]et me be . . . your

²⁵ Josephine Butler, ed., *Woman's Work and Woman's Culture: A Series of Essays* (London: Macmillan, 1869), xxxiii.

inferior,' " Cobbe wrote. " 'So long as you allow I possess moral responsibility and sufficient intellect to know right from wrong . . . I am quite content. It is *only* as a moral and intellectual being I claim my civil rights. Can you deny them to me on that ground?' "[26] The same point had been made by Anna Jameson, Caroline Norton, and Eliza Lynn in 1855: women might be the weaker vessels, but they nonetheless had the right to the fruits of their own labor. J. S. Mill used a stronger image to express his outrage over the confiscation of a woman's property upon marriage, arguing in *The Subjection of Women* that the "wife's position under the common law of England is worse than that of slaves in the laws of many countries: by the Roman law, for example, a slave might have his peculium, which to a certain extent the law guaranteed to him for his exclusive use," while a married woman in England had *no* income of her own.[27]

The existence of two completely different sets of rules governing the property of married women was also a standing condemnation of the common law in feminists' eyes. Under equity, any woman rich enough to have the legal documents drawn up could have her "separate property" or "separate estate" protected by a trust. Advocates of married women's property reform pointed to the common practice among the well-to-do of creating equitable trusts for their daughters prior to marriage as evidence that Members of Parliament thought that their own daughters, sisters, and wives should have their own property, albeit under the control of a trustee. Indeed, if a wife had a "chose in action" (such as a debt owed her) which was under the jurisdiction of the Court of Chancery, the Court would not let her husband reduce her chose in action to possession (that is, collect the debt, which he had a legal right to do and which would then be his), until he had settled a portion of the funds on his wife. This was called the wife's "equity to a settlement." The rule in such cases was to settle half of the property on the wife and children, and the remainder on the husband, although the amount could vary according to circumstances.[28] Although the practice of "equity to a settlement" reflected the notion that equity courts were supposed to *protect* women and children from those who

[26] Frances Power Cobbe, "Criminals, Idiots, Women and Minors: Is the Classification Sound?" (Manchester: A. Ireland, 1869), reprinted from *Fraser's Magazine* (December 1868), 5, 27.

[27] J. S. Mill, *The Subjection of Women*, in *Essays on Sex Equality*, ed. Alice Rossi (Chicago: University of Chicago Press, 1970), chap. 2, 158–59.

[28] Sir Thomas Barrett-Lennard, *The Position in Law of Women* (London: Waterlow & Sons, 1833), 78; Herbert N. Mozley, "The Property Disabilities of a Married Woman and Other Legal Effects of Marriage," in Butler, *Woman's Work*, 195–96.

might take advantage of them—including in this case husbands—it nonetheless gave married women who could appeal to equity a legal recourse unknown to their poorer sisters. Proponents of reform argued that it was an affront to English justice that there should be two distinct systems of property law, with equity governing the property of upper-class women and the common law that of working-class wives. What was needed was a single statutory scheme which would give *all* women the same capacity to manage their own affairs that was at present enjoyed only by the rich.

Reformers invoked the practical plight of working-class wives as well as theoretical considerations of justice to make the case for eliminating gender distinctions in property law. Several essays published in *All the Year Round*, edited by Charles Dickens, attempted to show that many poorer women were at the mercy of lazy and dissolute husbands, who acquired their wives' property upon marriage and proceeded to squander it on drink, horses, or mistresses. "Slaves of the Ring" told the story of Lucy Bloxham, a poor landlady's daughter who married the son of a country squire only to find that he lacked the accomplishments and self-discipline to maintain himself and his wife, so that "Lucy's nimble fingers" and then "her natty little milliner's shop" were their sole source of income. Despite the fact that Lucy Bloxham earned enough to support them and even to put away savings, "there is little doubt that the Gazette and the workhouse will be the ultimate fate of both." Polly Comber was similarly destitute, "cursed with a husband who left her, years ago, but who turns up periodically to break up her home, to sell the bits of furniture she has gathered together laboriously, to seize upon her earnings, and then to wallow in the mire again, leaving her to begin her nest-building for herself and the little children anew." Giving such women control of their property, said the author, was "an attempt at emancipating slaves who are in our midst."[29]

Many of these workers for legal reform hoped that the changes they sought would not only help the poor but would also spur changes in the marriage relationship itself. Although they differed on much else, they agreed that the corruption of contemporary marriage stemmed from the fact that many women married from economic and social necessity rather than from choice; many writers implicitly compared marriage to prostitution. Eliza Lynn Linton, no unqualified friend of women, argued in "Womanly Dependence" that if married women

were independent of man's support, and could feed and clothe themselves unhelped, and maintain their own social status unassisted, they could make better terms for themselves and compel a

[29] *All the Year Round* (4 July 1868), 86–88.

more just and liberal treatment. . . . As it is, men have the right to demand from their wives absolute attention to their wishes, because they are their property, their dependent creatures whom they feed and clothe in return for certain services.[30]

Women fortunate and wise enough to have formed love matches would not desire financial independence from men. But other women, not so fortunate, needed to be able to control their own property. As she had in protesting Caroline Norton's fate in the 1850s, Linton did not advocate married women's property reform as a logical consequence of women's fundamental equality with men, but rather as a form of self-protection against men in an imperfect world.

Julia Wedgwood, writing on suffrage, pointed out that the "social framework" made marriage "woman's only career."[31] Josephine Butler remarked on "the insipidity or the material necessities of so many women's lives [which] make them ready to accept almost any man who may offer himself."[32] The *Victoria Magazine* decried women's poverty, which "makes any change welcome; the custom that makes marriage the only means by which a woman's relations can free themselves of the burden of her maintenance."[33] Both Frances Power Cobbe and John Stuart Mill called marriage a "Hobson's choice" for a woman, that is, she must marry or have no useful, socially recognized, and remunerative occupation.[34] John Boyd Kinnear explicitly described marriage as a kind of harlotry. By confining women's aspirations to marriage, society increased the pressure to get married until it occupied all of a woman's energy. To anyone who doubted this harsh judgment Kinnear said that he need only

frequent the fashionable London drive at the fashionable hour, and there he will see the richest and most shameful woman-market in the world. Men stand by the rails, criticising with perfect

---

[30] Eliza Lynn Linton, "Womanly Dependence," in *Ourselves: A Series of Essays on Women*, 2d ed. (London: G. Routledge & Sons, 1870), 226–27.

[31] Julia Wedgwood, "Female Suffrage, Considered Chiefly with Regard to Its Indirect Results," in Butler, *Woman's Work*, 261.

[32] Butler, Introduction to *Woman's Work*, xxx.

[33] *Victoria Magazine* 10 (January 1868): 198.

[34] Frances Power Cobbe, "What Shall We Do with Our Old Maids?" in *Essays on the Pursuits of Women*, ed. Frances Power Cobbe (London: Emily Faithfull, 1863), 64; J. S. Mill, *Subjection of Women*, chap. 1, 156. The praises of celibacy which appeared at the time were a reaction to this notion of marriage as a woman's only career. Josephine Butler would not believe that "it is every woman's duty to marry in this age of the world" (Butler, Introduction to *Woman's Work*, xxxv). See also Martha Vicinus, *Independent Women: Work and Community for Single Women, 1850–1929* (Chicago: University of Chicago Press, 1985).

impartiality and equal freedom while women drive slowly past, some for hire, some for sale—in marriage—these last with their careful mothers at their side, to reckon the value of the biddings and prevent the lots from going off below the reserved price.[35]

The chilling picture of Edith Skewton and her mother in Charles Dickens's *Dombey and Son* (1848) involved a mother and daughter involved in just such a marriage auction.

Men's and women's unequal resources, particularly women's inability to be economically independent, led feminists to assert that legal and social constraints made marriage a relation of domination and subordination, regardless of the attitudes or wishes of the marriage partners. It was this power relationship that they set out to expose and to change. Indeed, the transformation of marriage was a deep and abiding goal of Victorian feminists. The feminists' determination to change a relationship of dominance and submission to one of equality was better understood by some of their opponents than by some of their liberal allies, who paid attention only to the language of individual rights used in arguments for property law reform.

Cobbe believed that what was really at the bottom of the opposition to married women's possession of their own property was the feeling that "a woman's whole life and being, her soul, body, time, property, thought and care, ought to be given to her husband; that nothing short of such absorption in him and his interests makes her a true wife; and that when she is thus absorbed even a mediocre character and inferior intellect can make a man happy." Even supposing, asked Cobbe, that such a marriage were desirable, was this the way to attain it? "Is perfect love to be called out by perfect dependence? Does an empty purse necessarily imply a full heart?" The law treated husband and wife like tarantula spiders, one of whom gobbled up the other after mating. (Cobbe did not seem to be aware that it is the female tarantula who consumes the male.) Cobbe proposed the alternative model of loving friends, sharing a common house and a common purse.[36]

Josephine Butler was convinced that the opposition to married women's property reform was motivated by "a secret dread" that women's claims would "revolutionize society [and] our *Homes*."[37] John Stuart Mill believed that "[women's] disabilities [in law] are only clung to in order to maintain their subordination in domestic life; be-

[35] John Boyd Kinnear, "The Social Position of Women in the Present Age," in Butler, *Woman's Work*, 354.

[36] Cobbe, "Criminals, Idiots, Women and Minors," 18–20.

[37] Butler, Introduction to *Woman's Work*, xxv.

cause the generality of the male sex cannot yet tolerate the idea of living with an equal."[38] Priscilla Bright McLaren maintained that men resisted married women's property reform because "it was a question of power. They could not bear that the wife should have power."[39]

Feminists envisioned a transformation that would substitute marital "friendship" for spousal hierarchy. As Wedgwood put it, "All mutual affection is so good a thing that we only estimate the power of this form of it by comparing it with a marriage which is also a friendship; ... how much marriage loses in being made the sole opportunity of communion between the two halves of mankind." The exclusion of women from the work of the world, "men's work," prevented men and women from meeting on shared ground, and the unequal intellectual as well as economic resources that men and women brought to marriage "indicate a disastrous side of our stage of civilization."[40] Butler asserted that what people need is "*love* itself—the love which is based on a deep respect—instead of those mimicries and desecrations of the name of love which prevail."[41]

John Stuart Mill composed the most sustained reflection on the necessity for transforming the relationship of husband and wife into a true friendship. The rather visionary fourth chapter of *The Subjection of Women* was devoted to "the ideal of marriage," which was "a union of thoughts and inclinations" that created a "foundation of solid friendship" between husband and wife.[42] For Mill, the "true virtue of human beings is the fitness to live together as equals." Such equality required that individuals "[claim] nothing for themselves but what they as freely concede to every one else," that they regard command as "an exceptional necessity," and that they prefer whenever possible "the society of those with whom leading and following can be alternate and reciprocal."[43] Women were to be regarded as equals not only to fulfill the demand for individual rights and to enable them to survive in the public world of work, but also in order that women and men could form ethical relations of the highest order. Men and women alike had to "learn to cultivate their strongest sympathy with an equal in

[38] J. S. Mill, *Subjection of Women*, chap. 3, 181.

[39] NAPSS, *Transactions* (1880), 199.

[40] Wedgwood, "Female Suffrage," in Butler, *Women's Work*, 262, 260–61.

[41] Butler, Introduction to *Woman's Work*, xxxiii.

[42] J. S. Mill, *Subjection of Women*, chap. 4, 231, 233. On Mill's ideal of marital friendship, see Mary Lyndon Shanley, "Marital Slavery and Friendship: John Stuart Mill's *Subjection of Women*," *Political Theory* 9 (May 1981): 229–47.

[43] J. S. Mill, *Subjection of Women*, chap. 2, 174–75.

rights and in cultivation."[44] This picture of reciprocity and even of the shifting of responsiblity according to need was all the more remarkable because some feminists, such as Jameson and Cobbe, believed in the natural and inevitable complementariness of male and female personalities and roles.[45]

This ideal of marital friendship stood in sharp contrast to Mill's descriptions of marriages of his day. Men's legal treatment of women was not only unjust, but self-defeating and even self-destructive. Most women were confined to domestic concerns and had no opportunity for the self-development that comes from citizen activity. As a result women became dull, petty, or unprincipled.[46] The cost to men was less apparent but no less real; in seeking a reflection of themselves in the consciousness of these stunted women, men deceived, deluded, and limited themselves. The most corrupting element of male domination of women was that men learned to "worship their own will as such a grand thing that it is actually the law for another rational being." A boy might be "the most frivolous and empty or the most ignorant and stolid of mankind," but "by the mere fact of being born a male" he was encouraged to think that "he is by right the superior of all and every one of an entire half of the human race: including probably some whose real superiority to himself he has daily or hourly to feel." Such self-worship, which arose at an early age, warped a boy's natural understanding of himself and his relationship to others. By contrast women were taught "to live for others" and "to have no life but in their affections," and then further to confine their affections to "the men with whom they are connected, or to the children who constitute an additional indefeasible tie between them and a man."[47] The result of their upbringings was that women and men came to marriage with distorted sensibilities and an inability to speak and act openly and truthfully. The corruption of the relationship was shared by both superior and subordinate, by master and slave, and the harm engendered by unequal relationships was not confined to the home. A man who worshipped his own will as a law for his wife developed habits of dom-

[44] Ibid., chap. 4, 236.

[45] As early as 1833 Mill had expressed (in a letter to Thomas Carlyle dated October 5) his belief that "the highest masculine and feminine" characters were without any real distinction. See *Earlier Letters*, ed. Francis E. Mineka, vol. 12 of *The Collected Works of John Stuart Mill* (Toronto: University of Toronto Press, 1963), 184 (hereafter referred to as *C.W.*).

[46] J. S. Mill, *Subjection of Women*, chap. 2, 168; chap. 4, 238. See also Mill's speech on the Reform Act of 1867, 3 Hansard 189 (20 May 1867), 824.

[47] J. S. Mill, *Subjection of Women*, chap. 2, 172; chap. 4, 218; chap. 1, 141.

ination that became hard to curb in other situations. A woman whose life was confined to her affections risked losing her ability for more abstract reflection; she could neither contribute to public discussion nor help her husband and children take principled stands.

Despite the radical nature of the feminists' critique of marital domination and subordination, by and large they accepted the notion that, in a marriage, women were responsible for the care of household and children, and men for providing the family income. Cobbe believed that once marriage had been reshaped by new laws, the education and the moral virtues of men and women, like their legal rights, would be identical, but their duties would of necessity differ. They would learn that "no longer must morality be divided between them; Truth and Courage for him, and Chastity and Patience for her; but that she, too, must be true as an honourable *man* is true, and brave in her own sphere of duty as he is brave in his."[48] Mill also accepted the traditonal division of labor within the household, despite his pleas for marital equality and friendship. "When the support of the family depends . . . on earnings, the common arrangement, by which the man earns the income and the wife superintends the domestic expenditure, seems to me in general the most suitable division of labour between the two persons"; it is not "a desirable custom, that the wife should contribute by her labour to the income of the family."[49] Women should take care of any children of the marriage; repeatedly Mill called it the "care which . . . nobody else takes," the one vocation in which there is "nobody to compete with them," and the occupation which "cannot be fulfilled by others."[50] It seemed to Mill that it would be unusual, although not impossible, for a woman to combine household duties and a public life: "Like a man when he chooses a profession, so, when a woman marries, it may be in general understood that she makes choice of the management of a household, and the bringing up of a family, as the first call upon her exertions . . . and that she renounces . . . all [other occupations] which are not consistent with the requirements of this."[51]

Most advocates of women's rights agreed with Cobbe and Mill that legal equality of opportunity would solve the problem of women's subjection, even while the sexual division of labor in the household and the inequality of income remained intact. In this expectation they

[48] Frances Power Cobbe, "Celibacy v. Marriage," in *Essays on the Pursuits of Women*, 55–57.

[49] J. S. Mill, *The Subjection of Women*, chap. 2, 178–79.

[50] Ibid., chap. 2, 178, 183; chap. 4, 241.

[51] Ibid., chap. 4, 179.

were quite wrong. Household duties and repeated pregnancies made continuous or full-time work outside the home impossible for most married women. This meant that only by claiming part of her husband's income did a married woman have any financial resources, and these were scarcely her "independent" means. Similarly, women did not achieve equal educational opportunity when they were finally admitted to the universities. Without access to professional employment women were cut off from firsthand knowledge of business or public affairs. Should a married woman's husband die or leave her, the full extent of her economic vulnerability was clear; only by remarrying could she again lay claim to part of a man's income.

A good deal of criticism has been aimed at Victorian feminists—Mill in particular—for accepting the sexual division of labor in the household and the inequality of economic and other resources which that entailed.[52] This criticism, while partially justified, overlooks the nature of the feminists' commitment to equality in marriage, which was of a different and higher theoretical order than their acceptance of a continued sexual division of labor in the family. Their belief that equality was a precondition to marital friendship was a profound theoretical tenet, resting on the assumption that among adults relationships of equality were better and more desirable than those of inequality; the human spirit could not develop to its fullest potential when kept in subordination to another human being. In contrast, their belief that friendship could be attained and sustained while women bore nearly exclusive responsibility for the home might be modified or even abandoned if experience proved it to be wrong. In this sense the feminists' belief that marital equality could exist while women took primary responsibility for the home was like Mill's view that the question of whether socialism was preferable to capitalism could not be settled by verbal argument alone but must "work itself out on an experimental scale, by actual trial."[53] The view that equality might exist where married men and women moved in different spheres of activity was a proposition

[52] See, for example, Julia Annas, "Mill and the Subjection of Women," *Philosophy* 52 (1977): 179–94; Leslie F. Goldstein, "Mill, Marx, and Women's Liberation," *Journal of the History of Philosophy* 18 (1980): 319–34. Richard W. Krouse, "Patriarchal Liberalism and Beyond: From John Stuart Mill to Harriet Taylor," in *The Family in Political Thought*, ed. Jean Bethke Elshtain (Amherst: University of Massachusetts Press, 1982), 145–72, is more sensitive to the inherent tension in Mill's thought about women in the household.

[53] J. S. Mill, *Chapters on Socialism* (1879), in *Essays on Economics and Society*, ed. John M. Robson, in *C.W.*, 5:736.

subject to demonstration; marital equality itself was a moral imperative.

The feminists' attack on the common law rules governing married women's property was firmly rooted in liberal principles such as the sanctity of private property and the equality of rights under the law. The reliance on liberalism was a double-edged sword: on the one hand, it was difficult for Parliament to reject measures that claimed to rectify unequal legal treatment (although Parliament frequently managed to find ways to do so); on the other hand, feminists spoke and wrote as if the enactment of legal equality by itself would bring about equality between husband and wife, ignoring the profound effect of the sexual division of labor both inside and outside the home on men's and women's occupations and resources.

If their analysis of what was needed to *achieve* equality was partial and flawed, feminists' belief in the necessity of equalizing all of men's and women's legal rights retained a radical and subversive force. Women deserved higher education, full property rights whether married or single, the same grounds for divorce as men, and the vote. Under a regime of legal equality, men would no longer develop habits of self-indulgence and command, women would no longer be schooled in self-abnegation. Men and women would be partners in building families grounded in mutual respect and reciprocity, and would join in building more just institutions through public activity. These visionary goals, however, while motivating all of the feminists' efforts to reform marriage law, were seldom if ever heard when the married women's property bill was debated in Parliament.

PARLIAMENT AND MARRIED WOMEN'S PROPERTY REFORM: 1868–1870

Some feminists in Parliament, notably John Stuart Mill, Jacob Bright, and George Shaw Lefevre, shared the perspective of Butler, Wolstenholme, Cobbe, and others on the need to reform and reshape marriage. The main arguments heard in Parliament for a married women's property law, however, shifted the focus of the argument away from the relationship of husband and wife to an almost exclusive focus on the treatment of the poor under English law. Among feminists outside Parliament, married women's property might be a "woman's issue," but in the corridors of Westminster it was legislation for the laboring classes.

The married women's property bill was debated during three sessions before it became law in August 1870. The bill which was finally adopted departed so substantially from the measure originally sought by its proponents that they were reluctant to accept it. The Act did not provide that a married woman's property should be treated as if she were a feme sole, but only that certain kinds of property should be treated as a married woman's "separate estate." Only some of a wife's property was removed from her husband's control, and that by creating a fictional trust rather than by giving a married woman the same ability to control her property as her single sisters enjoyed. The friends of married women's property reform scarcely knew whether to regard the Married Women's Property Act of 1870 as a victory or a defeat, for while they had won recognition that the common law rules worked insupportable hardship on some women, they had failed to gain parliamentary endorsement of their contention that a woman's loss of her independent legal personality upon marriage was unjustifiable.

The arguments put forward as the bill moved through Parliament did not vary greatly from year to year. The opening debate in 1868 laid out the general lines of argument for that and subsequent years. George Shaw Lefevre, acting on behalf of the Social Science Association, introduced the married women's property bill in April; it was drafted by Richard Pankhurst, and cosponsored by John Stuart Mill and Russell Gurney. In introducing his bill, Shaw Lefevre reminded his listeners that one of the most telling arguments in Mill's speech for women's suffrage during the previous year had been the hardship caused by the present property laws. He believed that a married women's property law would be one of the first laws women would pass were they to gain the franchise, and he trusted that this Parliament would rectify the grievances of those who could not speak for themselves in Parliament. Shaw Lefevre then outlined the differences between equity and the common law with respect to marital property, noting that the recourse to equity had developed to the point where by means of marriage settlements, "the wealthy classes, almost without exception, escaped from the operation of the Common Law." No man of property would allow his daughter to marry without a settlement, "no matter how favourable appearances might be." The "humbler classes," however, could not take advantage of equity, and "the consequences were often disastrous." Of 3.2 million wives in England, some eight hundred thousand were employed, or one in every four. Working-class women did not have the property to make a marriage settlement, and they did not legally possess their own wages. Extending the Divorce Act's provisions for protection orders would not help such women, because many would not bring their domestic quarrels before a third party, and even if they did overcome their reticence, by the time the protection order was issued the damage would often be done.

Shaw Lefevre therefore did not propose to extend the exceptional procedures of equity, "eating into the principle of the Common Law but leaving that law still in the fundamental groundwork of the system," but to alter the common law itself. Some would consider this an extremely dangerous step, one that would "teach married couples that there might be a separation of interests," but he denied it. The "whole doctrine of separate estates as now allowed by Chancery under marriage settlements" gave wealthy wives separate property without creating division between husband and wife. Shaw Lefevre concluded by stating that there was no call to decide "whether women were or were not the equals of men"; time and experience would settle that issue. This bill aimed rather at "raising the status of women of the lower classes" by giving them control of their earnings and savings. After his statement the bill passed its first reading without discussion.[54]

Subsequent debate on the second reading highlighted the lines of contention between parliamentary supporters and their opponents. Supporters continued to emphasize the need of working-class women for protection of their earnings. Opponents largely ignored these arguments and instead attacked the ideas about marriage put forward outside of Parliament, raising the specter of the great danger of altering domestic relations and the relative authority of men and women in the home. Mr. Lopes, a staunch opponent of women's rights, was convinced that the bill would materially alter the "existing relations between husband and wife, and introduce discomfort, ill-feeling, and distrust where hitherto harmony and concord had prevailed."[55] Sir John Karslake, the Conservative attorney general who had led the opposition to Mill's suffrage amendment, called the married women's property bill "the most revolutionary measure that had been introduced to the House" during his service there; it proposed "to put a married woman on the same footing as a man," and he was "not prepared to assent to it."[56] The bill passed the House of Commons by only one vote and was referred to a Select Committee chaired by Shaw Lefevre. The Committee reported it favorably, but the session was too far advanced for Parliament to proceed any further, and the bill was withdrawn.

A general election was held in December 1868, and in 1869 the complexion of Parliament had changed notably. The Liberals, profiting

---

[54] 3 Hansard 191 (21 April 1868), 1015–24.

[55] 3 Hansard 192 (10 June 1868), 1352.

[56] Ibid., 1355, 1367–69.

from the expanded franchise of the Reform Act of 1867, swept the Conservatives out of office. More than one-third of the members were new to Parliament. Although Mill lost his seat, many Radicals and supporters of women's rights were elected for the first time, including Charles Dilke, Sir George Jessel, Osborne Morgan, and A. J. Mundella. Shaw Lefevre was appointed secretary to the Board of Trade in the Liberal government, and since he felt that holding office prevented him from introducing the married women's property bill, the Married Women's Property Committee asked Mr. Russell Gurney, the Recorder of London and a Conservative, to take charge of the measure. The bill Gurney introduced, with Jacob Bright and Thomas Headlam as cosponsors, was the same as that of 1868.

In 1869 Lopes and other opponents in the Commons had progressed to the point of conceding that there was a need to protect the *earnings* of married women. But they strenuously objected to the clause in the bill's preamble which stated that the "Law of Property and Contract with respect to married women is unjust in principle." It was not, they contended: since "the wife was the weaker vessel, . . . there ought to be only one head of the house, and . . . the husband was the proper head." Given the concession by Lopes that protection must be found for the wages of working women, it is not surprising that proponents of the married women's property bill continued to insist that this was a *poor* women's bill, and that they did not touch on its implications for the understanding of the marriage contract or the relationship of husband and wife. Only the Liberal solicitor general, Sir John Coleridge, "declined to treat this as a 'poor woman's question.'" The married women's property question, said Coleridge, "was 'a woman's question,'" pure and simple. "He could not see why a woman's property should not be protected just as much as a man's was."[57]

But despite his office, Coleridge did not set the terms of discussion. At the close of debate the bill was referred to a Select Committee, chaired by Gurney. The stipulation that "a married woman shall be capable of holding, acquiring, alienating, devising, and bequeathing real and personal estate, of contracting, and of suing and being sued, as if she were a feme sole," was immediately qualified by restrictions.

---

[57] 3 Hansard 195 (14 April 1869), 774–75, 797. Coleridge had worked with Richard Pankhurst as counsel to women seeking the parliamentary franchise under the Reform Act of 1867, a plea that was rejected by the Court of Common Pleas in *Chorlton* v. *Lings* (1869). In 1889, to the consternation of many feminists familiar with his earlier efforts on women's behalf, Coleridge presided over the Court of Appeal when it rejected Lady Sandhurst's claim that her election to the London County Council could not be invalidated simply on the grounds that she was a woman.

Nothing in the bill was to empower a married woman to alienate any property that she received as a legacy, except by will (which was invalid without her husband's agreement), thus protecting a husband's rights "as tenant by the curtesy [*sic*]" to part of his wife's property if she predeceased him, as well as protecting a child's inheritance. Further, while retaining the provision that a married woman might sue and be sued, the new bill stated that a married woman's contract would make her liable to the extent of any "personal property (if any)" that she might possess, but not personally liable (and hence not subject to working off the debt or to debtors' prison). This was a concession to those who thought married women needed not equality, but protection, for it made a married woman less liable for her debts than other citizens were for theirs.[58]

The amended bill also stipulated that husband and wife could not sue one another for tort, except in cases of property, thus guarding against the kinds of interspousal disputes that opponents of the bill so feared. It also made the wife liable for debts she contracted as the agent of her husband, perhaps in an attempt to assuage the fears of those who claimed the bill would give married women property rights without corresponding financial responsibilities. Further, it empowered the Poor Law Guardians to issue an order against a wife possessing property of her own for maintenance of her husband if he became chargeable to the parish. The bill also gave married women with property the same responsibility for the maintenance of their children that widows had. But perhaps the most telling change between the original and amended bills was in the preamble. Whereas the original bill had asserted that the common law with respect to married women's property "is unjust in principle, and presses with peculiar severity upon the poorer classes of the community," the amended bill stated simply that "it is desirable to amend the law of property and contract with respect to married women." The dilution of the claim was an unmistakable indication that the majority of Parliament regarded the common law as inexpedient, perhaps, but not unjust.[59]

When the amended bill reached the House of Lords, Lord Penzance, who introduced the bill, declared his commitment to maintaining what he repeatedly referred to as "the proper authority of the husband in his own house." In a transparent reference to John Stuart Mill he remarked that he "understood that there had been a recent discovery by profound thinkers that there was no moral or intellectual difference

[58] 32 Vict., Bill 122, secs. 1 and 2.
[59] 32 Vict., Bill 122, secs. 8–13 and preamble; and 32 Vict., Bill 20, preamble.

between the sexes such as lead to the subordination of the one to the other." But this belonged to the realm of "ingenious theories" rather than that of "practical truth." The husband was "the protector and support of the wife, and the latter [should be] subordinate to and reliant upon him." Their lordships' task was to reconcile "the paramount authority of the husband" with "a reasonable protection to women who are tyrannized over and down-trodden." Lord Cairns stated that the law "ought to provide for those who could not afford the expensive luxury of a settlement" without going so far as to have "the whole law relating to husband and wife . . . thrown into confusion."[60] It was too late in the session to fully debate any measure, so the Lords consented to the second reading as an indication that they supported some change in the property laws to aid working-class women.

The legislative session of 1870 produced a married women's property law, but it was a far cry from the measure the feminists had originally proposed. Gurney introduced his bill, which was essentially the same as the amended bill of 1869, and Henry Cecil Raikes, a staunch opponent of women's rights, introduced a rival property bill. Raikes's bill would have created a cumbersome mechanism by which a husband would have acted as trustee for his wife's property, with the wife having the power to apply to a County Court for the purpose of having the property vested in another trustee if she felt aggrieved by her husband's management. Or, if the wife had earned more than half the support of her family for the preceding six months, she would be regarded as a feme sole with respect to those earnings. Both of these awkward provisions showed how tenaciously Raikes held to the idea that, except under extraordinary circumstances of demonstrable male incompetence, wives should not be independent of their husbands. Raikes's and Gurney's bills came up for their second reading together, and the debate was a triumph for Gurney. Proponents of Gurney's bill emphasized the need of poor women to control their own earnings, while advocates of Raikes's measure emphasized how little their bill departed from the common law. Coleridge congratulated Gurney on the advance the issue had made since the previous year: then, he noted, Mr. Raikes had moved rejection of the bill, but now he came forward with a bill of his own. Coleridge hoped he would not give offense or transgress the rules of the house if he said that this "was a great example of a Raikes progress." The Commons then agreed to the second

[60] 3 Hansard 198 (30 July 1869), 979–84, 985–86.

reading of Gurney's bill without a division and voted down Raikes's bill by a decisive vote of 208 to 46.[61]

The sentiment in the House of Commons was not, however, echoed in the Lords. There the married women's property bill encountered even more vehement opposition than it had the preceding year. Lord Cairns, a highly respected lawyer who had served briefly as solicitor general and attorney general before being elevated to the peerage and appointed lord justice of appeal in Chancery, had charge of the bill. In 1867 Cairns had been selected to chair the Royal Commission whose reports became the basis of the Judicature Act of 1873. Cairns had served as Disraeli's lord chancellor during the brief session of 1868 and was an immensely powerful law lord, steeped in the rules and practices of equity. As Cairns announced, he "had not taken charge of the Bill from any desire to set up abstract theories of philosophical principles with regard to the rights of married women," but simply to provide that a married woman would be entitled to money or property gained by her own industry. He saw a clear distinction between a woman's right to money she had earned by her own labor and that from any other source (it did not seem to occur to Cairns that if this theory were applied to the finances of the members of the House of Lords, it would have had radical implications).[62] At the end of his remarks Cairns indicated that he thought the married women's property bill should be sent to a Select Committee for revision.

Other Lords who spoke were hostile to the very idea of the bill, certain that it would, as Lord Penzance said, "subvert the principle on which the marriage relation had hitherto stood." Lord Penzance's objections to the bill revealed a remarkable mistrust not only of women's ability to manage property but of their emotional and sexual fidelity. A married woman with liberty to contract might set up business without her husband's consent or even knowledge, "so that a man might be startled by the information that his wife had determined to set up a rival shop in his neighborhood"; indeed, he might even find that "she had entered into a partnership with her cousin, who need not be a woman," a remark which the Lords greeted with approving laughter.[63] Lord Westbury, who as Sir Richard Bethal had vehemently opposed Erskine Perry's bill of 1857, declared that passage of the bill would mean "an entire subversion of domestic rule which had prevailed in this country for more than 1,000 years." Again he raised the specter of

[61] 3 Hansard 201 (18 May 1870), 878–94.
[62] 3 Hansard 202 (21 June 1870), 621–22.
[63] 3 Hansard 202 (21 June 1870), 603–4; *Times* (London), 23 June 1870, p. 9.

women's sexual infidelity by warning that if the law passed, "if there was some person for whom she had greater affection than for her legitimate lord, she might lavish the proceeds upon him." Even the Earl of Shaftesbury, the great social reformer, who desired a measure to ease the lot of poor women, warned ominously and suggestively that for the upper classes this bill "struck at the root of domestic happiness, introducing insubordination, equality, and something more."[64] (Considering the fact that virtually every woman of their lordships' acquaintance possessed her own property in an equitable trust, the suggestion that a woman in control of money would be an unfaithful wife was decidedly odd. The explanation of the difference in the Lords' attitudes towards their wives' separate estates and towards Gurney's bill may be that trusts in equity were largely created *by men* for women for the latter's protection and did not belong to women by right.) At the end of the debate the bill was referred to a Select Committee chaired by Lord Cairns. The Married Women's Property Committee, appalled by the tenor of the debate, requested that they might give evidence before the Select Committee; they were told that the Committee would not hear witnesses, but would simply modify the bill.[65]

The bill that was reported by the Select Committee showed the influence of the rules of equity on Lord Cairns's mind. The bill struck out the words "her own property," providing instead that three kinds of property would be treated as a married woman's "separate property": first, her earnings; second, investments in savings banks, government annuities, public stocks and funds, incorporated or joint-stock companies, various loan societies, and life-insurance policies; third, all property coming to her as the beneficiary of someone who died intestate, and legacies of less than £200.

If there was any principle behind the Lords' revisions it seemed to be that the earnings of poor women should be protected; the way the Lords chose to do this was to stretch the rules of equity to cover such earnings. Nonetheless, the Act did not even provide adequate protection for the earnings of married women, as Elizabeth Wolstenholme pointed out. Only those wages and earnings a married woman acquired after passage of the Act were to be regarded as her "separate property," not money she had earned before her marriage or before the Act became law.[66] As for money deposited in a savings bank, friendly society, or other such institution, it could only be treated as a

---

[64] 3 Hansard 202 (21 June 1870), 606–7, 610.

[65] MWPC, *Final Report* (1882), 18.

[66] NAPSS, *Transactions* 14 (1870), 549–52.

married woman's "separate property" if she had made special application to have her account so registered. The stipulation that all property inherited by intestate succession was to be a married woman's separate property, but that only bequests of less than £200 were to be so regarded, has puzzled some latter-day commentators. The provision for intestate bequests, like the use of the term *separate property*, reflected the deep influence of equity concepts on the Lords' deliberations. The courts of equity had authority to make settlements of bequests of greater than £200 even in the absence of a stipulation that the bequest was for a married woman's "separate use." But women of the lower classes would be unlikely to receive legacies of such size, and therefore this stipulation was meant to give poorer women the same kind of control over any small legacies they might receive as richer women could get by an appeal to equity for larger sums.

At the same time that they refused to accept the notion that a married woman could be treated as a feme sole with respect to her property, the Lords did retain some of the provisions from Gurney's bill which created new financial responsibilities for wives. The Act imposed on a wife the same Poor Law liability to maintain her husband and children as a man had to maintain his wife and children, although there was no obligation on the woman to support the family except when the husband could not do so. The Lords also retained the provision that a wife was responsible for her prenuptial debts, ending the husband's common law liability, while at the same time they deleted the clause allowing her to retain possession of her prenuptial property. (The confusion caused by this careless drafting is examined in chapter 4.)

Although some feminists had previously advocated greater responsibilities as well as greater rights for married women, in the context of the Lords' bill Wolstenholme and Becker argued that a married woman should not be compelled to support her husband even if he was destitute, because the wife's right to support derived from the household services she performed. They saw with much greater clarity than had Cobbe and Mill that the traditional division of labor by which wives provided domestic services and husbands provided support gave men and women very different financial resources. If women really were free to earn money as men did, then they too should be responsible for the financial support of the family, but in 1870 most women were *not* able to earn money, and a husband's obligation of spousal support was a reflection of the injustice of the larger economic structure of society. Similarly, the Lords' extension of Poor Law obligations to wives as well as husbands might look like a recognition of the principle of spousal equality, but as Wolstenholme and Becker observed, the Lords imposed equal legal obligations on people with unequal economic and social resources.[67]

The Lords' amendments were so extensive, and so thoroughly rejected the principle of equal property rights for married women, that the Married Women's Property Committee seriously considered opposing the revised bill in the House of Commons. Shaw Lefevre's judgment typified that of many committee members when he remarked some years later that the bill was so badly drawn, faulty, and absurd in many of its details that it was virtually "unintelligible."[68] Since the bill would relieve the actual distress of at least some women, however, the committee decided that it should become law, and that they would continue their campaign for a recognition of a married woman's right to hold any property she might have in her own name, to contract, and to sue as if she were a feme sole. (The committee was also undoubtedly influenced by the prospect of the imminent outbreak of the Franco-Prussian War, which would drive matters like marriage law reform off the legislative agenda.) The Commons passed the bill with the Lords' amendments on August 3, almost without discussion, and the measure received the Royal Assent six days later.

The campaign to alter the laws governing married women's property, which began in 1867, was closely related to the women's suffrage campaign launched in the same year. The suffrage and married women's property campaigns were connected not only by many of the same activists, but by a shared ideology as well. Advocates of both causes believed that the notion that women belonged at home stunted women's spirit and talents and deprived them of their rightful voices as citizens. To counteract this assumption, married women must be freed from the bonds of coverture, and at the same time, women must be given the vote to enable them to move and speak effectively in the public realm. The removal of women's disabilities based upon coverture went hand-in-glove with the abolition of women's disabilities based upon sex: alone, neither would free married women from dependency upon and subordination to men.

There was one moment, in the spring of 1870, when suffrage and married women's property came before Parliament in quick succession and revealed the complexity of the difficulties that lay ahead for marriage law reformers. Just two weeks before its initial consideration of

[67] Lydia Becker, "The Political Disabilities of Women," *Westminster Review* 41 n.s. (January 1872): 58; and Elizabeth Wolstenholme Elmy, NAPSS, *Transactions* 19 (1875), 268–69.

[68] 3 Hansard 214 (19 February 1873), 679.

the married women's property bill that year, the Commons had debated the first women's suffrage bill (as distinguished from Mill's amendment to the Reform Act of 1867)—Jacob Bright's "Women's Disabilities Removal Bill," which would have allowed women to vote on the same terms as men. It briefly appeared that the Commons might vote both to give women the parliamentary franchise and to overturn coverture as it affected married women's property rights.

The joy in feminist circles must have been as intense as it was brief. On May 12, Gladstone, the prime minister, declared his opposition to the suffrage bill as the house went into Committee, making it a matter of party loyalty. The bill was defeated by a majority of 126. (There is no record of the reason for Gladstone's opposition, but it was probably due to his fear that the newly enfranchised women would vote Conservative, as well as to his hostility to changing roles for women.) On May 18 the Commons defeated Raikes's diversionary bill and passed Russell Gurney's married women's property bill, which the government did not oppose. Although the Commons was willing to let a married woman control her own property as if she were a feme sole (albeit subject to various restrictions), members were not willing to go into the lists against the government over her right to vote. The difference was not due solely to Gladstone's influence. In voting for the married women's property bill members regarded themselves as protecting wage-earning women, particularly poor women, from incompetent, lazy, or unprincipled husbands; in voting for Bright's suffrage bill they would have explicitly endorsed women's equal civic status. After their flirtation with that idea on May 7, substantial majorities consistently voted against the second reading of women's suffrage bills for the next decade, and after accepting Lord Cairns's very limited married women's property measure in August, did not pass a full married women's property law until 1882.

THE compromises embodied in the Married Women's Property Act of 1870 were repeated in subsequent laws dealing with married women's rights. Feminists would demand a recognition of the principle of spousal equality, and Parliament would respond by protecting the most vulnerable women from exploitation and abuse. Protecting women, however, is not the same thing as giving them the resources with which to protect themselves, something Parliament refused to do. After two years of struggle feminists had gained a married women's property law but failed to win legislative recognition of the principle that a married woman had a right to a legal status independent of and equal to that of her husband. It took proponents of change twelve more years to procure a semblance of the married women's property measure they desired, and even then they did not gain recognition of the principle that a married woman should be treated as a feme sole with respect to her property and contracts. The spring of 1870 was filled with hopes which, had they been realized, would have had a major impact on women's legal position and political history in England. As it was, however, suffrage was defeated in the Commons and the married women's property bill was butchered in the Lords. Having pulled back from both of these recognitions of women's rights, Parliament would thereafter tread cautiously in extending legal rights to married women.

In the course of these struggles the link between women's disfranchisement and their subordinate position in marriage law was made very clear. The strongest argument against women's suffrage was that women were not "independent" persons and had to be represented by male relatives (husbands or fathers). Maintaining women's dependency in marriage was a prop for their political as well as their domestic subordination. Denying women the franchise, in turn, perpetuated the notion of female dependency.

The struggle to pass the Married Women's Property Act of 1870 confirmed feminists in their belief that widespread cultural attitudes about women's place in the home were at the heart of women's subordination in family and polity. During the 1870s feminists vigorously attacked a wide range of laws that reflected in various ways Parliament's assumption that women should be defined, at least in part, by their domestic and reproductive functions. Once again the principle of equality, the insistence on a single standard or "moral law" for men and women, provided the feminists with their most potent weapon against public policies which rested on that assumption.

· 3 ·

THE UNITY OF THE MORAL LAW: PROSTITUTION, INFANTICIDE, AND EMPLOYMENT

> Could it be possible that a woman should come forward to declare that "man is eminently, *essentially*, and primarily, a child-begetting animal," the degrading immorality of the assertion would be recognized at once. . . . We protest this doctrine. Reproduction is not the essential aim of existence for either half of the human race. To declare it such is to deny the unity of the moral law. . . . The faculties of reason and conscience are the signs of the *human* nature, and the right of the human being to voluntary and responsible self-government.
>
> —Josephine Butler et al.,
> *Legislative Restrictions on the*
> *Industry of Women* (1874)

The disappointment they suffered over the married women's property bill in 1870 did not deter feminists from pursuing their aims in Parliament. During the 1870s the group of activists centered around Manchester, which included Ursula and Jacob Bright, Lydia Becker, Josephine Butler, Richard Pankhurst, and Elizabeth Wolstenholme, took up in rapid succession a number of legislative measures which they felt consigned women (particularly married women) to the home, excluded them from the world of work and public life, and dealt with them as if their most important characteristics were their sexual and reproductive capacities. This chapter analyzes three such campaigns of the 1870s—repeal of the Contagious Diseases Acts, opposition to the compulsory registration of baby nurses, and opposition to protective labor legislation for women—each of which was closely related conceptually to the struggle to reform marriage laws.

In the course of each of these struggles feminists, several of whom were working on all of these issues simultaneously, began to develop an analysis of the interlocking nature of women's domestic and civil subordination. Women were kept from the vote and from most remunerative employment because it was assumed that their proper place was in the home, bearing and raising children. Every woman, married or not, was regarded as a mother, or, more crudely, as a reproductive machine. A woman's sexual and reproductive capacities, not her other abilities, assigned her both her proper sphere in society and her rights under the law.

It was not simply that laws and legislators seemed to regard all women as potential mothers, but that in treating men's and women's sexual and reproductive capacities differently, the law sanctioned the sexual double standard. This had been true of the Divorce Act, which made women's adultery grounds for divorce but did not hold husbands accountable for their sexual transgressions unless they were also bestial, incestuous, or brutal wife-abusers. The Contagious Diseases Acts of 1864, 1866, and 1869 mandated the examination and detention of prostitutes in an effort to curb the spread of venereal disease, but left their male customers untouched. Similarly, the Infant Life Protection Act of 1872, meant to protect the lives of infants born out of wedlock, did so by policing mothers and baby nurses, not by enforcing fathers' financial responsibilities. The Factory Acts of 1874 and 1878, while not touching the question of sexual morality per se, presumed that adult women should be treated differently from men because in addition to being "weak," they were potential mothers. The implicit assumptions about sexuality and reproduction embedded in each of these statutes reinforced the economic and political, as well as the social and sexual, domination of women by men.

Liberalism provided the feminists with the "equal rights" arguments they used before Parliament in their efforts to alter these laws. They argued that the law should treat similarly situated individuals in the same way: prostitutes should not be detained unless prostitution was made a crime for prostitutes and their customers alike; parents, including unmarried parents, should equally bear responsibility for their children according to their means; and the labor of adult men and women should be regulated in identical fashion. These reforms would not by themselves have eliminated male dominance in marriage, because they did not give women access to the same economic resources as men had, nor touch the sexual division of labor in the family. But the principle of equality under the law was a powerful tool with which feminists exposed and denounced the law's tendency to assume that men had a right to sexual access to women both inside and outside of marriage. As feminists saw it, the sexual double standard greatly restricted women's public activity, wrongly excused male profligacy and adultery, and placed the burden for children born out of wedlock on the woman's shoulders. By keeping women out of most remunerative occupations and putting economic independence beyond their reach, men forced women not only into economic dependence but sexual subservience as well. In denying women the vote, an all-male Parliament assured the perpetuation of the unequal distribution of resources between men and women.

This interlocking system of sexual, economic, and political domination was what feminists referred to when they spoke of a male "sex class," and when they insisted that women of all economic classes shared a common "sisterhood" based on their exclusion from these forms of male power. W. Lyon Blease's description of "sex solidarity" in the early twentieth-century women's movement applied to earlier feminists as well. It meant "the realization by each woman of the fact that she was an individual apart from each man, and it meant also the realization by all women of the fact that they were a class apart from all men, with common interests different from, and often opposed to, those of the other sex."[1] Given their perceptions of the mutually reinforcing nature of women's economic and sexual subordination, it is no wonder that feminists fiercely resisted the tendency to incorporate assumptions about women's sexuality and maternal capacity into any laws. As long as women were defined by their maternal capacity, the laws would shut them out of or deter them from entering public life and remunerative jobs. As long as women and not men had to bear the responsibility for sexual and reproductive activity, the law would unfairly burden one parent with the financial and moral responsibilities that clearly belonged to both.

Parliament was not used to hearing arguments concerning sexual hierarchy in the domestic and public realms, much less that public policy systematically sanctioned men's sexual exploitation of and economic power over women. Indeed, most of these notions were never put forward in parliamentary discussions. Women's rights advocates nonetheless forced public officials to consider, if only briefly, the role that assumptions about women's sexuality and motherhood played in the treatment of women as prostitutes, unwed mothers, and workers under English law. The feminists' attack on the legislation examined here drew upon the principle of equal treatment under the law for men and women and was closely related both theoretically and politically to their campaigns to reform marriage law.

[1] W. Lyon Blease, *The Emancipation of Women* (London: Constable, 1910), 167, quoted in Sandra Stanley Holton, *Feminism and Democracy* (New York: Cambridge University Press, 1986), 27–28.

CHAPTER 3

THE CAMPAIGN TO REPEAL THE CONTAGIOUS DISEASES ACTS

The campaign to repeal the Contagious Diseases Acts (C. D. Acts), passed during the 1860s in order to curb the spread of venereal disease in the military, addressed the issue of women's sexual subordination to men both in society as a whole and in marriage. The C. D. Acts passed in 1864 and 1866 had been routinely enacted as military health measures. They empowered police in specified towns having sizable military installations (such as Portsmouth, Southampton, Devonport, and Chatham) to apprehend women suspected of being common prostitutes and to order them to submit to medical examination in order to determine if they were infected. If a woman refused to submit to the exam, she could be taken before a magistrate who could force the examination to take place. If she was found to be diseased, the woman could be detained in a hospital for up to six months. The Harveian Medical Society and other groups interested in public health, believing in the efficacy of the measures and wanting to curb infection, campaigned to apply the Acts to nonmilitary districts in the north. A third Act, passed in 1869, sparked a controversy that led, after more than a decade of struggle, to the repeal of the C. D. Acts in 1886.

Both the extensionist and repeal camps contained their full share of social reformers. Many medical men were strong advocates of the C. D. Acts, seeing a clear relationship between their work on sanitary reform (sewage, water supply, housing, epidemiology) and their efforts to regulate harmful practices such as prostitution, child labor, and baby farming (discussed below). All were intended to improve social order and the health of the urban poor. Repealers were a diverse lot, including some doctors, nonconformists and evangelists, political Radicals, working-class men, and feminists.[2]

Although extensionists and repealers coexisted for a while in reform organizations such as the Dialectical Society, the Statistical Society of London, and the Social Science Association, the deep division between them became evident during the annual meeting of the Social Science Association in 1869 in Bristol. The health section had scheduled papers in support of the Acts, one by Berkeley Hill (son of Matthew Davenport Hill) and one by Paul Swain of the Devonport hospital. Women were excluded from the session, and their exclusion strikingly revealed

---

[2] Judith Walkowitz, *Prostitution and Victorian Society* (Cambridge: Cambridge University Press, 1980), 79–85, 99–104.

the effect of both sex class and economic class. Although the topic of the session was whether to extend the practice of the physical examination of women's bodies, men judged the topic to be inappropriate for female ears. They also implicitly drew a distinction between "ladies," whose ears could not bear hearing of venereal disease, and prostitutes, whose bodies could be apprehended and examined.

Supporters of the Contagious Diseases Acts had prepared a resolution in favor of extension, which they submitted after the papers were read. A heated debate broke forth, the proposal was defeated, and the session instead adopted a resolution, drafted by repealers, "that the National Association for the Promotion of Social Science protest the Acts and resist their extension."[3] Elizabeth Wolstenholme, who attended the conference and found out immediately what had happened at the session, quickly wrote to Josephine Butler and urged her to organize a women's campaign against the Acts. By the end of December 1869, the Ladies' National Association (LNA) had been established, headed by Butler, and a "Ladies' Protest" had been published in the liberal *Daily News*.[4]

The Ladies' Protest set forth the central arguments advanced by the LNA. On a practical level, there was no evidence that the C. D. Acts had succeeded in eradicating venereal disease. Furthermore, they were a gross violation of women's civil liberties, since a woman could be apprehended on the mere suspicion of being a prostitute. The Acts, perhaps more clearly than other legislation, revealed the multifaceted nature of women's subordination to men. Many women were driven to prostitution because they could not earn money (or not enough money to support themselves and a child) by other means.[5] The military forces, which sought access to "clean" women, were all male, as was the Parliament which so readily enacted their proposals. The medical profession, which provided the intellectual rationale for the Acts as well as the examining doctors, was almost entirely male. The feeling of a male "sex class" using its collective strength against women was captured by a woman who complained to Butler:

[3] NAPSS, *Transactions* (1869), 428–51.

[4] Text given in Patricia Hollis, ed., *Women in Public: The Women's Movement 1850–1900* (London: George Allen & Unwin, 1972), 208–9.

[5] This leaves aside the question of whether the act of prostitution itself, of a woman selling the sexual use of her body to a man, is one of female subjection. Some liberals regard the renting of one's body for sexual purposes as being like the selling of one's labor; others regard such a sexual contract as illegitimate in itself, at least in a society structured as ours is. See Carole Pateman, *The Sexual Contract* (Stanford: Stanford University Press, 1988), chap. 7.

It is *men*, only *men*, from the first to the last, that we have to do with! To please a man I did wrong at first, then I was flung about from man to man. Men police lay hand on us. By men we are examined, handled, doctored, and messed on with. In the hospital it is a man again who makes prayers and reads the Bible for us. We are up before magistrates who are men, and we never get out of the hands of men.[6]

The C. D. Acts, by attempting to make resorting to prostitutes safe for men, revealed the ways in which the state accepted and sanctioned women's subordination. The Acts assumed that male sexual access to women was both legitimate and necessary; since the military did not allow its enlisted men to marry, it had to facilitate their access to prostitutes. The "Ladies' Protest" expressed its authors' deeply felt view of the immorality of the Acts: "Moral restraint is withdrawn the moment the State recognises, and provides convenience for, the practice of a vice which it thereby declares to be necessary and venial."[7]

The notion that male lust legitimated state regulation of prostitution had implications for marriage as well. At the same time that a wife could be divorced for a single act of adultery, the state was attempting to insure that any man, including her husband, could engage in illegitimate sexual relations without adverse effects on his health. John Stuart Mill, who testified in 1871 before a Royal Commission on the Administration and Operation of the Contagious Diseases Acts, pointed out that while a diseased woman could be forcibly hospitalized against her will for up to nine months, the state imposed no penalty on a diseased man. Where was the justice in examining and detaining prostitutes while letting their customers escape without even an examination? (The military contended that examination was too "degrading" for the men. Since prostitutes were already "fallen," authorities did not worry about degrading them.) The fact that Parliament would enact, and would resist repealing, legislation like the C. D. Acts, was a forceful practical refutation of the anti-suffragist argument that since Parliament regarded it as a sacred duty to protect women, there was no need for women to have the vote. Feminists pierced the rhetoric that Parliament was protecting women and pointed out that in no conceivable way were poor women "protected" by the Acts.

The sexual double standard that lay at the heart of the Acts also corroded the mutual confidence essential to marriage and was a fun-

[6] *Shield*, 9 May 1879, quoted in Walkowitz, *Prostitution and Victorian Society*, 128.
[7] "The Ladies' Protest," quoted in Hollis, ed., *Women in Public*, 208–9.

damental assault on the possibility of right relations between men and women within marriage. To the astonishment, one might say almost the incomprehension, of the Royal Commissioners, Mill argued that transmitting syphilis to a spouse who did not know one was infected should constitute grounds for divorce.[8] For an infected husband to engage in sexual relations with a wife ignorant of his disease was the grossest violation of the mutual respect and trust that properly lay at the heart of marriage. He, Butler, and other feminists saw in the Contagious Diseases Acts not only a threat to "fallen women" or those likely to be mistaken as such, but to *all* women, not only to women on the streets but to those properly married.

William Fowler submitted the first repeal bill in 1870, and repeal bills were introduced nearly every year in the 1870s, although after the defeat of Gladstone's government in 1874 they stood little chance of passing until the return of the Liberals in 1880. Anticipating (incorrectly, as it turned out) speedy repeal of the Acts, the *Women's Suffrage Journal* in 1871 urged women not to forget that "so long as women are unrepresented [in Parliament], their work is but half done."[9] For the first two years of its publication the *Women's Suffrage Journal* reported on the progress of the repeal campaign, but from 1872 on it rarely referred to the C. D. Acts, and always did so with oblique references to "oppressive and immoral legislation." The suffrage societies knew that many who would support votes for women could not tolerate discussions of the "great social evil." Indeed, in 1874 Jacob Bright's defeat for reelection muted a developing controversy between suffrage workers who actively supported repeal and those who could not bear the impropriety of association with such an issue. Members of the old London National Suffrage Society had declared earlier in the year that they would no longer be represented by Bright because he was becoming identified with " 'the agitation to which we will not further refer.' "[10]

Feminists brilliantly critiqued the sexual double standard and its role in maintaining women's exclusion from public life in their assault on the C. D. Acts. Acceptance of prostitution implied social acceptance of irrepressible male sexuality and social, indeed legislative, accommo-

[8] "Evidence of John Stuart Mill, taken before the Royal Commission of 1870 on . . . the Contagious Diseases Acts of 1866 and 1869" (London: National Association for the Repeal of the Contagious Diseases Acts, 1871); especially questions 20,045–58.

[9] *Women's Suffrage Journal* 2 (July 1871): 72–73.

[10] Ray Strachey, *The Cause: A Short History of the Women's Movement in Great Britain* (1928; reprint, London: Virago, 1978), 269.

dation of male sexual needs. The dignity and status of "respectable" women depended upon the existence of an underclass of "fallen" women. As feminists pointed out time and again, this assumed that there were three kinds of women—celibate spinsters, wives, and prostitutes—each group defined by the nature of its relationship to men. As long as male sexual license was tolerated, however, not only prostitutes but every woman was a potential victim of male sexual aggression.

The reason some women became prostitutes, according to the feminists, was the result of economic pressures created by women's exclusion from remunerative occupations. Men closed women out of most jobs, seduced those made desperate by poverty, and then condemned the "fallen woman" to the life of a social outcast. "[S]o long as men are vicious and women have no employment," Butler testified before the Royal Commission in 1871, "this evil [prostitution] will go on."[11] The notion that prostitutes were economic victims of the same male monopoly of employment that they had been battling for over a decade increased the feminists' sense of "sisterhood" with women of the streets. Some of them suggested that marriage, as long as it remained a "Hobson's choice" in a world which offered women no other respectable "career," was itself a form of prostitution.

In assailing the double standard of morality which assigned women to the category of either wife or prostitute, feminists did not intend to imply that all women should be as sexually active as prostitutes or many Victorian men. Rather, like Butler, they both protested the existence of "a slave class of women for the supposed benefit of licentious men" and urged men to rise to the standard of sexual control expected of respectable women.[12] Most feminists did not want to deny women's special moral sensitivity or relinquish their responsibility for the home and the moral education of children. They insisted, rather, that these were not the *only* components of women's nature, and that domestic duties did not exhaust women's proper activities. By the same token, while feminists did not argue that men should be the guardians of domestic order, they did demand that men learn to exercise self-restraint and to approximate women's standards. The C. D. Acts were, in their eyes, a glaring manifestation not only of men's victimization of women, but of an all-male Parliament's unwillingness either to protect women or to grant them equal rights with men.

[11] *Report from the Royal Commission on the Administration and Operation of the Contagious Diseases Acts 1866–9 (1871)*, PP, 1871 (C.408–I), XIX, 447, quoted in Susan Kent, *Sex and Suffrage in Britain, 1860–1914* (Princeton: Princeton University Press, 1987), 68.

[12] Josephine Butler, *Personal Reminiscences*, 42, quoted in Kent, *Sex and Suffrage*, 66.

BLAMING WOMEN FOR INFANT MORTALITY

Passage of the Infant Life Protection Act of 1872 [37 & 38 Vict., c. 38] seemed to some feminists to be another attempt by a male Parliament to blame women alone for a grave social evil, in this case the high rate of infant mortality. For two years Parliament had debated bills pro- posing to curb infant deaths by requiring women who took in infants to nurse to register with the local authorities. Baby nurses would be licensed only if they had adequate training and appropriate housing for the care of children. While most of Parliament and the public saw the measures as being designed to save innocent lives, Wolstenholme, Butler, Becker, and a few others regarded them as an attempt to blame the high infant death rate on women's negligence, exonerating men from any responsibility for infant death. They regarded the Infant Life Protection Act, like the Contagious Diseases Acts, as a product of male bias in the medical profession and in Parliament, which tended to blame and punish women for problems created by men's sexual and social irresponsibility.

By 1871 concern over infant mortality had been building for a dec- ade. Census figures revealed that while the general death rate was fall- ing, the infant death rate remained steady at around 150 deaths per 1,000 live births from 1840 until the end of the century.[13] At the end of the century infant deaths accounted for fully one-quarter of all the deaths in the nation.[14]

At greatest risk were children born out of wedlock. Children of unwed mothers were rarely supported by a father's income, and an unmarried woman was likely to be dismissed from domestic service and other jobs when her pregnancy was discovered. Even had they known the value of cow's milk or of sterile feeding tools, most unwed mothers were too poor to procure them. Mortality statistics reflected the high risks associated with out-of-wedlock birth. In Marylebone Vestry district between 1843 and 1858, 516 of 1,109, or 46 percent of infants born out of wedlock, died before they reached the age of twelve months. In Sheffield during the mid-1870s, children born out of wed- lock died at a rate of 582 per 1,000 live births, while 162 per 1,000 of children born to married couples died.[15]

---

[13] B. R. Mitchell and Phyllis Deane, *Abstract of British Historical Statistics*, 37–38, cited in F. B. Smith, *The People's Health: 1830–1910* (London: Croom Helm, 1979), 65.

[14] Anthony Wohl, *Endangered Lives: Public Health in Victorian Britain* (Cambridge: Harvard University Press, 1983), 11.

[15] *Lancet*, 22 October 1859, 415–16, and 21 July 1877, 101, cited in F. B. Smith,

The causes of infant mortality were complex, and articles by medical officers and other public health workers trying to isolate the main contributors to infant death filled the pages of the *Transactions* of the National Association for the Promotion of Social Science, of the *Journal* of the Statistical Society, and of medical journals like the *Lancet*. In January 1867, a deputation from the Harveian Medical Society waited upon the Home Secretary and laid before him twenty recommendations relating to infanticide, children born out of wedlock, and baby farming. "Baby farming" referred to the practice of placing infants in the care of women or couples who often took in many such children at one time. Baby farmers did not serve as wet-nurses, but fed the babies bottles or pap. While some baby farmers acted as temporary "foster parents," many of them knew that they were expected to let the infants in their care die.[16]

The range and variety of the Harveian Society's proposals reflected the complexity of the factors contributing to infant mortality. They proposed: compulsory registration of all births, including stillbirths; provision for a single woman who had been certified by a physician to be pregnant to make a declaration of the father before a magistrate; admission of pregnant women to the workhouse at the end of their eighth month of pregnancy; authorization of the Poor Law Guardians to recover from the father of a child born out of wedlock a weekly sum towards its maintenance; registration of all baby nurses; exclusion of infants from burial clubs or life assurance policies (in order to insure that the parents would have no incentive for its death); and government intervention to remove the conditions leading to out-of-wedlock births, including overcrowding in dwellings and the gang system in agriculture. The Home Secretary was noncommittal, and the pressure of passing the Reform Act of 1867 drove infant mortality from the legislative agenda of that year.

Three years later, concern with infant mortality moved from the pages of professional and medical journals to the daily newspapers, with its focus narrowed to the abuses of baby farming. In June 1870, a coroner's jury investigating the deaths of two infants whose bodies were found in the street were presented with evidence that sixteen infants had been found dead in the area over the last several weeks. One

---

People's Health, 69–70. The actual mortality rates were in fact probably higher, because registration of births was not mandatory until 1874, and even after that date midwives conveyed supposedly "stillborn" infants to the cemetery without bothering to register them.

[16] J. Brandon Curgenven, *On Baby-Farming and the Registration of Nurses* (London, 1869), 3.

of the children had been wrapped in a blue cloth and a piece of brown paper with "Mrs. Waters" written on it. The police traced the paper to Margaret Waters of Brixton and her sister, Mary Ellis. Mrs. Waters, a widow, regularly placed ads in the newspapers offering to "adopt" children for a fee of four or five pounds. A typical ad read: "Adoption—A respectable married couple wish to adopt an infant from the month of birth. Good home. Premium 4£." Some forty children were suspected of having passed under Mrs. Waters's care, nearly all of whom died of starvation and the administration of opiates. The jury convicted her of the murder of one child, and she was sentenced to death. Her sister pleaded guilty to receiving money under false pretences and was sentenced to eighteen months of hard labor.[17]

The Waters case and subsequent revelations of equally sordid cases generated pressure for some measure to halt what was generally regarded as outright infanticide. Early in the session of 1871, Mr. Charley, M.P. for Salford and a member of the Infant Life Protection Society, submitted a bill proposing the compulsory registration of all those who took in babies to nurse or tend and government inspection of their establishments.[18] Although favorable to the goals of the bill, the government objected to the expenditure that inspection would involve. Jacob Bright, prompted by the fear that poor women, unable to pay the registration fee, would be closed out of yet another occupation, questioned whether those who took care of children only during the day while their parents were at work should be required to register. In the face of these objections, Mr. Charley withdrew his bill, and a Select Committee was appointed to examine the issue. Acting on the *Report* of the Select Committee, Mr. Charley submitted a revised bill in 1872. It dropped the registration fee and excepted day nurseries and those which took in only one child from registration. Licensed baby nurses were to keep registers in which they were to record the names of all infants entrusted to their care, and of all those who died. The coroner was to be given notice of any death within twenty-four hours under penalty of law.[19] The bill passed virtually without opposition, although it was generally regarded as a rather ineffectual measure, as it attacked only the worst cases of baby farming, leaving to one side altogether the unsanitary dwellings, ignorance, and poverty that were the major causes of infant mortality.

No sooner had Mr. Charley submitted his bill in 1871 than Eliza-

[17] *Times* (London), 16, 21, 23 June; 2, 7, 9, 28 July; 11, 13 August; 3, 22, 23 September, 1870.
[18] 3 Hansard 204 (16 February 1871), 318.
[19] 3 Hansard 209 (6 March 1872), 1486–89.

beth Wolstenholme, Josephine Butler, and Lydia Becker formed "The Committee to Amend the law in points wherein it is Injurious to Women" (CALPIW).[20] The CALPIW's first activity was to issue a pamphlet, *Infant Mortality: Its Causes and Remedies*, a biting critique of the infant life protection bill and the proposal to curb baby farming by registering women who took infants into their homes. The CALPIW tried to refocus the discussion of infant mortality away from the negligence of women (both as mothers and nurses) to male irresponsibility in sexual and family matters. The critique had much in common with the LNA's attacks on the C. D. Acts: Mr. Charley's proposed measure smacked of undue state interference in women's lives, prompted and encouraged by medical men, and it penalized women alone for the deaths of infants who had been conceived, as often as not, because of male seduction and betrayal.[21]

Wolstenholme, Butler, and Becker were concerned that compulsory registration would drive women—both mothers doing factory labor and daily child-minders—from work, and urged that only baby farmers who took in children overnight be compelled to register. They also opposed state inspection as a burden on the ratepayer. In a passage that resonated with Butler's sense of moral mission they contended that compulsory registration would tend to weaken the sense of individual responsibility "to conscience and to God in which virtue, national as well as personal, has its root."[22] Their most interesting and telling criticism, however, was that regulating baby farmers left untouched the true causes of infant mortality: the ignorance and poverty of women, the seduction of young girls, and the difficulty of unmarried mothers in finding employment by which to maintain themselves and their children.

Children died not because their mothers were unfeeling or irresponsible, said CALPIW, but because their mothers could not afford to support them. Hence children died under their mothers' care as well as at the hands of baby farmers. Eradicating poverty would take generations, but there were statutory measures which could help ensure that fewer children born out of wedlock would suffer such gross deprivation as to lead to death. First, Parliament could raise the "age of consent" to protect very young girls from seduction. It was a felony to seduce a girl under ten years, a misdemeanor to seduce one under

---

[20] The history of the CALPIW can be traced in the pages of the *Women's Suffrage Journal*, 1871–1873.

[21] Committee to Amend the Law in Points wherein it is Injurious to Women (CALPIW), *Infant Mortality: Its Causes and Remedies* (Manchester, 1871).

[22] Ibid., 8.

twelve years. If Parliament would make it a criminal offense to have sexual relations with an unmarried girl under seventeen, the illegitimacy rate would fall, and with it the infant mortality rate. The state of the law against seduction was particularly indefensible, said CALPIW, since it was a felony to seduce an heiress under twenty-one or even to marry one without her parents' consent. Parliament was willing to protect property by making the seduction of rich young women a crime, but it was not willing to extend the same protection to other young girls once they reached the age of ten. Property, it appeared, was more sacrosanct than children's welfare.

Second, the Poor Laws governing a father's support of his out-of-wedlock children were inadequate. Only if the father was named within twelve months of the child's birth, or if he was proved to have supported it during that time, could he be made to contribute towards its support. The maximum he could be charged was a half crown (two shillings six pence) weekly, except during the infant's first six weeks of life, when he could be ordered to pay five shillings. It was impossible to order a father to pay arrears for more than thirteen weeks, no matter how long he went without paying support, and all his obligations ended when the child reached age thirteen or the mother remarried. The cost of obtaining the support order fell on the mother, the parish officers being forbidden to take action against the father unless the child had become chargeable to the parish.[23]

Even children born within marriage suffered grievously when their parents—particularly their mothers—were poor. "It is of no use for members of Parliament and medical men to say—hand them over to nurses whom we will license and duly inspect. Neither at home nor abroad can mothers whose wages average less than nine shillings a week provide properly for their children's maintenance."[24] Compulsory education, including industrial training, higher wages for both men and women, and a means by which wives could enforce maintenance from their husbands, would do more to lower infant mortality than registering baby farmers.

Wolstenholme, Butler, and Becker concluded that Parliament's approach to curbing infant mortality, like its effort to reduce the spread of venereal disease, blamed women for problems that were clearly the

[23] Ibid., 21–22. In July 1871, Wolstenholme on behalf of CALPIW had sent a Memorial to James Stansfeld, president of the Poor Law Board of Guardians, protesting the provisions relating to fathers of children born out of wedlock, and asking that parents bear joint responsibility for a child's welfare up to the child's sixteenth birthday (*Women's Suffrage Journal* 2 [August 1871]: 85–86).

[24] CALPIW, *Infant Mortality*, 25.

responsibility of men and women and were often not in an individual's hands but caused by society's exclusion of women from adequately paid work. However, the infant life protection bill, age of consent laws, and even the Poor Laws sanctioned male sexual license. Taken together, they drove the writers to "the conviction that all these measures have sprung from the same poisonous root,—the notion that vice is necessary to men, and being necessary, should go unpunished and unchecked." In addition to imposing severe penalties on the seducers of the young and requiring fathers to support their offspring, CALPIW urged, Parliament must reject every proposal based on "the doctrine of the necessity of vice."[25] The infant life protection bill diverted attention from both female poverty and male irresponsibility.[26]

The CALPIW's condemnation of the sexual double standard and of the state's complicity in maintaining men's sexual access to women has led some commentators, such as F. B. Smith, to refer to its authors as "Feminist purity campaigners."[27] The label is superficial and misleading. The social purity movement, as it has been called, emerged in the late 1870s and grew in strength after the publication of W. T. Stead's "The Maiden Tribute to Modern Babylon" in the *Pall Mall Gazette* in 1885. The social purity movement condemned many forms of illicit sexual behavior, such as youthful sexual expression, prostitution, and white slavery. Many purity crusaders moved from attacking criminal activity such as organized child prostitution to trying to stamp out voluntary sexual activity among the unmarried, which they saw as "vice," particularly among the lower classes. After the repeal of the Contagious Diseases Acts in 1886, "practically everyone associated with the repeal cause jumped on the purity and vigilance bandwagon." This collaboration was short-lived for Butler and her friends on the LNA executive, however, for they soon condemned the methods of the Na-

[25] Ibid., 23.

[26] Not all feminists agreed with CALPIW's opposition to Mr. Charley's bills. *Woman*, a magazine edited by Amelia Lewis, took note of CALPIW's pamphlet in an essay of 20 July 1872. During that year *Woman* endorsed suffrage, married women's property, greater custody rights for mothers, and severe penalties for wife-beaters. But while it was sympathetic to CALPIW's assertion that the bill "attacks a symptom of the disease instead of going to its root," *Woman* asserted that the appropriate question was whether the measure would be effectual "within its own limited sphere of operation[.] If even some infant lives were saved, the measure would be worthwhile." Nonetheless, *Woman* emphatically agreed that "one of the most fruitful causes of infanticide is to be sought in the hardships of the present Bastardy Law in its dealings with the mother of illegitimate children," and urged the law's amendment along precisely the lines proposed by CALPIW (*Woman* [20 July 1872]: 450–51).

[27] F. B. Smith, *People's Health*, 70.

tional Vigilance Association as attacks on "the poorest, most helpless and most forlorn of womankind."[28] CALPIW's attack on male sexual irresponsibility and the infant life protection bill occurred in the context not of the later campaign against vice but of the effort of the early 1870s to safeguard women's civil rights and promote women's economic and political autonomy.

Wolstenholme, Butler, and Becker formed CALPIW because they saw that a more flexible organization with a broad definition of its purpose was needed in addition to the suffrage, married women's property, and C. D. Acts organizations. CALPIW's analysis insisted upon the close interrelationship between systems of sexual and political domination. Just as it was important for married women to control their own property as part of doing away with their legal subjection in marriage, so it was important for married and unmarried women alike that no woman be regarded as the "sexual property" of any man. CALPIW seems never to have involved more than a handful of members in its active work, but it nonetheless developed a powerful analysis of male sexual, economic, and political domination, and of the complicity of the laws in maintaining women's subjection.[29]

THE FEMINIST CASE AGAINST THE FACTORY ACTS

While feminist criticism of the infant life protection bills was a short-lived incident in the public health movement of the later nineteenth century, feminist opposition to factory legislation has received the scorn of several generations of labor historians. B. L. Hutchins and A. Harrison, Fabian Socialists, expressed their anger in *A History of Factory Legislation*, published in 1903. As they saw it, feminist opposition to the factory legislation came from misguided members of the middle class who made the mistake of "transferring their own grievance to a class whose troubles are little known and less understood by them; in supposing that while they pined to spend themselves in some 'intolerable toil of thought,' Mary Brown or Jane Smith should also pine to spend herself in fourteen hours a day washing or tailoring." The feminist movement was "dominated by this middle-class preconception of the woman being denied her 'opportunity,' " rather than by

[28] *Personal Rights Journal*, January 1889, quoted in Walkowitz, *Prostitution and Victorian Society*, 252.

[29] Subscription lists to CALPIW can be found in the *Women's Suffrage Journal*, 1871–1873.

an understanding of the dynamics of class conflict.[30] Certainly many feminists demonstrated a lamentable ignorance of the needs and goals of labor and the trade unions. Politically, their ignorance strained the incipient alliance between working-class men and feminists that had developed in some areas during the campaign to repeal the Contagious Diseases Acts. But feminist opposition to the Factory Acts had a logic of its own, and was informed by their critique of the ideology of the home and their vision of a new marital and domestic order. That logic merits more attention than it has yet received.

The Mines Regulation Act of 1842, which prohibited women from working underground in the mines, was the first statute to regulate women's, as well as children's, labor; throughout the nineteenth century Parliament considered it inappropriate to regulate men's hours of labor by statute. After great efforts to limit women's and young people's labor in the textile industry to ten hours a day, the Factory Act of 1850 restricted them to ten and a half hours a day or sixty hours a week.[31] Subsequent acts brought additional industries under regulation, often with slightly different stipulations. By the 1870s the multiplicity of rules covering the hours and conditions of labor meant that workers within the same district or industry might be covered by a wide variety of regulations, making violations difficult to detect. Factory inspectors and medical officers urged Parliament to bring all regulated industries under a single statute, to reduce women's and young persons' hours of work, and to tighten the regulations on home workshops, where the most appalling kinds of sweated labor took place.

In 1874 A. J. Mundella introduced the bill that became the Factories (Health of Women) Act which restricted women's factory labor to fifty-six hours a week [38 & 39 Vict., c. 44]. In 1878, acting on the recommendations of a Royal Commission appointed to investigate the possible consolidation of the Factory Acts, Parliament passed the Factory and Workshops Consolidation Act of 1878, also sponsored by Mundella [41 & 42 Vict., c. 16]. The 1878 Act brought all regulated industries under one statute and stiffened enforcement of workshop regulations by making enforcement the responsibility of factory inspectors rather than local authorities. But the government failed to stop opponents of regulation, including feminists as well as manufacturers, from passing amendments to the bill that left workshops where

---

[30] B. L. Hutchins and A. Harrison, *A History of Factory Legislation* (1903; reprint, New York: Burt Franklin, 1970), 184.

[31] A stimulating analysis of the Mines Regulation Act is Jane Humphries, "Protective Legislation, the Capitalist State, and Working Class Men: The Case of the 1842 Mines Regulation Act," *Feminist Review* 7 (Spring 1981): 1–33.

no children or young people worked and home workshops that employed only family members virtually unregulated.

The chief argument used by parliamentary opponents of regulation was the political economists' contention that the state had no business interfering in the contracts of adult workers, and it was this, of course, which infuriated activists and historians concerned with the plight of labor. The feminists' main parliamentary spokesman on labor legislation was Henry Fawcett, a professor of political economy at Cambridge and a disciple of John Stuart Mill. His young wife, Millicent Garrett Fawcett, and his sister-in-law Elizabeth Garrett Anderson were deeply involved in suffrage work. Fawcett was committed both to laissez-faire economic principles and to women's rights. Because he did not believe in state regulation of labor contracts for men, he opposed any legislative restrictions on the hours women might work. He contended that the Commons had "no right to interfere with the labour of adults," and that "the working classes can settle such a question as this far better for themselves than the State can settle it for them." To limit the hours of women and not of men would lend credence to the assumption that women, like children, "are not free agents."[32] That assumption was pernicious and wholly unacceptable to Fawcett.

Feminists outside of Parliament also voiced laissez-faire arguments, not so much because they opposed state regulation per se, as because they felt compelled to insist that women must be regarded as being equally as competent and autonomous as men. Ben Elmy (the crepe silk mill owner from Congleton who married Elizabeth Wolstenholme in 1874) appeared before the Royal Commissioners investigating the Factory Acts and testified that he advocated the removal of "any restriction applying to grown women which does not apply to grown men. . . . I think that there should be free trade and free labour."[33] The *Women's Suffrage Journal* editorialized that "the time and hands of a poor woman are her capital. Her natural right is to have her whole time at her own disposal, and to have the right of free contract for the work of her hands."[34] A letter from "A Lady Weaver" to the *Kidderminster Shuttle* which was reprinted in the *Women's Suffrage Journal* asserted that "I have a right to sell my labour at any price I like, and when and where I like: and the liberty I claim for myself I will gladly give to others."[35] The *Englishwoman's Review* ran frequent articles in

[32] 3 Hansard 217 (30 July 1873), 1291–94.

[33] Royal Commission on the Consolidation of the Factory and Workshops Acts, "Minutes of Evidence," PP, 1876, XXX, qs. 14,195–96.

[34] *Women's Suffrage Journal* 9 (March 1878): 38.

[35] *Women's Suffrage Journal* 5 (November 1874): 150.

the same vein.[36] It was contentions such as these which convinced trade unionists and labor historians that feminists lacked any understanding of the dynamics of industrial capitalism.

While certain feminists espoused laissez-faire economic principles in public discussions, more widespread and vehement feminist opposition arose from the fact that the Acts treated women as weak, childlike, and in need of protection. Feminists opposing the Acts saw them as one more attempt to define all women, whether married or single, as essentially domestic and reproductive creatures. Factory inspectors, medical examiners, and other professionals argued that too-long hours and certain forms of work would wreck a woman's health and that of her children.

As early as 1859 Dr. John Simon, a leading medical officer, attacked female factory labor as "a sure source of very large infant mortality, both diarroeal and convulsive." Where mothers worked in factories, "infants who should be at the breast are commonly ill-fed or starved, and have their cries of hunger and distress quieted by those various fatal opiates which are in such request at the centre of our manufacturing industry."[37] In 1864 Mrs. Raynard, whose Bible women were forerunners of the female health visitors, said in an address to the Social Science Association that "the wife or mother going abroad to work is, with few exceptions, a waste of time, a waste of property, a waste of morals, and a waste of health, and life, and ought in every way to be prevented."[38] The 1873 *Report to the Local Government Board* by J. H. Bridges and T. Holmes included a recommendation that nursing mothers be barred from factory work:

> consideration of the subject of infant mortality in factory districts, has led us to the conviction that some means should be taken for restricting the employment of mothers of suckling infants. . . . It does not appear to us impracticable, and if practicable, it certainly appears desirable, to make some arrangements by which mothers of young infants shall either be employed for half-time, or be excluded from the factories altogether.[39]

[36] See, for example, Helen Blackburn, "Law and Women-Earners," *Englishwoman's Review* 50 (June 1877): 253; *Englishwoman's Review* 54 (October 1877): 464–72; and "The Night Cometh When No 'Woman' Can Work," *Englishwoman's Review* 58 (February 1878): 97–98.

[37] PP, 1860, XXIX, "Second ARMOHPC [Annual Report of the Medical Officer to the Privy Council], for 1859," 64, quoted in Wohl, *Endangered Lives*, 26.

[38] Wohl, *Endangered Lives*, 28, citing W. C. Dowling, "The Ladies Sanitary Association and the Origins of the Health Visiting Service," (M.A. thesis, London University, 1963), 84ff.

[39] PP, 1873, LV, *Report to the Local Government Board*, 60–61.

At the eighth annual Trades' Union Congress (TUC) held in Glasgow in October 1875, Mr. Henry Broadhurst, secretary of the powerful Parliamentary Committee, said during a discussion of the factory and workshops consolidation bill (which the TUC endorsed), that women were wrong to oppose restrictions on women's labor. "In the union to which he belonged (the masons') they had always devoted themselves to the reduction of the number of hours, and . . . that had always led to the improvement of their condition and the increase of wages. To shorten hours had ever been found the best way to improve the condition of both men and women." At this point Emma Paterson, founder of the Women's Protective and Provident League, England's first women's union, interjected, "By union," to which Broadhurst replied "Certainly by union if possible, but if not by union, then by some other means." He then immediately added that "the proper position of married women was the home," and mentioned approvingly the fact that "the effect of the improvement which had taken place in the condition of working men had been to withdraw from the labour movement the competition of married women."[40] At the tenth annual TUC Congress in 1877, Broadhurst argued that "it was their duty as men and husbands to use their utmost efforts to bring about a condition of things where their wives should be in their proper sphere at home, seeing after their house and family, instead of being dragged into the competition for livelihood aginst the great and strong men of the world."[41] Proponents of regulation urged that women's hours be restricted because women were weaker than men and because they pushed men's wages down, but the most widely-heard argument was that women had to quit the factory in order to safeguard their children's health.

Feminists who opposed extension of the Factory Acts' provisions respecting women's labor had no complaint with regulation of children and young persons, and many advocated restrictions of the hours of all adult workers. Bad working conditions, after all, might wreck a man's health as well as a woman's, a fact which was obscured by the argument that a woman's work should be regulated not for her sake alone but so that she could bear healthy children. Feminists' ire was sparked by the notion that in the name of infant health the government

[40] Trades' Union Congress, *Report of the Eighth Annual Trades' Union Congress*, Glasgow, 11–16 October 1875 (n.p., n.d.), 14. For biographical information on Mrs. Paterson, see Harold Goldman, *Emma Paterson: She Led Women into a Man's World* (London: Lawrence & Wishart, 1974).

[41] Trades' Union Congress, *Report of the Tenth Annual Trades' Union Congress* (Manchester: Co-operative Printing Society, 1877), 18.

would regulate *all* women's work and *only* women's work—again, women were being regarded as essentially reproductive beings. Feminists viewed the proposals for maximum hours legislation for women as yet another instance of the damaging parliamentary preoccupation with women's domestic and maternal roles.

These concerns were evident in testimony by delegations of women before the Royal Commission on the Consolidation of the Factory and Workshops Acts in 1875. Many of these deputations were got up by what the "Minutes of Evidence" described as "ladies connected either with business, or with public and philanthropic work, bringing them into relations with . . . working women." Some of these women were members of the Vigilance Association for the Defence of Personal Rights and for the Amendment of the Law in points wherein it is Injurious to Women, an amalgamation of the Vigilance Association, founded by Josephine Butler in 1870 to work for repeal of the C. D. Acts, and CALPIW. They went into the cities where the Commissioners were to hold hearings and organized meetings of middle-class and working-class women to drum up local opposition to the Acts among female workers.[42]

On July 17, a delegation composed of working- and middle-class women testified before the Royal Commissioners in Leeds. It consisted of Miss Wilson and Mrs. Scatcherd (both active in a number of women's causes), Miss Roberts (a saleswoman in a shop), Mrs. Wood, Mrs. Ellis, Miss Conron, and Mrs. Marsden (all power loom weavers). The chief speaker for the delegation was Lucy Wilson of Leeds, who was a member of the Executive Committee of the Married Women's Property Committee from 1876–1882, a leader in the LNA, and a member of the Executive Committee of the Vigilance Association. She told the Commissioners that one of the ideas that lay behind the factory bill was the notion that married women should be barred from factory work because "women ought to attend to their families." The Commissioners were obviously annoyed with this approach, reminding her that no proposal to ban married women's work was actually before them. But Wilson persisted, arguing that such a ban was the ultimate goal of restrictions on women's labor, a not unreasonable fear in the light of certain medical officers' pronouncements. Mrs. Oliver Scatcherd, a member of the suffrage and C. D. Acts repeal campaigns, also voiced

[42] Royal Commission on the Consolidation of the Factory and Workshops Acts, "Minutes of Evidence," *PP*, 1876, XXX; *Sixth Annual Report of the Vigilance Association for the defence of personal rights* . . . (London: The Women's Printing Society, 1876), 9, mentions the efforts of the Executive Committee to bring working women to give evidence before the Royal Commission.

the fear that the aim of factory legislation was to restrict the employment of married women, as did Mrs. Ellis, a power loom weaver.[43]

The consistency with which women testifying before the Commissioners made the leap from the actual proposal to restrict women's hours of labor to the fear that Parliament would ban married women from factory work reflected the feminists' conviction that the ideology of the home could be used to undercut advances in women's (particularly married women's) legal rights. Mrs. Scatcherd's testimony made it plain that to many feminists the Married Women's Property Act of 1870 felt like a most tenuous achievement; she argued that a married woman's right to control her own property had been "so very recently conceded" that every precaution must be taken not to "cripple" further a married woman's ability to earn money. Lucy Wilson asked the Commissioners to consider the fact that banning married women would work economic hardship on their families. Moreover, restrictions on women's hours of labor "alter the conditions of marriage for women if you reduce them to an inability to maintain themselves." Legislation that diminished a married woman's ability to support herself threw her back into a situation of unavoidable dependency on her husband. And if the Factory Acts prevented unmarried women from maintaining themselves, they would have "a tendency to compel women to marry for a maintenance" rather than for love, an echo of the notion that marriage was like prostitution, an economic necessity for women deprived of other employment.[44]

A pamphlet on *Legislative Restrictions on the Industry of Women, Considered from the Women's Point of View*, written by Josephine Butler, Elizabeth Wolstenholme, Emilie A. Venturi, Ada Smith, and Dinah Goodall, reflected the same conviction that parliamentary opinion about the factory bills was influenced by false preconceptions about women's domestic obligations. (Venturi, a sister-in-law of James Stansfeld, was active in women's rights work in London, and Smith and Goodall were factory workers from Nottingham and Leeds.) As a consequence, the result of protective legislation would be "not to protect, but to oppress women." Limiting the hours they could work would make it harder for women to find employment and to earn a living. Moreover, if women's hours were to be curtailed because of their maternal responsibilities, the proposed reduction of women's hours of labor might smooth the way to the "restriction of married

[43] *PP*, 1876, XXX, qs. 13,183, 13,187–89, 13,242–43, and 13,262.
[44] *PP*, 1876, XXX, qs. 13,190–91.

women to the condition of half-timers . . . preparatory to their ultimate exclusion from factory labour."[45]

Butler and her colleagues were also skeptical about the claim that the proposed restrictions were aimed solely at preserving the health of married women rather than at increasing the "comfort of the married man." To reduce a woman's hours of labor because women were overworked was simply to reduce her *paid* labor, they said. Since "one of the chief reasons given for this reduction is, that 'the comfort of home is greatly affected by the prolonged absence of the mother of the family,' it is fair to infer that the one hour spared from paid labour at the factory, is spared in order that the mother may employ it in unpaid labour at home."[46] There was good evidence for their view. Inspector Brewer stated that one advantage of regulating the hours of women's work would be that women would have time in the evening to look after their homes: "[T]he men often naturally want some little attention, and they often say to me that they would like to sit down and have a bit of supper with their wives."[47] Charles Parnell, who in general *opposed* restrictions, asserted that Parliament might limit the hours of *married* women as they "ought to be afforded an opportunity of attending to their household duties."[48] Given the repeated expression of such views, it was understandable that Butler and her colleagues concluded that the state was not protecting women from overwork, but shifting the locus of their work back into the home.

The authors of *Legislative Restrictions on the Industry of Women* were more sympathetic to the argument that factory work by mothers was harmful to nursing infants. But to restrict married women's labor in the name of saving infant life would affect innumerable women who were not nursing, and it might have precisely the opposite effect from that intended. They quoted Jessie Boucherett's observation that " 'Half a day's work means, of course, half a day's pay, and half a day's pay is quite insufficient for the maintenance of a woman and her family.' "[49] A woman should be able to judge and choose what constituted the best course for her and her family.

Finally, the most pernicious aspect of the appeals to infant health as a justification for restricting women's hours of factory work was the assumption that childbearing and nursing were women's primary du-

---

[45] Butler et al., *Legislative Restrictions on the Industry of Women, Considered from the Woman's Point of View* (n.p. [1874]), 8.

[46] Ibid., 6–7.

[47] *PP*, 1876, XXX, q. 6466.

[48] 3 Hansard 238 (21 February 1878), 94.

[49] Butler et al., *Legislative Restrictions*, 8.

ties. The authors quoted a parliamentary speech by George Hastings, secretary of the Social Science Association and on all other issues a staunch ally of the feminists, in which Hastings asserted that it was legitimate to regulate the labor of adult women and not that of men because men's and women's

> destiny in life is dissimilar. Man . . . is eminently a working animal, one intended to earn wages to maintain himself and those dependent upon him; whereas a married woman is eminently, essentially, and primarily a child-bearing animal, and it is from that point of view that public policy must look upon her and insist that that view should occupy the foremost place in any legislation affecting her destinies.

To base public policy on a view of woman as the nurser of infants, retorted Butler and her colleagues, "reduces her to the level of a cow." The same kind of outraged moral sensibility that underlay Butler's campaign against the C. D. Acts and CALPIW's denunciation of the bastardy and the seduction laws burst forth again here, directed at the notion that Parliament could legitimately legislate for women on the basis of their sexual functions. "Reproduction is not the essential aim of existence for either half of the human race."[50] Women were not to be legislated for as if they were "essentially" sexual or maternal beings but rather as individuals with all the capacities and capabilities of the adult citizen. The moral law was one and must apply to both men and women alike.

WHEN feminists focused attention on such seemingly disparate matters as preventing the spread of venereal disease in the armed forces, lowering the infant mortality rate, and protecting the health of women and children working in factories, they brilliantly exposed the pervasiveness of the assumption by social scientists and Parliament alike that legislation concerning women should be based on their reproductive functions. The practice of referring to women simply as "the sex" reflected this tendency to regard women as dominated and defined by their sexuality. By the early twentieth century the preeminent anti-suffrage argument was that women, on account of their reproductive systems, were "too emotional, too unstable, too lacking in intellectual capacity to participate in the running of government."[51] Moreover, as Josephine Butler put it, as long as a woman could be referred to as "the

[50] Ibid., 17–18.
[51] Kent, *Sex and Suffrage in Britain*, 54.

101

sex" while no one would regard a man as *"essentially*, and primarily, a child-begetting animal," Parliament would continue to distinguish between men and women in social legislation, the franchise, and marriage law.

When feminists argued that women factory workers should be treated no different from men, that prostitutes and their customers should both be subject to legal sanctions, and that mothers and fathers of an out-of-wedlock child should be equally liable for its maintenance, they drew upon the liberal notion of equality to refute the idea that gender constituted any difference between men and women which the law should recognize. This "androgynous" position was not one they espoused in every situation. When the Criminal Law Amendment Act was before Parliament in 1885, feminists did not suggest that women, like men, should be chargeable with the seduction of minors or with rape. They never proposed that women had an obligation to bear arms for the country. And when arguing to expand mothers' rights to custody of their children, as we will see in chapter 5, some feminists invoked the notion that mothers had a *superior* claim to custody because of their unique maternal functions. But these can be thought of as the limiting cases; even in our own day feminists are deeply divided over whether "equality" in military service, sexual assault, and custody is properly achieved by gender-neutral laws.[52]

For Victorian feminists the achievement of equal rights in the public realm was integrally related to their determination that Parliament cease legislating for women on the basis of their sexual and reproductive capacities. The abstract individualism of liberal theory served them well; it made evident the broad range of issues on which the law treated women as beings defined by their sexuality. Until the law ceased to regard women as defined by their social roles as wives or mothers and treated women as equal citizens with men, feminists knew that marriage law reform would be elusive and partial at best. In the name of justice in both the family and the polity, feminists in the mid-1870s renewed their struggle for a comprehensive married women's property law.

[52] See Wendy W. Williams, "The Equality Crisis: Some Reflections on Culture, Courts, and Feminism," *Women's Rights Law Reporter* 7 (Spring 1982): 175–200.

· 4 ·

AN AMBIGUOUS VICTORY: THE MARRIED
WOMEN'S PROPERTY ACT OF 1882

> No question of social or domestic concern can surpass
> this in importance, . . . no interest can transcend this
> in magnitude and it is of supreme moment to the well-
> being of society that the most intimate and sacred of
> human relationships should rest on those broad foun-
> dations of equality and justice of which the recogni-
> tion of the property rights and responsibilities of a
> married woman may be held to be the cornerstone.
>
> —Married Women's Property Committee,
> *Report of the Executive Committee*, 1876

Passage of the Married Women's Property Act of 1882 was arguably
the single most important change in the legal status of women in the
nineteenth century. It capped thirty years of organized agitation, extending back to Caroline Norton's pamphlets on the Divorce Act and
Barbara Leigh Smith Bodichon's married women's property petition of
1856. In enabling married women to act as independent legal person-
ages, it not only gave them the legal capacity to act as autonomous
economic agents, but struck a blow at the whole notion of coverture
and the necessary subordination of a woman's will to that of her husband. Although in practical and theoretical terms the Married Wom-
en's Property Act of 1882 was not the total reformation of the law that
feminists had sought, the *Final Report* of the Married Women's Property Committee (MWPC) rejoiced in "this peaceful overthrow of a char-
tered Wrong in the name of a moral Right; . . . this first great victory
of the principle of human equality over the unjust privilege of Sex; this
bloodless and beneficent revolution."[1]

Feminists involved in the married women's property agitation hoped
that this "revolution" would bring women's suffrage as well as married women's property rights in its wake. Prior to passage of the Married Women's Property Acts of 1870 and 1882, coverture provided a
rationale for barring married women from voting for all but local officials: a wife was presumed to be under her husband's protection and
represented by him. Married women's property bills, by undercutting

---

[1] Married Women's Property Committee (MWPC), *Final Report* (1882), 34.

coverture, therefore threatened not only to give married women control of their property but also to make it more difficult to exclude women from suffrage in the future. As England moved toward passage of the Reform Act of 1884, which enfranchised agricultural workers by eliminating all but the most minimal property qualification for the vote, women's disfranchisement became a salient issue in any discussion of women's rights.[2] The suffrage question complicated the struggle for married women's property rights throughout the 1870s and early 1880s by exacerbating the fear that married women's economic rights would undermine male political hegemony as well as men's control in the family. As we shall see, Parliament was willing to extend a helping hand to married women, but giving married women equal legal status with their husbands was too great a threat both to marital hierarchy and to political order to be acceptable to most Victorian legislators.

THE "CREDITORS' BILL": THE MARRIED WOMEN'S PROPERTY ACT (1870) AMENDMENT ACT OF 1874

Very soon after the passage of the Married Women's Property Act of 1870, Elizabeth Wolstenholme and Lydia Becker wrote a letter to the *Times* of London announcing the determination of the Married Women's Property Committee to continue its struggle for a truly comprehensive property law. Wolstenholme and Becker captured the Janus-faced aspect of the legislation of 1870. They acknowledged that while with "regard to the number of women whose position is favourably affected by it, it is a real and great gain," they could not but regret "that our legislators should have abandoned the vital principle of the original measure," retaining instead "the general rule of confiscation of a wife's property by the simple act of marriage." Because of this they declined to accept the Act of 1870 "as even a temporary settlement of the question," announced that they would "keep our organization intact and in working order," and set about to raise £150 for the continuing effort.[3] In September 1870, Wolstenholme struck the theme that she would reiterate for over a decade: "The only measure which can satisfy us is one which shall secure to women the same rights to their own property and earnings which are enjoyed by men."[4] In order to keep chances alive for a bill that would give married women the

---

[2] On the extension of the franchise in England, see Neil Blewett, "The Franchise in the United Kingdom, 1885–1918," *Past and Present* 32 (1965): 27–56.

[3] *Times* (London), 25 August 1870, p. 11.

[4] NAPSS, *Transactions* (1870), 552.

same rights as men, the Married Women's Property Committee continued to meet, published annual *Reports* throughout the 1870s, and printed and circulated pamphlets that it felt would advance its principles to a wide audience.

The first parliamentary initiative on married women's property after the passage of the Act of 1870, however, was taken not by friends but by opponents of women's rights. The Married Women's Property Act provided that a husband should not be responsible for his wife's antenuptial debts, as under traditional law, but that instead "the wife shall be liable to be sued for, and any property belonging to her for her separate use shall be liable to satisfy, such debts as if she had continued unmarried." Feminists had urged Parliament to impose such liability on wives as one part of giving married women the status of femes soles with respect to their property. When the Lords revised the Commons' bill, they stipulated that only a woman's earnings and property settled on her by a marriage settlement were to be designated as property for her "separate use"; other property became the husband's upon marriage, as it always had. The statute of 1870 thus created a situation in which a husband was absolved of responsibility for his wife's prenuptial debts even though he might have received her property upon marriage, while she was liable for those debts but might have surrendered all her property to her husband.

As cases appeared of creditors unable to collect debts incurred by married women when they were single, Mr. Alexander Staveley Hill (joined by those staunch opponents of women's rights, Henry Lopes and Henry Raikes) introduced a Married Women's Property Act (1870) amendment bill in 1872 to rectify the abysmal drafting of the Act of 1870. The bill provided that the husband and wife could be sued jointly for the wife's antenuptial debts, and that the husband would be liable to the extent of the property he received from his wife at marriage. The wife would be liable, as she was under the Act of 1870, to the extent of her separate property. The Married Women's Property Committee held a special meeting and decided to oppose the bill. It was a bill for creditors, not for women (indeed, the bill in no way altered women's rights or responsibilities). The correct way to solve the problem of liability, said the Married Women's Property Committee, was to give married women control of all their property and liability for all their debts, not to take the "retrograde" step of reimposing liability for wives' antenuptial debts on their husbands.[5]

Parliamentary friends of the Committee, in the meantime, were able

[5] MWPC, *5th Annual Report* (1872), 4–5.

to defeat Hill's bill. When it came forward on July 17, John Hinde Palmer announced his opposition to the bill and proposed that it be postponed for three months.[6] Taking advantage of the new "half-past-twelve rule" which did not allow a private member's bill to be taken up after 12:30 A.M. if opposition had been announced, he was able to kill the bill for that session.[7]

In September the Married Women's Property Committee, meeting in conjunction with the annual meeting of the Social Science Association, denounced Hill's bill and voted to send a memorial to Gladstone urging the government to repeal all common law property disabilities of married women. It asserted that

> these limited and partial mitigations of a rule of law, which is in itself unjust, are wholly inadequate to remedy the evils inevitably arising from the acceptance of injustice as the basis of legislation between husband and wife. . . .
>
> Your Memorialists therefore earnestly request that you [introduce] a comprehensive measure which shall remedy all defects and hardships of the existing law, by establishing for all women the same rights and liabilities as to property and contract as appertain by law to men.[8]

Although the Memorial was forwarded by Sir John Coleridge, the attorney general and the presiding officer of the meeting, Gladstone did not reply.[9]

In 1873 the issue of whether Parliament would pass a full married women's property reform law or settle instead for Hill's "creditors' bill" was squarely joined. Palmer introduced a comprehensive bill drafted by Richard Pankhurst, and Hill reintroduced his bill. Both measures came up for their second readings in February. At that time, Palmer reminded the house of the arguments made for married women's property on previous occasions and reaffirmed the principle that "a married woman should be capable of acquiring, holding, alienating, devising, and bequeathing real and personal estate,

---

[6] Russell Gurney, the sponsor of the married women's property bills of 1869 and 1870, had been appointed one of the arbitrators of American and British claims under the Treaty of Washington, and so could not act for the Married Women's Property Committee in Parliament. He selected John Hinde Palmer, a Liberal barrister who had been a strong supporter of the Education Act of 1870, as his replacement (Lee Holcombe, *Wives and Property: Reform of the Married Women's Property Law in Nineteenth-Century England* [Toronto: University of Toronto Press, 1983], 187).

[7] Ibid., 185–86; MWPC, *5th Annual Report* (1872), 5–7.

[8] MWPC, *5th Annual Report* (1872), 11.

[9] MWPC, *6th Annual Report* (1873), 3.

of contracting and of suing and being sued, as if she were a *femme sole*." He "expected to hear the stock objections against this Bill," but it was based on the only principle consistent with "common sense, justice, and equity." Mr. Gregory responded that if the "stock arguments against this measure . . . were rightly founded, he did not see why he should avoid their repetition." And then he and other opponents paraded them forth, even resurrecting the old canard that a wife would set up a business in competition with her husband, and take "a partner whom she called a cousin—her partner need not be a woman, and might not be a cousin at all."[10]

Palmer's bill passed its second reading by a vote of 124 to 103, but was thereafter lost in a maze of obstructionist tactics and parliamentary indifference. After being reported out of committee, it was "counted out" six times (that is it failed for lack of a quorum), it was postponed fifteen other times due to the half-past-twelve rule invoked by Lopes and other opponents, and was then postponed six more times. It and Hill's proposed measure both died for lack of time in the parliamentary session.[11]

The next year, however, Parliament did pass a measure to make a husband responsible for his wife's prenuptial debts to the extent of the assets he had received from her upon marriage. Disraeli led the new, Conservative Parliament, elected after Gladstone dissolved Parliament in January 1874. Some eighty members who had supported thoroughgoing married women's property reform between 1868 and 1873 were absent from the new Parliament, and the Married Women's Property Committee decided a comprehensive bill would not pass. They therefore decided not to further oppose the creditors' bill, which they did not regard as pernicious *per se*, but as a palliative rather than a comprehensive measure.

[10] 3 Hansard 214 (19 February 1873), 667–89.

[11] MWPC, *6th Annual Report* (1873), 4–5. Parliament's failure to enact the comprehensive married women's property bill in 1873 was particularly telling, because that same year Parliament enacted the Judicature Act, the most prominent legislative accomplishment of the session. Section 22 of the Judicature Act provided that whenever the rules of law and equity were in conflict, those of equity would take precedence. Lee Holcombe has argued that these reforms meant that in time, through judicial decisions guided by the Judicature Acts, the old common law rules governing married women's property would have been superseded by those of equity governing a married woman's separate estate (Holcombe, *Wives and Property*, 190). But her claim is not clear; such decisions had not appeared by passage of the Married Women's Property Act of 1882, and it is hard to see how the Judicature Act could have been made to apply to anything but a woman's "separate estate." Parliament's willingness to overhaul the legal system while refusing to pass a married women's property law is, however, a striking indication of how unpalatable they found the latter.

CHAPTER 4

Ironically, the "creditors' bill" which became the Married Women's
Property Act (1870) Amendment Act of 1874 [37 & 38 Vict., c. 50]
was introduced by Samuel Morley, a Liberal representing Bristol and
in general a supporter of women's causes. Morley was a wealthy,
large-scale hosiery manufacturer, a great philanthropist, and the principal proprietor of the liberal London newspaper, the *Daily News*.
Morley presided at the 1869 annual meeting of the Married Women's
Property Committee, chaired a meeting in 1875 to establish a Congre-
gational Committee for the Repeal of the Contagious Diseases Acts,
chaired the newly-founded City of London Committee for Repeal in
1877, and gave money to the custody law reform campaign of the
1880s.[12] Despite his ties to Wolstenholme and the Brights, Morley did
not share their conviction that to pass a measure not based on first
principles was worse than leaving the law as it was. Although the Married Women's Property Committee had excoriated Hill the year before,
they never mentioned Morley's name in connection with the bill. Morley's bill was approved by the attorney general, was amended only
slightly by a Select Committee after its second reading, and passed
Parliament within two months. As Arthur Arnold, a strong supporter
of a comprehensive married women's property bill, remarked on the
easy progress of the bill, "That tradesmen—electors and fathers—
should be cheated, was to Parliament intolerable," while that married
women should be deprived of all their property except their earnings
was not.[13]

Passage of the Acts of 1870 and 1874, as many had predicted, undercut any efforts for more thoroughgoing reform.[14] From 1873 to
1878 no comprehensive married women's property bill was debated in
the House of Commons. Not only was Parliament in general inclined
to leave well enough alone, but Lord Cairns, the member of the House
of Lords chiefly responsible for rewriting the bill sent up by the Commons in 1870, was clearly hostile to any more extensive measure. He
was now Disraeli's lord chancellor, and as long as he was in office,
married women's property reform had little hope of success. Changes
in the manner of conducting parliamentary business also undercut efforts for a more comprehensive bill. By the mid-1870s private mem-

---

[12] MWPC, *2nd Annual Report* (1869) and *4th Annual Report* (1871), 5; Paul McHugh,
Prostitution and Victorian Social Reform (New York: St. Martin's, 1980), 197, 142;
Elizabeth Wolstenholme Elmy, *The Infants' Act, 1886: The record of a three years' ef-
fort for Legislative Reform, with its results* (Manchester, 1886), 49.

[13] Arthur Arnold, *Social Politics* (London: C. Kegan Paul, 1878), 360, quoted in Holcombe, *Wives and Property*, 191.

[14] MWPC, *7th Annual Report* (1876), 4.

bers' bills not acceptable to the government had very little chance of success. The government increasingly controlled the allocation of time for debate, and the half-past-twelve rule meant that unless a measure received time from the government prior to that hour, it could be blocked by a single opponent. This had frustrated proponents of reform in 1873, even before Disraeli took office. The Married Women's Property Committee realized that their best hope for reform would be to return a Liberal government at the next election, and to convince that government to sponsor a married women's property bill.

THE "WIDOWS AND SPINSTERS" BILL: SUFFRAGE AND MARRIED WOMEN

Further complicating the task of passing married women's property laws was the fact that both proponents and opponents of reform linked married women's property and the question of women's suffrage. Thanks to an amendment offered by Jacob Bright that passed late at night without discussion, the Municipal Corporations (Franchise) Act of 1869 had given women the right to vote in local elections on the same terms as men. Women's exercise of the local franchise rarely came under attack, even from virulent antifeminists; local conditions, schools, and Poor Law boards seemed an extension of women's traditional charitable work and within women's proper area of concern. It was quite a different matter, however, with national politics.[15]

The first women's disabilities removal bill, as suffrage measures were called, was presented to Parliament during the spring of 1870, at the same time as the House of Commons was considering the married women's property bill. Richard Pankhurst had drafted the suffrage bill, which said in part

[15] The distinction between local and national was not always clear. "When, as a result of population growth, a rural district council became an urban district council, or an urban district council became a borough council, then all the rules and electoral arrangements changed as well. Whenever a local council aspired to grander things, women lost out," as they did when London vestries became London boroughs. Furthermore, the web of governing bodies was made even more complex for women by the fact that Parliament refused to make any declaratory law as to whether married women could vote for and sit on all local boards. "From 1869 single women ratepayers always had the vote for everything; and a few married women ratepayers had the vote for some things, like parishes and poor law boards. But each type of local authority had different qualifications for its candidates, and the result was a bemusing tangle of electoral law" (Patricia Hollis, *Ladies Elect: Women in English Local Government 1865–1914* [Oxford: Oxford University Press, 1987], 45, 43).

That in all Acts relating to the qualification and registration of voters or persons entitled or claiming to be registered and to vote in the election of members of Parliament, wherever words occur which import the masculine gender, the same shall be held to include females for all purposes connected with and having reference to the right to be registered as voters, and to vote in such elections, any law or usage to the contrary not withstanding.[16]

The bill carried its second reading on May 4 by a majority of 33, but a week later, Gladstone declared his opposition to the measure and the bill was then defeated by a majority of 126 on going into committee. Despite the unchanging disapproval of Gladstone, Jacob Bright brought forward similar bills in 1871, 1872, and 1873, all of which failed to win a majority on the second reading. The submission of each of these bills spurred suffrage workers in Manchester, London, and throughout the country to strenuous efforts of letter writing and petitioning. In the process, the suffrage societies matured from small groups of like-minded people to efficient lobbying organizations.

In 1874, however, the suffrage ranks split. The rift was not terribly damaging politically, as no bill stood much chance of passing, but it was full of meaning for those engaged in women's rights work. In the election called in January 1874, which brought Disraeli to power, many friends of women's causes lost their seats, including Jacob Bright. Although Bright reentered Parliament in 1876, in 1874 his defeat meant that the suffrage organizations had to find another parliamentary spokesman. They turned to William Forsyth, Q.C., Conservative member for Marylebone. To the consternation of the feminists outside Parliament, Forsyth added a clause to the suffrage bill which provided that no *married* woman should be entitled to vote in a parliamentary election.

The clause, popularly known as the "widows and spinsters" proviso, was not only an affront to married women, but seemed quite unnecessary. Up to then supporters of women's suffrage had asked in the legislation they sponsored that women be given the vote on the same terms as men. The Reform Act of 1867 had enfranchised virtually all urban householders and ratepayers (that is, all occupiers of dwelling places taxed for the poor rates, and all occupiers of lodgings rented for £10 a year). Since most married women neither owned nor leased their own homes nor paid rates in their own names they would not, in any event, have been qualified for the vote. Furthermore, in 1872 the Court of Queen's Bench had ruled in *Regina* v. *Harrald* that although the

---

[16] *PP*, 1870, XXXI, 799.

Municipal Corporations (Franchise) Act of 1869 had given women the right to vote on the same terms as men, the common law doctrine of coverture disqualified *married* women from exercising the municipal franchise. If a court were to apply the same reasoning to a women's parliamentary suffrage bill, an explicit statutory revocation of coverture with respect to the franchise would be necessary to allow married women to vote.[17] Nonetheless, the Married Women's Property Act of 1870, weak as it was, had made it theoretically possible for some married women to earn and save enough to become householders. That remote possibility required, in Mr. Forsyth's view, an explicit stipulation that they would not thereby be admitted to the parliamentary franchise. He was willing to empower women to participate in civic affairs, but not if it gave wives the same right to vote as their husbands. A widows and spinsters bill not only added fewer female voters to the rolls, but it did not offer even an indirect challenge to male authority in the household.

Lydia Becker spoke for most suffrage workers and other feminists when she wrote to Mr. Eastwick (the seconder of Bright's earlier suffrage bill), on March 4, 1874, deploring the new bill's departure from previous women's suffrage bills:

> I earnestly hope Mr. Forsyth does not wish to alter the wording of our Bill. It would be a fatal error, as it seems to me. We should limit ourselves strictly to the disabilities of *sex* and leave the marriage question alone. We ought not to introduce the matter of marriage into the electoral law. If married women cannot vote under the Municipal Franchise Act of 1869, it is nothing in the wording of the Statute which disqualifies them, but the common law disabilities of marriage. It would be very unwise to raise the question of the expediency of maintaining these disabilities in a debate on the question of removing the disabilities of sex.[18]

Before long, however, Becker and the *Women's Suffrage Journal* had decided to support Mr. Forsyth's bill, although continuing to object to the married women's proviso, a condition "which we deem indefensi-

---

[17] Even qualifications for the local vote for women were confusing. "The law was ambiguous. The test case of *Regina* v. *Harrold* in 1872 had disenfranchised married women ratepayers in the boroughs. Did it also apply to school boards? Poor law boards? The presumption was yes to the first and no to the second, but no one was sure" (Hollis, *Ladies Elect*, 45).

[18] Helen Blackburn, *Women's Suffrage: A Record of the Women's Suffrage Movement in the British Isles with Biographic Sketches of Miss Becker* (London: Williams & Norgate, 1902), 135.

ble."[19] As the *Women's Suffrage Journal* said, it was truly regrettable "on grounds of principle, that a statutory penalty on marriage should be introduced into the electoral law." If it was not going to be possible to rid the law of the effects of coverture soon, it was better that Parliament be responsible to at least some women, "even if all such women were *Femmes soles*."[20] Some commentators have suggested that Becker accepted the widows and spinsters bill because she was unmarried. But in other contexts, as this book demonstrates, Becker cared deeply for married women's rights; an explanation more consonant with her ideological convictions is that she could not bear to let the session pass without a suffrage bill and could get no member of Parliament to sponsor a comprehensive measure.

Other feminists found Forsyth's clause totally unacceptable. Becker carried the majority of the Central Committee of the National Society for Women's Suffrage with her, arguing that because it would grant *some* women the vote, the widows and spinsters bill was the thin edge of the wedge that would someday admit all women to the suffrage. Richard Pankhurst, Ursula and Jacob Bright, and Elizabeth Wolstenholme were among those who refused to endorse the bill. They argued that the widows and spinsters bill strengthened rather than weakened the ideology of separate spheres by creating a dichotomy between married women and all other women and men, between being a wife and being a citizen. Fifteen years later this disagreement over principle and strategy would lead the Pankhursts, Elizabeth Wolstenholme and her husband Ben Elmy, Josephine Butler, and others to form the Women's Franchise League to protest the policy of the national suffrage societies of advocating parliamentary suffrage only for unmarried women or those "not under coverture."[21]

The disagreement within feminist ranks in 1874 concerned not only the widows and spinsters clause but also the relative importance of the suffrage and married women's property agitations. On March 1, just three days prior to her letter to Mr. Eastwick, Becker wrote to Wol-

[19] *Women's Suffrage Journal* 5 (May 1874): 69. Becker did get Forsyth to change the language from "married woman" to "woman under coverture." This linked married women's electoral disability to the existence of the common law rules, not to marriage itself; if the common law rules were abolished, married women would be entitled to vote (Blackburn, *Women's Suffrage*, 137).

[20] *Women's Suffrage Journal* 5 (April 1874): 53.

[21] Women's Franchise League, *Report of the Proceeding at the Inaugural Meeting: London, July 25, 1889* (London: Hansard Publishing Union, n.d.). The original Executive Committee and officers consisted of Mrs. Fenwick Miller, Mrs. M'Ilquham, Mr. H. N. Mozley, R. M. Pankhurst, Mrs. Pankhurst, Mr. P. A. Taylor, Mrs. P. A. Taylor, Mrs. Alice Scatcherd, Mrs. Agnes Sunley, and Mrs. Wolstenholme Elmy.

stenholme urging the Married Women's Property Committee to suspend its activities until after women's suffrage was won.

I should be strongly averse to any attempt to re-open the question [of married women's property] in the House of Commons *until women have votes. I am convinced that any such attempt would only retard the period of a settlement of the question on a just basis.* To my mind the question lies between seizing the opportunity of going in for a just Bill while Parliament is considering the question, or letting the whole matter lie over till the Suffrage Bill is passed. *If we look at the Parliamentary strength of the questions we see at once how far behind is* M.W.P. . . . It is a remarkable fact, brought out by your analysis, that *not one* member of the Government has given a vote on our side in any other women's question—and that a *majority* vote for the suffrage. That is an *unmistakable indication of which question is the right one to push while the present Government retain office.* I fear it will be difficult to raise funds for M.W.P. with no Bill. I will try to get something from Mrs. Watts again and then I think the best plan would be to pay off our liabilities and rest on our oars.[22]

Probably due to this dispute, Becker, who had been a driving force of the Married Women's Property Committee in its earliest days, resigned from its Executive Committee in 1874, leaving its work very much in the hands of Elizabeth Wolstenholme and Ursula Bright.

In retrospect, these members of the Married Women's Property Committee who opposed Mr. Forsyth's clause took the truer position. On the most pragmatic level, Forsyth's sacrifice of principle did not succeed in making women's suffrage acceptable to a majority of the House of Commons. Contrary to Becker's prediction, a more comprehensive married women's property act was obtained forty years *before* women got the vote. On a more theoretical level, disabilities due to sex *were* distinguishable from those based on marital status. To allow a statutory exclusion of married women to be attached to a suffrage bill was to concur in the retrograde decision of *Regina* v. *Harrald* and to concede that marriage should make a difference in the civil status and legal capabilities of women. That was precisely what those fighting for a married women's property act denied.

The most vehement opposition to women's voting came from those who could not tolerate the notion of divisiveness and loss of male au-

---

[22] Lydia Becker to Elizabeth Wolstenholme, 1 March 1874, quoted in E. Sylvia Pankhurst, *The Suffragette Movement* (London: Longmans, Green & Co., 1931), 48–49.

thority within the family. During the debate on the suffrage bill of 1873, Mr. Bouverie argued that "our social system and habits were bound up with the distinction between the occupations and pursuits of the sexes, which was the foundation of much of our national happiness and glory, and he would have no part in beginning to destroy it."[23] Mr. Leatham contended that "our object ought to be to enfranchise independent voters; but the female sex must in the nature of things remain in a position of dependence."[24] Just two months earlier, during the debates on Hill's creditors' bill, George Osborne Morgan had remarked that "he could not help thinking that it was opposed by some hon. Members not so much because of what, in reality, would be its effect, as because of that to which they feared it would lead—the development of the 'women's rights' question, and looming behind that a Parliament in petticoats."[25] His observation pierced the rhetoric about who would be legally responsible for what marital expenses and debts and exposed the link between domestic and political power, between married women's property rights and women's suffrage. The married women's property bill—unlike the marriage settlements that Members of Parliament routinely created for their daughters—and the women's suffrage bills focused attention directly on the general principle of married women's legal status and independence, a principle which the majority of Parliament was quite unwilling to concede.

The fears of opponents of Mr. Forsyth's clause were realized when parliamentary *supporters* of women's suffrage implied that it was proper and desirable to exclude married women from the vote. Arguing *for* the suffrage bill of 1878, Mr. Serjeant Sherlock found "the limiting of the Bill to widows and ladies who are not married is perfectly intelligible. It does not endanger the domestic arrangements and the harmony that ought to exist in a family."[26] At the very moment when some feminists were making every effort to pass statutes to overturn the effects of coverture, the widows and spinsters bill would have lent statutory sanction to the common law doctrine. The limited franchise bill contradicted the lesson that marriage law reformers had been trying to teach, that the political and domestic subordination of women were inextricably related and mutually reinforcing. It is no wonder that Pankhurst, Wolstenholme, and the Brights regarded the restrictive clause in the suffrage bill as anathema.

[23] 3 Hansard 215 (30 April 1873), 1219.
[24] Ibid., 1227.
[25] 3 Hansard 214 (19 February 1873), 667–89.
[26] 3 Hansard 240 (19 June 1878), 1837.

The "Magna Carta" for Women:
The Married Women's Property Act of 1882

Feeling disheartened and temporarily defeated after the passage of Hill's Married Women's Property Act (1870) Amendment Act of 1874, the Married Women's Property Committee did not meet in 1874 or 1875. These were also the years of the rift between Lydia Becker on the one hand and Elizabeth Wolstenholme, Ursula Mellor Bright, and Richard Pankhurst on the other over the "widows and spinsters" suffrage bill. In addition, during the winter of 1875 Elizabeth Wolstenholme married and gave birth to a son, events which would in any case have deflected her energies from married women's property work, but which were surrounded by what must have been draining drama and controversy.

Prior to her marriage at age forty to Ben Elmy, a silk crepe manufacturer, Elizabeth Wolstenholme ran a girls' boarding school in Congleton, Cheshire, where Elmy's factory was located. They shared an active involvement in women's rights causes, and indeed were so committed to the principle of women's rights that they refused to marry before living together. Eventually, according to Sylvia Pankhurst, "Mrs. Jacob Bright induced the two to marry, on the plea that their continued refusal would be harmful to the suffrage cause."[27] Despite Bright's intervention, a storm of controversy errupted in December 1875, when it became clear that Wolstenholme Elmy had become pregnant before her marriage.

The displeasure and dismay caused by this fact was brief but intense. On December 10 Millicent Garrett Fawcett of the London suffrage society wrote a heavy-handed letter to entreat Wolstenholme Elmy

> to retire from the secretaryship of the M.W.P. Com*ee* and . . . my reasons for doing so are to be found in the circumstances connected with your marriage and what took place previous to it. . . . At the present moment more than half the life and energy of the M.W.P. Com*ee* is suspended, and a large section of workers feel they must dissociate themselves from it as long as you are the secretary. By retiring you could in some measure repair the injury which the circumstances connected with your marriage have inflicted on the women's movement.[28]

[27] Pankhurst, *Suffragette Movement*, 31.
[28] Millicent Garrett Fawcett to Elizabeth Wolstenholme Elmy, 10 December 1875, Butler Collection, Fawcett Library, London.

James Stuart, a Fellow of Trinity College, Cambridge, an advocate of higher education for women, and an active supporter of repeal of the C. D. Acts, also urged Wolstenholme Elmy to resign the secretaryship of the Married Women's Property Committee. He agreed with Fawcett that Mr. Shaw Lefevre, the parliamentary spokesman for the Committee, would have to be told about Wolstenholme Elmy if she did not resign the secretaryship and "let matters take their course."[29] Josephine Butler, for her part, deplored Fawcett's threats, but also felt Wolstenholme Elmy should resign her office.[30]

The disapproval of most feminists was not long-lasting, however, and indeed the greatest concern of the active feminists seems to have been that Wolstenholme Elmy not *hold office* until the scandal blew over. Isabella Tod and the Irish section disassociated themselves temporarily from the Married Women's Property Committee over the matter, but a resolution brought forward to expel Wolstenholme Elmy from the Vigilance Association never came to a vote. Even Fawcett, despite her harsh words, told Wolstenholme Elmy that she would have opposed any such resolution, since it was one thing to be a member of an organization, and "another thing to be put forward as secretary and therefore a representative of the movement in the eyes of the public."[31] While she resigned her offices temporarily, Wolstenholme Elmy soon again directed the Married Women's Property Committee and later the child custody campaign; her co-workers seem to have followed Butler's advice to let "this wretched affair . . . drop into oblivion" as soon as possible.[32]

By early 1876 Wolstenholme Elmy and Ursula Bright were back at work together on the married women's property campaign.[33] Their

[29] James Stuart to Millicent Garrett Fawcett, 13 December 1875, Butler Collection, Fawcett Library.

[30] Josephine Butler to H. J. Wilson, 19 December 1875, Butler Collection, Fawcett Library.

[31] Millicent Garrett Fawcett to Elizabeth Wolstenholme Elmy, 10 December 1875, Butler Collection, Fawcett Library.

[32] Josephine Butler to H. J. Wilson, 19 December 1875, Butler Collection, Fawcett Library.

[33] According to Lee Holcombe and Olive Banks, Wolstenholme Elmy did not resume her duties as secretary of the Married Women's Property Committee until 1880. This is contradicted, however, by her communications to the *Women's Suffrage Journal*, the *Englishwoman's Review*, and the *Times*, as well as by the pamphlets issued by the Married Women's Property Committee bearing her name and address as secretary. Her name did not appear as a member of the Executive Committee until 1880, which may be the source of the error. See Holcombe, *Wives and Property*, 80; and Olive Banks, *The Biographical Dictionary of British Feminists* (New York: New York University Press, 1985), vol. 1 (1800–1930), 225–28.

strategy was to persuade leaders of public opinion to press Members of Parliament to amend the law. They submitted progress reports and pleas for funds to the *Women's Suffrage Journal* and the *Englishwoman's Review* on a regular basis; in January and February, the *Women's Suffrage Journal* advised that petitions to be sent to members of Parliament were available from Elizabeth Wolstenholme Elmy of Congleton.[34] The two women kept the issue alive in legal circles by circulating pamphlets such as "The Early History of the Property of Married Women" by Sir Henry Maine, a renowned legal scholar and professor of jurisprudence at Oxford, and "The Married Women's Property Committee, the Hon. Mrs. Norton and Married Women," by Arthur Arnold, both published in 1873.[35] They also made certain that a session of nearly every annual meeting of the Social Science Association was devoted to married women's property reform.[36] They tried to keep the issue before Parliament by private Members' bills which had no realistic chance of passing, but which provided a focus for petitioning campaigns. It is hard to know how much good this ceaseless gathering of signatures accomplished. The parliamentary history suggests that married women's property measures passed when they received the sponsorship of influential members of the legal profession, and not on account of petitions by lay-people. But the petitioning undoubtedly served to hold together the ranks of the active feminists, to recruit new supporters, and to define issues in ways favorable to the feminists. The Committee reported that they "regarded their petition work as having been of the highest educational value, so many of the signatures having only been given after long and deliberate consideration."[37]

The day-to-day work of the Married Women's Property Committee was shouldered by Wolstenholme Elmy, who worked out of her home in Congleton. Although initially she was unpaid, between 1875 and 1880 she received a yearly salary of about £100, which rose to about £200 in 1881 and 1882.[38] It appears that her papers from this period were destroyed during World War I, which makes it impossible to reconstruct her work in detail, but general patterns emerge from available sources.[39] Wolstenholme Elmy's mastery of both legal detail and

---

[34] *Women's Suffrage Journal* 7 (January 1876) and 11 (February 1876): 23.

[35] Holcombe, *Wives and Property*, 186.

[36] Papers were read by Wolstenholme Elmy in 1876 and 1880, John McLaren in 1877, and John Boyd Kinnear in 1879 and 1880 (NAPSS, *Transactions*).

[37] MWPC, *Final Report* (1882), 52.

[38] MWPC, *6th Annual Report* (1873), *7th* (1876), *10th* (1880), and *Final* (1882).

[39] Mr. Frank Stockton of Congleton recalls being called to the Elmy home during World War I by Frank Elmy, Elizabeth and Ben's son, to assist in loading large amounts

legislative procedure was prodigious. In articles in the *Women's Suffrage Journal* and the *Englishwoman's Review*, papers before the Social Science Association, and letters to the *Times*, she carefully explained the inadequacies of existing law and details of various bills. She oversaw the printing and distribution of over half-a-million pamphlets, and it was she who drew up the petitions for various bills, circulated them to women's rights workers to collect signatures, and kept the tabulations of the sixteen hundred petitions with some sixty thousand signatures that were forwarded to Westminster. She frequently wrote dozens of letters a day, giving notice of upcoming debates, explaining procedures, and exhorting workers to further efforts.[40]

Ursula Bright, who took over from Lydia Becker as treasurer of the Married Women's Property Committee in 1875, bent her efforts to raising money. She was eminently successful. When she assumed office the Married Women's Property Committee was in debt by more than £158, but only two months after Bright issued her first appeal for funds, the debt was retired, and that year the Committee raised an additional £300. The total subscriptions exceeded those of any previous year by £180, and the number of subscribers rose from sixty to ninety.[41] The yearly budget of the Committee was about £300, although with victory in sight under a Liberal government, expenditures totaled £1145 for 1881 and 1882.[42]

Bright was also invaluable in working with the parliamentary supporters of married women's property reform. She had personal links to several Members of Parliament: her husband, Jacob; her husband's brother John; her sister's husband, Duncan McLaren; their son Charles; Duncan McLaren's son John, by his first marriage; and the McLaren's nephew, Walter McLaren. All of these men sat at various times in the House of Commons, and all except John Bright were strong supporters of women's rights legislation. Ursula Bright moved in parliamentary circles more easily and gracefully than Wolstenholme Elmy, who was the wife of a financially pressed silk manufacturer.[43]

---

of paper into carts during a "paper drive" for the war. He noticed peculiar writing on a bundle of manuscripts, and was told they had been written by Frank's mother, who wrote with both hands (letter to the Congleton *Chronicle*, signed "Oxymel," 17 August 1984, and personal interview with author, August 1984).

[40] MWPC, *Final Report* (1882). Wolstenholme Elmy refers to her prodigious correspondence in many letters to Harriet M'Ilquham, for example, those of 11 April 1890, 19 April 1891, and 11 February 1895, Wolstenholme Elmy Collection, British Library.

[41] MWPC, *7th Annual Report* (1876), 9–12.

[42] MWPC, *Final Report* (1882), 52, 55.

[43] Wolstenholme Elmy discussed the family's finances in letters to Harriet M'Ilquham, 1 April, 11 May, and 10 June 1889, Wolstenholme Elmy Collection, British Library.

Bright also travelled frequently between her homes in Alderly Edge, Cheshire, and Onslow Square, London; she served as a liaison between the full Married Women's Property Committee, which met in London, and Wolstenholme Elmy and other members who lived in the area of Manchester.

Despite the renewed activity of 1876, no date for a parliamentary debate was obtained that session. At the year's end hopes were pinned on Coleridge's promise to introduce a comprehensive married women's property bill in the House of Lords during the next session.[44] (He had become Lord Coleridge in 1874.) Their entrusting the bill to Coleridge reflected the political realities confronting the Married Women's Property Committee. The Conservative government had little interest in the matter of married women's property reform, and by the mid-1870s a bill without government support had almost no chance of becoming law, or even of obtaining a second reading in the House of Commons. Therefore, to keep the issue alive, the Married Women's Property Committee resorted in 1877 to having it debated in the House of Lords, although with little expectation of further progress.

The debate on Coleridge's bill was brief in the extreme, for no sooner had he introduced the bill than Lord Cairns, now Disraeli's lord chancellor, rose in opposition. Reminding the Lords that they had dealt with this same matter in 1870, Cairns said that they had not been prepared then to sanction the "complete revolution in the institutions of society" that had been contained in the comprehensive married women's property bill, and he saw no reason to reopen the question now: "It was settled seven years ago that married women were not to be unmarried so far as their property was concerned, and that they were yet to retain the marriage tie in other respects. The Act of 1870 had worked admirably, and, moreover, it remedied every grievance upon which any person could put his finger."[45] Lord Selborne (the former Roundell Palmer) who had served as attorney general under Russell and as lord chancellor under Gladstone from 1872–1874, also urged Coleridge to withdraw the bill. Significantly, however, since Selborne would pilot the Married Women's Property Act of 1882 through the House of Lords, he indicated that he thought that "there were several points in reference to which the existing law required revision and amendment," although these involved so much detail and required "so large an amount of consideration and discussion" that they could not

44 *Women's Suffrage Journal* 7 (November 1876): 155, and (December 1876): 128.
45 3 Hansard 235 (21 June 1877), 80.

be dealt with at present. In the face of opposition from such distinguished and powerful jurists, Coleridge withdrew his bill.[46]

Lord Cairns's pronouncement that the Married Women's Property Act of 1870 remedied "every grievance upon which any person could put his finger" was belied by many court decisions applying the Act. In 1878 the case of *Hancock* v. *Lablache* caused the *Times* as well as feminist writers to call for amendment of the Act of 1870.[47] The case involved the singer Madame Lablache, who purchased a locket from Messrs. Hancock, jewellers, pledging to pay for it by installments from her wages, which were her separate property. After paying two installments, she left £14 unpaid, and Messrs. Hancock sued her for the balance. Her attorneys maintained that as a married woman she could not be sued unless her husband was joined in the action. To Messrs. Hancock's consternation, as well as to that of feminists watching the case, the defense was successful. To recover the debt, Messrs. Hancock would have to sue the wife and husband jointly, but Madame Lablache's husband could not, as it turned out, be found. Such a state of the law made it extremely difficult for wives to get credit. As the *Women's Suffrage Journal* observed, "It is probable that this inconvenience might have gone on for an indefinite period so long as women only were the sufferers." But now that a man had been victimized there was hope of amendment: "The demand for change will be seen to be irresistible when it is backed by the appeal, 'Am I not a Man and a Creditor?' "[48]

Later that same year another case drew public attention to the Act of 1870. One Thomas M'Carthy was charged with stealing a gold watch, the property of his wife, Mary Ann. (The watch, along with other property, had been settled upon her for her absolute use by a marriage settlement.) Mrs. M'Carthy had been granted a decree of judicial separation by the Divorce Court in May 1878. Six months later, Mr. M'Carthy entered his wife's house and removed the watch, along with a chain that belonged to his daughter. Mrs. M'Carthy sued her husband for theft, arguing that the language of section 11 of the Act of 1870, which stipulated that a married woman should have in her own name the same remedies, civil and criminal, *against all persons whomsoever*, as if she remained unmarried, gave a wife such a capacity. The magistrate, Mr. Headlam, however, ruled that the husband could not be prosecuted for theft of the watch because a wife could not

[46] Ibid., 71–81.
[47] *Times* (London), 11 March 1878, p. 9.
[48] *Women's Suffrage Journal* 9 (April 1878): 55–56.

enter such a charge against her husband. The *Women's Suffrage Journal* remarked that "bad husbands may learn from Mr. Headlam's decision that they may rob their wives with absolute impunity, even of that which the law declares to be the wife's own, and in spite of a decree of judicial separation."[49] The reach of coverture seemed very long indeed, despite the Act of 1870.

To the Conservative government that held office from 1874 to 1880, cases such as these did not constitute compelling reasons for change.[50] Although the government had promised during the debate in 1877 to deal comprehensively with married women's property in the future, the future always receded into the distance. In 1878 Sir John Hibbert, on behalf of the Married Women's Property Committee, introduced a comprehensive married women's property bill in the House of Commons, but he was asked by the Chancellor of the Exchequer to relinquish his time in order to consider the Army Discipline Bill. Then, on December 16, Peter A. Taylor asked the attorney general, Sir John Holker, if in the light of the incapacity of the Married Women's Property Acts to protect married women's property, as recently manifested in the M'Carthy case in Manchester, the government planned to propose any further legislation. The attorney general replied that "no amendment of the Law was necessary."[51] Ursula Bright followed with a letter to the attorney general asking that the law be amended, because it was producing such anomalous results. His noncommital answer questioned "whether it was wise to make a difference in the law as applicable to the husband and the wife."[52] Efforts by George Anderson

---

[49] *Women's Suffrage Journal* 9 (December 1878): 198–99. See also the decision of Lord Coleridge at the Manchester Assizes that a wife could not sue for damages for torts unless joined by her husband (*Women's Suffrage Journal* 11 [March 1880]: 53).

[50] The only measure affecting married women's property to be passed after 1874 was the Married Women's Property (Scotland) Act [40 & 41 Vict., c. 29]. The Married Women's Property Act of 1870 had not applied to Scotland, and the law there still consigned all of a woman's real and personal property as well as her earnings to her husband. The home secretary, Richard Assheton Cross, made it abundantly clear that the government would not support any Scottish bill if it went beyond the law of England. The Married Women's Property (Scotland) Act of 1877 protected a wife's wages and made a husband responsible for his wife's prenuptial debts only to the extent of the property he received from her upon marriage, although it did not protect inheritances or money invested in saving banks. The Married Women's Property Committee regarded the Scottish bill as hopelessly limited, but there was little they could do except to agree to the terms the government offered and take whatever solace they could in the hope that a few women might be helped by the measure. See MWPC, *8th & 9th Annual Reports* (1879), 3–4.

[51] 3 Hansard 243 (16 December 1878), 853.

[52] MWPC, *10th Annual Report* (1880), 8–10.

in 1879 to get a more comprehensive married women's property bill for Scotland debated in the House of Commons came to naught, and he eventually withdrew the measure. All this was, as the Married Women's Property Committee acknowledged, "arduous and at times depressing work."[53]

In the midst of these doldrums, one of the most dramatic election campaigns in English history took place, with Gladstone personally stumping the country in his "Midlothian campaign" of 1880. Party control of Parliament again changed hands, and when the Liberals took office George Osborne Morgan, a staunch supporter of married women's property reform, was appointed judge advocate general. With optimism somewhat restored, John Hinde Palmer promptly introduced a Married Women's Property Bill for England, and George Anderson introduced a similar bill for Scotland. The English bill provided that a married woman would be a feme sole with respect to her property, wages, and earnings, and with respect to her ability to contract, to sue and be sued, and to bear responsibility for her torts. The Scots bill was intended "to do exactly for the property of married women in Scotland" what the English bill proposed to do. The attorney general, Sir Henry James, indicated the government's support for the general principle of the bills, and both measures passed without a division.[54] It was late in the session, however, and George Campbell, a Liberal M.P., announced his opposition to the measures, invoking the half-past-twelve rule. Palmer withdrew his bill and Anderson's was dropped in committee. It was clear that passage of a married women's property bill would require not only a Liberal majority in the Commons, but also government sponsorship of the measure in order to obtain the necessary time for debate.

In January 1881, a delegation from the Married Women's Property Committee led by Palmer and including Arthur Arnold, Jacob Bright, and Sir Arthur Hobhouse waited on Lord Selborne, now the lord chancellor, to discuss the possiblity of governmental support for married women's property reform.[55] At first glance, Selborne did not seem a likely ally. He had seconded Lord Cairns in urging Coleridge to withdraw his bill in 1877, and in a speech he delivered as president of the Juridical Society in 1870 he had said that a measure that made wives independent of their husbands would not be "conducive to domestic peace and the harmony of families."[56] The delegation of 1881

---

[53] MWPC, *8th & 9th Annual Reports* (1879), 3.

[54] 3 Hansard 252 (9 June 1880), 1533–45.

[55] *Times* (London), 8 January and 24 January 1881.

[56] *Times* (London), 27 January 1870, p. 10.

emerged, however, with "the satisfaction of finding how substantial was his Lordship's agreement" with them, and with his commitment to confer with them about possible reforms that Parliament might enact.[57] As Lee Holcombe notes in her study of the Married Women's Property Acts, it was "extremely doubtful" that the conservative-minded Lord Chancellor "had become a convert to the cause of women's rights."[58] But Selborne had been a distinguished member of the Royal Commission to study the reorganzation of the law and the courts, and as lord chancellor had guided the Judicature Act of 1873 through Parliament. His altered position seems to illustrate the truth of A. V. Dicey's observation that "men trained in and for this kind of employment [the law] acquire a logical conscience; they come to care greatly—in some cases excessively—for consistency."[59] By 1881 married women's property law reform probably appeared to Selborne as simply a specific instance of the fusion of the common law and equity that he had championed for so many years.

Married women's property bills for Scotland and England were introduced in Parliament in January 1881 and passed their second readings without a division after the sponsors agreed that they should each be sent to a Select Committee.[60] The Scots bill passed the House of Commons in April; Lord Selborne took charge of the measure in the Lords, and the Married Women's Property (Scotland) Act of 1881 received the Royal Assent on July 18 [44 & 45 Vict., c. 21]. The English bill did not make its way through the parliamentary maze with equal success. After the Select Committee reported the bill in March, it ran into the obstructionist tactics of Charles Nicholas Warton, Conservative M.P. for Bridport. His opposition, and the absorption of great amounts of time on the Irish question, led to a series of postponements which finally resulted in Palmer's withdrawal of the bill.

Yet despite this temporary setback, the tide had turned. Sometime during the second half of 1881 the law officers of the government agreed to support a married women's property bill during the next parliamentary session. Although he suffered a stroke at the end of the session in 1881, Lord Selborne recovered quickly and agreed to introduce the married women's property bill in the House of Lords, just as he had done with the Scots bill the year before.[61]

[57] MWPC, *Final Report* (1882), 31

[58] Holcombe, *Wives and Property*, 198.

[59] A. V. Dicey, *Lectures on the Relation between Law and Public Opinion in England during the Nineteenth Century* (1905; reprint, London: Macmillan, 1930), 364.

[60] 3 Hansard 257 (13 January 1881), 706–14.

[61] Holcombe, *Wives and Property*, 200.

Unlike most previous married women's property bills that had originated in the House of Commons, therefore, the married women's
property bill of 1882 was first brought forward in the House of Lords
and was at long last a government measure.[62] It was readily approved
by the Lords, and with the exception of some last-minute obstruction-
ism in the House of Commons, its passage lacked drama and suspense.
Osborne Morgan, the judge advocate general, introduced the bill in
the Commons. On June 8, at 1:30 A.M., it received its second reading
without any substantive debate and without a division.[63] Sir George
Campbell and Mr. Warton then gave notice of opposition, both condemning the bill as fostering "social revolution" within the English
family. Campbell added that he felt compelled to speak, because while
"the 'women righters' had been exceedingly energetic, . . . the friends
of the poor married man were indolent, so that the case of the poor
married man was hopeless." The value of government sponsorship was
readily apparent, for as Campbell and Warton continued to give notice
of objection, the government agreed that the committee stage of the
bill should be held early in the day so that it could not be blocked by
the half-past-twelve rule. In committee, the house quickly passed some
technical amendments that Osborne Morgan brought forward. In a
last-ditch effort to stave off the "social revolution" he so dreaded, Mr.
Warton unsuccessfully proposed that the date on which the Act would
become effective be postponed from 1883 to 1885 in order to "give
people who were contemplating matrimony the time to change their
minds when they found the law altered."[64] No clearer reflection of the
attitude that marriage was only worthwhile to a man if it gave him
authority over his wife and her purse could be imagined. It is no wonder that the *Women's Suffrage Journal* hailed the Act of 1882 as "the
Magna Carta" of women's liberties.[65]

Separate Estate vs. Feme Sole Rights:
The Persistence of Coverture and
the Denial of Suffrage

In his great study, *Lectures on the Relation between Law and Public
Opinion in England during the Nineteenth Century*, A. V. Dicey expressed a certain sense of amazement that in thirteen years the status
of a married woman under English law changed from one in which she

[62] 3 Hansard 266 (14 February 1882), 626.
[63] 3 Hansard 270 (8 June 1882), 615–17.
[64] 3 Hansard 273 (11 August 1882), 1603–12.
[65] *Women's Suffrage Journal* 13 (September 1882): 131.

"possessed at common law hardly any property rights whatever," to one in which she had "more complete and independent control of her property than is possessed by the married woman of France or Scotland." Dicey's explanation of what he regarded as rapid change was that rather than try to work any "sudden revolution" in the law, Parliament had been content to engage in "judicial legislation," that is, "the reproduction in statutory shape of rules originally established by the Courts." Although "the simpler mode of proceeding was to enact ... that a married woman should, as regards her property and rights or liabilities connected with property, stand on the same footing as an unmarried woman," Parliament instead made the property of a married woman "her 'separate property' in the technical sense which that term had acquired in the Courts of Equity." At long last the procedures that were "framed for the daughters of the rich, have at last been extended to the daughters of the poor."[66]

Dicey's analysis explained the legal rules embedded in the Act but obscured its political meaning. Missing from Dicey's account was an appreciation of the existence of a strong, alternative vision of what the law governing married women's property should be. In the course of moving from the hands of Richard Pankhurst, the author of the bill of 1868, to those of Lord Selborne in 1882, the married women's property bill had undergone subtle but nonetheless significant technical changes. The principle of Pankhurst's original bill was that with respect to her property a married woman should be able to act as a feme sole, and this continued to be the principle that feminists such as Becker, the Brights, and Wolstenholme Elmy advanced. They sought legal equality between husband and wife; what they got instead was an extension to all women of the protection and special status that wives with "separate property" had long enjoyed.

The shift from the feme sole language of Pankhurst's bill to what was in essence a statutory marriage settlement was gradual and incremental. The Married Women's Property Act of 1870 had stipulated that the earnings, savings, and legacies covered by the Act would be treated as a married woman's "separate property," adopting the protective language of equity rather than asserting a married woman's right to treat her property as if she were a feme sole. When, after a hiatus of five years, Coleridge introduced a comprehensive married women's property bill in the Lords, his bill used the language of feme sole rights. John Hinde Palmer's bill of 1880 also spoke of a married woman's ability to deal with her property "as if she were unmarried,"

---

[66] Dicey, *Law and Public Opinion*, 362, 387–88, 394–95.

but in debate Palmer referred to the "separate property" the bill would create for wives. Palmer's remarks blurred the distinction between common law rules and those of equity concerning property. The confusion was immaterial in the short debate of 1880, but it anticipated Parliament's abandonment of the notion that a married woman should be a feme sole with respect to her property. The bill of 1881 referred to a married woman's feme sole rights to her "separate property," thus indiscriminately and illogically combining terminology from the common law and equity.

The bill Lord Selborne introduced in 1882 contained what the lord chancellor called "mere trifling alterations" to Palmer's bill of the previous session. But as Dorothy Stetson has shown, those changes "completed the destruction of the concept of economic and legal equality and substituted limited rights of married women to separate property," which had been creeping into discussions about the bill for several years.[67] Her argument is well illustrated by a comparison of section 2 of the version reported from the Select Committee in 1881 with that of the government bill of 1882:

A married woman shall be capable of entering into and rendering herself liable on any contract, and of suing and being sued, either in contract or in tort, or otherwise, in all respects as if she were *feme sole*, and her husband need not be joined with her as plaintiff or defendant or be made a party to any action or other legal proceeding. (Committee version)

A married woman shall be capable of entering into and rendering herself liable *in respect of and to the extent of her separate property* on any contract, and of suing and being sued, either in contract or in tort, or otherwise, in all respects as if she were *feme sole*, and her husband need not be joined with her as plaintiff or defendant, or be made a party to any action or other legal proceeding brought by or taken against her; and any damages or costs recovered by her in any such action or proceeding *shall be her separate property*; and any damages or costs recovered against her in any such action or proceeding *shall be payable out of her separate property* and not otherwise. (Government bill; emphasis added)

The language that gave married women control of their property and enabled them to make contracts and wills by proclaiming that a

[67] 3 Hansard 267 (7 March 1882), 316; Dorothy Stetson, *A Woman's Issue: The Politics of Family Law Reform in England* (Westport, Conn.: Greenwood Press, 1982), 88.

married woman's property was to be her "separate property" or "separate estate" circumscribed a married woman's ability to use and be responsible for her property in particular and significant ways. A married woman did not acquire full contractual capacity; her contract did not bind her personally but only her separate property.[68] Even property a married woman acquired after incurring a debt was not liable to satisfy the debt, since it was not her "separate property" at the time she made the contract. The effect of "restraint on anticipation" also remained in full force if it was made part of a settlement or bequest. Contractual liabilities that a married woman incurred could not be satisfied out of property subject to such a restraint, even after the death of her husband. Under the Act of 1882 a married woman also did not acquire full testamentary capacity. If while she was married she made a will leaving all of her property to specified beneficiaries, that property would not include anything that she inherited from her husband if he predeceased her, for it would never have been her "separate property" in the technical sense of the term. She might bequeath it to whom she chose, but she would have to write a new will as a widow, that is, as a feme sole.[69] The Married Women's Property Act of 1882 also eliminated the section of the original bill that would have made a married woman responsible for her torts. This meant that married women were relieved of full responsiblity and liability for their actions. To recover damages from a married women for a tort, one still had to sue her husband.

When Ursula Bright in 1882 thanked the National Society for Women's Suffrage for their "Address" acknowledging her "labours of so many years" on the Married Women's Property Act, she urged them to abandon the widows and spinsters bill because now married women had the same property rights as their unmarried sisters.[70] Bright was right to reject the widows and spinsters bill, but the Married Women's Property Act had not in fact put unmarried and married women on the same legal footing with respect to their property. Members of Parliament had decided that women who were married to bad, irresponsible, or brutal husbands should have property rights so that they could

---

[68] *Draycott* v. *Harrison* (1886), 17 Q.B. 147, cited in Dicey, *Law and Public Opinion*, 392 n. 1.

[69] These and other anomalies in the Act of 1882 were finally removed by the Married Women's Property Act of 1893 [56 & 57 Vict., c. 63]. Thereafter a married woman could deal with her separate property as she chose, except for any restraint on anticipation.

[70] MWPC, *Final Report* (1882), 64–65.

manage their own affairs, but had not decided to annul entirely a husband's legal authority within marriage.

EVEN if Parliament had granted married women feme sole status with respect to their property and contracts, that alone would not have worked the "social revolution" that opponents of married women's property reform so feared. The material conditions of women's and men's lives would have continued to situate wives and husbands very differently with respect to the public world of work and politics as well as the private world of the family. Husband and wife could not meet as economic equals unless the wife enjoyed a large inheritance; few jobs were open to women and their pay was very low. Women could not move and act in public circles as men did, although in the last quarter of the nineteenth century women did serve on school boards and local government boards. The kinds of issues that women could address were prescribed by their supposed expertise in matters pertaining to the home and children, and public speaking by women was a matter of enormous controversy.[71] As long as women bore the exclusive or preponderant responsibility for looking after the household and children, they could not devote the time or energy to other activities that men did. Although a married woman's property law was a precondition for spousal equality, by itself it could not bring about that similarity of resources, training, and experiences that advanced feminists saw as necessary to a truly reformed marriage.

The limitations of equal rights legislation in procuring married women equal economic, social, and political power with their husbands should not be allowed to obscure the enormous accomplishment of the Victorian feminists. The radical nature of their demands was evident not only in Parliament's denial of feme sole status to married women, but also in government's repeated denial of women's claims to the parliamentary suffrage. The suffrage issue influenced all debates on married women's property. During the debate on the married women's property bill of 1880, the attorney general, Sir Henry James, stated on behalf of the government that Palmer's bill would be read a

[71] Brian Harrison, *Separate Spheres: The Opposition to Women's Suffrage in Britain* (New York: Holmes & Meier, 1978); Caroline Morrell, *"Black Friday": Violence against Women in the Suffrage Movement* (London: Women's Research & Resource Centre, 1981); Martha Vicinus, *Independent Women: Work and Community for Single Women, 1850–1920* (Chicago: University of Chicago Press, 1985); Sandra Stanley Holton, *Feminism and Democracy: Women's Suffrage and Reform Politics in Britain, 1900–1918* (Cambridge: Cambridge University Press, 1986); Kent, *Sex and Suffrage in Britain*; Hollis, *Ladies Elect.*

second time only if it was amended to remove some of the features of rendering a married woman a feme sole with respect to her property. Some of these affected domestic harmony: "The Bill, . . . it must be borne in mind, would effect a great revolution in the matters not merely within but outside the household of every married man." The fact that the bill imposed no limit on a married woman's powers to contract, he hinted, also threatened the political order.

> [A woman] might, for example, become the tenant of a house; and although he did not wish to refer for a moment to the political aspect of the question—for that was a subject which, in his opinion, ought to be kept apart from the Bill—he thought she must in those circumstances be liable to pay rates, because it was evident that the husband might have no money for the purpose.[72]

Despite the attorney general's demurrer, "the political aspect of the question" could not be dismissed from the parliamentary mind, especially after he raised it in debate. For several years supporters of women's suffrage had circulated petitions among *unmarried* female ratepayers, putting forward their special claim that they were taxed but unrepresented in Parliament.[73] If the married women's property bill that Parliament was considering made it possible for married women to enter into contracts as householders, they too would be able to cry "taxation without representation."[74]

The attorney general sought a way to give married women greater control of their property without conceding that they stood in the same relationship to their property as their husbands did to theirs. If women were independent property owners, what was to justify their exclusion from the political rights to which the laws of England conceded men of property were entitled? The answer obviously was that their sex would exclude them, but it was harder to justify discrimination based

[72] 3 Hansard 252 (9 June 1880), 1538.

[73] See the *Women's Suffrage Journal*.

[74] Many married women ratepayers could not vote even in local elections: "The burgess register, used for borough and county councils and school boards, by *R. v. Harrold* excluded all married women ratepayers from voting, until amended in 1914. The parish register until 1894 included married women who either owned property, such as cottages on which they paid rates, or occupied it, perhaps as shopkeepers. The 1894 Act ended the right of both owner and tenant to acquire a vote from the same property, and confined it to occupiers. As the husband occupied and acquired his vote from the matrimonial home, the married woman who had to be separately qualified, would normally only have a vote if she occupied a property for business purposes. The parish register was used for parish, district, and poor law elections" (Hollis, *Ladies Elect*, 44 n. 83 [references omitted]).

upon sex than to justify discrimination based upon marital status. To make the latter argument one did not have to deal with the awkward question of whether women were men's equals in ability or intellect; equal or not, men and women inhabited separate spheres that carried distinct rights and obligations. The different legal status of husband and wife was a manifestation of these separate spheres and of men's and women's distinct roles in the family and the polity.

The deletion of the language granting married women feme sole rights exposed the connection between married women's domestic rights and their political status. Married women were given protection, not independence, equity, not equality. Despite the great change in the law worked by the Married Women's Property Act of 1882, Parliament managed to retain the language of coverture and of a married woman's unique legal status. This engendered uncertainty and confusion, which left "ample room for assertion, peroration, and invective" concerning women on the floor of the Commons during consideration of the Reform Act of 1884.[75] But Parliament had no intention of enfranchising women. "Both sides of the House tacitly agreed not to press the right of married women with property to have a ratepayer vote of their own. The Tories would not challenge husbands' hegemony, the Liberals feared that such a vote would enfranchise the more affluent and tory."[76] The struggles over suffrage and the Married Women's Property Acts alike demonstrated the truth of the feminists' claims that women's domestic and political subjection were mutually reinforcing and shaped the fundamental structures of their society.

[75] *Englishwoman's Review* 14 (14 July 1883): 303–5.

[76] Hollis, *Ladies Elect*, 43 (reference omitted). See also Andrew Rosen, *Rise Up, Women!* (London: Routledge & Kegan Paul, 1974), 13.

· 5 ·

PARLIAMENT'S REJECTION OF
PARENTAL EQUALITY:
THE INFANT CUSTODY ACT
OF 1886

We ask, what evil beneath the sun
Has your life's co-partner, the woman done.

. . . .

Why for her must there be no right
But the man's gloved hand in its feudal might.

. . . .

[Why] wrest from the victim thus reviled
Her more than equal share in the child?

> —Emily Pfeiffer, "A Rhyme for
> the Time," *Contemporary Review*
> (June 1884)

To Victorian feminists there was no more wrenching proof of the evils
of men's monopoly of domestic and political power than a father's
nearly absolute right to the custody of his children. Under the common
law a father of minor children enjoyed such control of his children that
he could effectively bar his wife even from access to them. During his
lifetime he could take the children from the family home, and by nam-
ing someone other than his wife as their testamentary guardian he
could remove them from her care after his death. It is not surprising
that as soon as the struggle for the Married Women's Property Act of
1882 was completed, feminists turned their attention to reform of the
custody laws.

The result of their efforts, the Infant Custody Act of 1886 [49 & 50
Vict., c. 27], was not regarded by feminists as an unqualified success.
While it ameliorated the plight of some mothers, it did not embody the
feminists' central tenet of coequal parental responsibility and the strict
legal equality of husbands and wives. Like the Divorce Act of 1857,
the Custody Act was of greatest help to women who were no longer
living with their husbands, either because of legal separation or the
husband's death. It gave mothers and fathers an equal right to name
testamentary guardians or to have a court award custody after a legal
separation. In families that were intact and living together, however,

131

Parliament continued to allow fathers alone to exercise legal control over the children of the marriage. Despite the reforms of the Infant Custody Act of 1886, the legal construction of the Victorian family remained patriarchal at its core.

THE COMMON LAW REGARDING CUSTODY

The significance of the statutory changes concerning custody can best be judged against the background of the common law that they replaced. Parliament's first modification of common law rules had taken place in 1839, and only very slightly altered the assumption that children of a marriage "belonged" to their father. By contrast, a child born out of wedlock was in the exclusive custody of its mother; such a child was supposedly *fillius nulli*, the child of no (known) father. The custody of children born to a husband and wife, however, was placed exclusively in the husband's hands. If a father was not guilty of utterly gross or dangerous misconduct towards his children, his right to their custody and guardianship was practically absolute.

The basis of this right was variously described as springing from the father's "nurture" of the child and from "nature" itself.

> The father is the natural guardian and is *prima facie* entitled to the custody of his minor child. This right springs from two sources: One is, that he who brings a child, a helpless being, into life, ought to take care of that child until it is able to take care of itself; and because of this obligation to take care of and support this helpless being arises a reciprocal right to the custody and care of the offspring whom he must support; and the other reason is, that in the law of nature the affection which springs from such a relation as that is stronger and more potent than any which springs from any other human relation.[1]

No one who argued for the father's right to custody "by nature" ever satisfactorily explained why the father was to be considered the one who "brings a child . . . into life," or why his love for the child was to be weighed more heavily than the mother's. Nor, until the nineteenth century, did the mother's role in nurturing the child receive any consideration in law. Only as notions both of parenting and of the nature and needs of childhood changed did daily care and comforting of the young

[1] *Chapsky* v. *Wood*, 26 Kan. 650, 13 Cent L. J. 494, quoted in *Irish Law Times and Solicitors' Journal* 17 (8 September 1883): 473–74 as a good recent summary of the law of England.

seem as important as earning the money for the household, providing children with formal education, and securing a job for one's off-spring—all traditionally the province of the father.

Legal cases involving custody prior to the nineteenth century there-fore involved a father's rights vis-à-vis the state or third parties, not vis-à-vis the mother. Frequently such cases concerned a father's at-tempt to recover custody of children removed from his home by rela-tives. During the eighteenth century fathers deprived of their children recovered custody by applying for a writ of habeas corpus from the Court of King's Bench. After the child was delivered before the justices, they determined whether it was under "improper restraint." The test was simple: "Because 'proper and free' custody of a child was with its father, a child living outside the father's custody was [by definition] improperly restrained."[2] Lord Mansfield, chief justice of the Court of King's Bench, began to carve out exceptions to this rule in the latter part of the eighteenth century. In *Rex* v. *Delaval* (1763) the court was informed that a father who sought custody of his daughter was himself the subject of a criminal information which charged that he had fraud-ulently apprenticed the child for purposes of prostitution. Mansfield held that the court would release the child from improper restraint, and that it was not bound to deliver her to her father: "They [the jus-tices] may be left to their discretion, according to the circumstances that shall appear before them." Mansfield reiterated his belief in the discretionary authority of the court in *Blisset's Case* (1774), when he refused to place a child in the custody of her father after learning of the father's bankruptcy and hearing the mother's testimony concern-ing cruelty against herself and the child.[3]

In the United States, as Michael Grossberg has shown, the trend be-gun by Lord Mansfield continued as the courts gave themselves in-creased discretionary authority over child custody.[4] In England, Mans-field's reform was short-lived, for it became a victim of the conservative reaction in legal thought that followed the French Revo-lution. Lord Ellenborough, who became chief justice of the Court of King's Bench in 1802, was "a personification of this reaction," and his decisions in custody cases laid down the precedents followed in sub-

---

[2] Jamil S. Zainaldin, "The Emergence of a Modern American Family Law: Child Cus-tody, Adoption, and the Courts, 1796–1851," *Northwestern University Law Review* 73 (1979): 1054 n. 48.

[3] *Rex* v. *Delaval*, 3 Burr 1434, 97 Eng. Rep. 899 (K.B. 1763); *Blisset's Case*, Lofft 748, 98 Eng. Rep. 899 (K.B. 1774), cited in Zainaldin, "Emergence," 1054 n. 48.

[4] Michael Grossberg, *Governing the Hearth: Law and the Family in Nineteenth-Cen-tury America* (Chapel Hill: University of North Carolina Press, 1985), 238–42.

sequent years.[5] One of the earliest of these, *Rex* v. *De Manneville* (1804), illustrates Lord Ellenborough's fidelity to strict common law doctrine concerning paternal authority. Mrs. De Manneville had married a Frenchman living in England. She separated from her husband, taking their child with her, charging cruelty. Her counsel relied on the decision in *Blisset's Case* that the court had the discretion to consider the circumstances of the case and to deprive the father of custody if warranted by his conduct. Lord Ellenborough, however, remanded the child to its father, insisting that "by law" the father had possession. He acknowledged that the Court had discretionary authority, but would exercise it only upon a showing that the father intended to "abuse" or "sacrifice" the child.[6]

Rex v. *Greenhill* (1836) further illustrated the near-absolute nature of the father's claim. The mother of three girls, aged five-and-a-half, four-and-a-half, and two-and-a-half, had separated from her husband and kept their daughters with her. Her husband was living in an acknowledged adulterous relationship in London. He nonetheless took out a writ of habeas corpus, demanding that the girls be turned over to him. The Court of King's Bench ruled with no hesitation that "if the party be a legitimate child, too young to exercise a discretion, the legal custody is that of the father."[7] Chief Justice Denman explained that "there is . . . no doubt that, when a father has the custody of his children, he is not to be deprived of it except under particular circumstances," which did not include open adultery.[8] So thorough was the reaction against judicial discretion in custody cases that one commentator has observed that it "was more than merely a reinstatement of pre-Mansfield doctrine. The nineteenth-century English judges adopted a patriarchal paradigm of family relations and applied it to the law with such force and vigor that it had the effect of creating new paternal rights, the existence of which had only been vaguely hinted at by previous judges."[9]

These decisions were handed down by common law courts, but equity courts did not exercise much greater discretion in custody suits. In a case heard in 1827, where the father was living with a mistress and

---

[5] Zainaldin, "Emergence," 1060 n. 77.

[6] *Rex* v. *De Manneville*, 5 East 221, 102 Eng. Rep. 1054 (K.B. 1804), cited in Zainaldin, "Emergence," 1060 n. 77.

[7] *Rex* v. *Greenhill* (1836) 4 A. & E. 624, quoted in P. H. Pettit, "Paternal Control and Guardianship," in *A Century of Family Law 1857–1957*, ed. R. H. Graveson and F. R. Crane (London: Sweet & Maxwell, 1957), 57.

[8] 4 Ad. & E. at 639, 111 Eng. Rep. at 927, quoted in Zainaldin, "Emergence," 1060–61 n. 77.

[9] Zainaldin, "Emergence," 1063 n. 97.

the mother had on that account obtained an ecclesiastical divorce, the vice-chancellor of the Court of Chancery held that "the court has nothing to do with the fact of the father's adultery, unless the father brings the child into contact with the woman." The father's right was so absolute that the Court would not even grant the mother access to her children. The vice-chancellor did remark that "if any alternative could be found, I would most gladly accept it; for, in the moral point of view, I know of no act more harsh or cruel than depriving the mother of proper intercourse with her child."[10] But such wishes were ineffectual in the face of the law.

The father's right to the custody of children was in no way diminished by his death. If the father chose to name a testamentary guardian other than the mother in his will, the mother had no basis on which to appeal for custody. The father could "put forth his 'dead hand' to continue his rights, [and] appoint a person to act as guardian after his decease . . . to the exclusion of the mother."[11] If a father died intestate or without having named a guardian for his children in his will, the mother did become their guardian. But even then the father's "dead hand" affected the children's upbringing, since it was a firm rule of law that in the absence of an express statement to the contrary, children should be brought up in the religion of their father. Finally, a mother who survived her husband could not appoint a guardian by her own will, even when her husband had appointed no guardian. If she died while the children were still minors, they became wards of the Court, no matter what her expressed wishes with respect to their custody might have been.[12]

Those roused to consider England's custody law in the nineteenth century tended to agree with the American legal scholar who wrote in 1891 that "When the English Court of Queen's Bench and Common Pleas, discarding the earlier doctrine of Mansfield, adopted a system of deciding questions of custody according to fixed, general rules, irrespective of the true merits of specific cases, the result was a line of adjudication that . . . was shocking to the moral sense."[13] Confronted by this train of legal reasoning, reformers could not hope that alteration of the law would be made from the bench, as had happened in the United States, where judges, following the path indicated by Lord Mansfield, had assumed wide discretion in custody cases. English fem-

---

[10] *Ball* v. *Ball* (1827) 2 Sim. 35, quoted in Graveson and Crane, *Century of Family Law*, 57.

[11] *Irish Law Times and Solicitors' Journal* 18 (12 July 1884): 357.

[12] 3 Hansard 286 (26 March 1884), 812.

[13] Lewis Hochheimer, *Custody of Infants* (1891), sec. 22, quoted in Zainaldin, "Emergence," 1059 n. 73.

inists therefore turned to Parliament to break the near-absolute hold of fathers over their children and give mothers an equal share in custody of their common offspring.

"MISERABLE AND PALLIATIVE" MEASURES: THE INFANT CUSTODY ACTS OF 1839 AND 1873

Two statutory modifications of the common law rules governing custody took place prior to the organized feminist campaign for equal parental rights of the late 1870s and 1880s: the Custody of Infants Act of 1839 [2 & 3 Vict., c. 54] and the Infant Custody Act of 1873 [36 Vict., c. 12]. Feminists acclaimed the former as a pathbreaking first step for mothers' rights; the latter they denounced as a weak and diversionary measure. Both needed to be superseded if mothers were to receive just treatment.

The Custody of Infants Act of 1839

Passage of the Infants Act of 1839 was in large part due to the agitation of Caroline Norton, who fifteen years later was involved in the debates over the Divorce Act. In 1836 Caroline and her sons, but not her husband, were invited to spend Easter with her sister (Caroline's family had decided to cope with George's brutality by associating with him as little as possible). George forbade the trip, and, fearing that Caroline would disobey his order, when she was out of the house one day took the boys to his sister's house, where he had them stay. Caroline was admitted to the house but prevented from seeing them: "I could hear their little feet running merrily overhead while I sat sobbing below— only the ceiling between us and I was not able to get at them," she wrote to Lord Melbourne. "[I]f they keep my boys from me I shall go mad."[14] George removed the boys to his brother's house in Surrey, initiated his suit against Lord Melbourne for criminal conversation, and, upon losing that case, sent the boys to live in Scotland, refusing to tell Caroline where they were. All of this, she discovered, he had a perfect right to do; fathers, not mothers, were by law the custodial parents of their children.

Her plight moved Caroline Norton to undertake her first campaign for legal reform. She turned to powerful political friends, particularly Serjeant-at-Law Thomas Talfourd and Lord Lyndhurst, to sponsor

---

[14] *Letters of Caroline Norton to Lord Melbourne*, ed. James O. Hoge and Clarke Olney (Columbus: Ohio State University Press, 1974), 3, quoted in Margaret Forster, *Significant Sisters: The Grassroots of Active Feminism 1839–1939* (London: Secker & Warburg, 1984), 28.

legislation giving mothers the right to apply to Chancery for custody of their minor children. As part of her desperate effort to be reunited with her children, Norton published *Separation of Mother and Child by the 'Law of Custody of Infants' Considered* in 1837 and *A Plain Letter to the Lord Chancellor on the Infant Custody Bill . . .* in 1839, both pleading for legal recognition of mothers' rights to custody.[15] As was typical of her, Norton insisted that married women needed the "protection" of the law in cases where their husbands, their "natural" protectors, failed them. More boldly, she suggested that by withholding such protection the law reduced wives to the status of concubines: "To refuse the protection which would enable a blameless wife to continue her care of infants . . . merely on the plea that the law will not interfere with the husband, what is it but to deny the position of the woman as a rational and accountable creature? What is it but to adopt in a degree the Turkish creed, and consider her merely as the toy of the hour?"[16] Norton was aided by the shock that public opinion had recently received in the decision in *Rex* v. *Greenhill* (1836) to place three girls in the custody of their openly adulterous father.

Norton's efforts met with some success. The Custody of Infants Act of 1839 provided that a mother could petition in the equity courts for custody of her children up to the age of seven, and for periodic access to children age seven or older. A mother could not avail herself of even these limited rights if she had been found guilty of adultery either in an action for criminal conversation or in an ecclesiastical court. Furthermore, in order to take advantage of the provisions of the Act a woman had to be rich enough to enter a suit in Chancery. There was no recourse for a less well-to-do woman whose husband took away their children. Only mothers who were wealthy, blameless of sexual misconduct, separated from their husbands, and whose children were under age seven might get custody under the Act—a small group indeed. Even this minimal concession provoked a lengthy diatribe in the *British and Foreign Review* against Caroline Norton's character and the evils of the doctrine of sexual equality.[17]

No other statutory modification of the common law affecting custody was made for eighteen years. In 1857, Parliament approved

---

[15] Caroline Norton, *Separation of Mother and Child by the 'Law of Custody of Infants' Considered* (privately printed, 1837), and Pearce Stevenson [Caroline Norton], *A Plain Letter to the Lord Chancellor on the Infant Custody Bill . . .* (London: James Ridgway, 1839). Both are reprinted in *Selected Writings of Caroline Norton*, ed. James O. Hoge and Jane Marcus (Delmar, N.Y.: Scholars' Facsimiles and Reprints, 1978).

[16] Norton, *On the Infant Custody Bill*, 108.

[17] [Edwin Hill Handley], "Custody of Infants Bill," *British and Foreign Review* 7 (July 1838): 269–411.

clauses in the Divorce Act that provided that in making a decree for divorce or judicial separation the "Court may, from time to time, before making its final order, make such interim orders, and may make such provision in the final decree as it may deem just with respect to the custody of the children" (sec. 35). Custody awards were to be made at the judges' discretion, and even a guilty spouse could be given custody. The provisions of the Divorce Act and its amendments helped only women whose husbands were guilty of adultery in combination with incest, bigamy, or extreme physical cruelty. Nonetheless, the broad discretion granted to the Divorce Court contrasted sharply with the limited powers Parliament had given to Chancery eighteen years earlier.

The discretionary authority given to the Divorce Court reflected a growing concern with children's welfare. The lawyers drafting the Divorce Act believed that the welfare of the child, rather than either paternal or maternal rights, should determine custody decisions. Indeed, the Matrimonial Causes Act Amendment Act of 1859 [22 & 23 Vict., c. 61] extended the powers of the Divorce Court to permit the Court even after a final decree "from time to time, to modify any provision . . . as to custody" (sec. 4). Such modifications obviously would not be based on the initial marital fault that led to the divorce, but on conditions that would affect the child.[18]

The differences between the common law rules and the provisions of the Divorce Act are best explained, I think, as reflections of the fact that an action for divorce or separation involved a judicial judgment that a marriage had been irrevocably broken. A father's authority was thought to be essential for family unity, but if such unity was already shattered there was less incentive to keep the children tied to their father. In actions for habeas corpus or suits in Chancery, where no legal divorce had taken place, the courts continued to hold that the child of a marriage was in the custody of its father. Even if only nominally intact, the family was to be ruled by the male head-of-household.

The Infant Custody Act of 1873

Ironically, the first effort to alter custody law undertaken in the wake of the married women's property campaign did not meet with the ap-

[18] The Conjugal Rights (Scotland) Act of 1861 (24 & 25 Vict., c. 86) extended similar relief to Scotland. Section 35 of the Divorce Act of 1857 was the model for section 9 of the Scottish statute, with the variation that the power of the court in custody orders was restricted to "pupil" children of the marriage, that is, to children under the age of puberty (*Juridical Review* 12 [1900]: 241–42).

proval of most active feminists. From the outset of their efforts to overturn married women's legal disabilities, feminists insisted that mothers' lack of custody rights was an integral part of their marital subjection. John Stuart Mill pointed out that custody law was one of the most oppressive forms of a wife's subordination in marriage:

> [W]hat is her position in regard to the children in whom she and her master have a joint interest? They are by law *his* children. . . . No one act can she do towards or in relation to them, except by delegation from him. Even after he is dead she is not their legal guardian, unless he by will has made her so. . . . This is her legal state. And from this state she has no means of withdrawing herself.[19]

When William Fowler, M.P. for Cambridge, introduced a custody bill in 1872, feminists found that while the bill expanded mothers' rights to petition for custody of or access to their children, it did not give them equal rights with their husbands, and they denounced it.

Fowler's bill allowed mothers to petition in exceptional circumstances for custody of or access to their children under the age of sixteen (rather than age seven). It also stipulated that a separation agreement between a husband and wife would not be held invalid solely because it provided that the father would give up custody of the infant to the mother. (Such provisions had previously invalidated separation agreements on the grounds that a father could not legally relinquish his obligations and rights as a father; these were, in effect, inalienable.) Finally, the bill removed the bar to a mother's petition if she had been found guilty of adultery. By distinguishing between the mother's offense and the possible needs of the child, this provision reflected increasing acceptance of the notion that the correct criterion for custody decisions was the interest of the child, not the absolute right (or the fault) of either parent.

Fowler's bill ignored the principle of coequal parental rights essential to the feminists' conception of marriage law. Their dispute with Fowler, like their disagreement with Morley over the Married Women's Property Act of 1874, was a telling indication of how difficult it was for feminists to get their views adequately represented in Parliament even by their friends. Fowler was a Liberal and a Quaker. He had introduced the first Contagious Diseases Acts repeal bill in Parliament in 1870, and was a political ally of Josephine Butler. He was undoubt-

[19] John Stuart Mill, *The Subjection of Women*, in *Essays on Sex Equality*, ed. Alice Rossi (Chicago: University of Chicago Press, 1970), chap. 2, 160.

edly influenced by the depictions of the hardships and injustices of custody law with respect to women that he had heard in feminist circles.[20] But Fowler does not seem to have consulted his feminist allies out of Parliament before drafting his custody bill. In 1872 Elizabeth Wolstenholme wrote to the *Women's Suffrage Journal* asking women to withhold support from Fowler's bill because it was a shortsighted measure that ignored the equal legal rights of mothers and fathers to custody. A bill based on correct principles would recognize the "coordinate legal rights of mothers," declare father and mother joint guardians during their lifetimes, and grant custody to whichever parent survived the other.[21] An editorial that year also criticized Fowler's bill as a weak and inadequate measure.[22] In 1873 the critics' language was stronger still: the bill embodied the "vicious principle of leaving untouched . . . the deprivation of the parental rights of mothers"; it was a "miserable and palliative measure."[23]

This custody bill also provided a remedy only to the well-to-do who could afford a suit in Chancery. The *Englishwoman's Review* remarked that "we cannot say that we feel much sympathy with this measure as it stands at present. It provides only a complicated and costly remedy for such mothers as are rich enough to incur the expenses of a Chancery suit."[24] The Infant Custody Act of 1873 [36 Vict., c. 12], although it may have looked like a response to the feminist demand for equal rights in marriage, in fact angered leaders of the movement, who were skeptical of any lasting good coming from the Act. The editors of *Englishwoman's Review* did concede that "limited as it is, it will prove an inestimable boon to many women, hitherto outraged in their tenderest affections—their love for their children," but they expected little in the way of meaningful reform.[25] Events soon showed that they were right in their assessment.

[20] See, for example, *Women's Suffrage Journal* 2 (July 1871): 72. See also *The Law Journal* 6 (15 December 1871): 849–50, and *The Law Times* 55 (7 June 1873): 96 for discussions of custody law generated by the effort to pass the Judicature Act of 1873.

[21] *Women's Suffrage Journal* 3 (May 1872): 64.

[22] *Women's Suffrage Journal* 3 (July 1872): 93.

[23] *Women's Suffrage Journal* 4 (March 1873): 31.

[24] *Englishwoman's Review* 4 (April 1873): 147–49. John Hinde Palmer, who in 1872 had taken over for Russell Gurney as parliamentary leader for the married women's property campaign, responded to this criticism and introduced an amendment to allow mothers' petitions under the proposed act to be heard in County Courts, but it was defeated (3 Hansard 214 [6 March 1873], 1513).

[25] *Englishwoman's Review* 4 (July 1873): 226.

THE INFANT CUSTODY ACT OF 1886

The Persistence of the Father's Rights to Custody

Commenting on the working of the Infant Custody Act of 1873 a decade after its passage, one legal periodical observed that

> the judges, in exercising their discretion, have shown themselves hitherto very strongly imbued with the old common law theories, for the construction they have shown themselves disposed to place on the Act of 1873 has been that the mother is to be excluded from the custody of her child, except when such grave misconduct can be made out against the father as might affect the child injuriously.[26]

During the decade following passage of the Infant Custody Act the *Women's Suffrage Journal* and the *Englishwoman's Review* repeatedly reported custody decisions involving egregious denials of mothers' rights to the custody of their children. In one Scottish case where a wife had obtained a separation for cruelty but was refused custody of her four-year-old daughter as well as of her older children, Lord Ardmillan declared: "To leave his wife with the defender were to subject him to an influence exciting and tempting him to violence towards her. To leave his little child in his house is, or may well be, to introduce a soothing influence to cheer the darkness and mitigate the bitterness of his lot, and bring out the better part of his nature."[27] It did not seem to occur to Lord Ardmillan that a man who beat his wife might also abuse his daughter. Furthermore, as an author in the *Westminster Review* commented, "The desirability of 'cheering the darkness and mitigating the bitterness' of the wife's lot does not seem to have crossed the judicial mind at all."[28] The ignoring of women's feelings and claims in this decision was extreme (one notes that the separation was granted not because the husband was brutal but because the wife was "an influence . . . tempting him to violence"), but the judge violated no legal principle in his decision.

Following the passage of the Married Women's Property Act of 1882, hopes were high that Parliament would find the case for other

[26] *Irish Law Times and Solicitors' Journal* 18 (12 July 1884): 356.
[27] Session Cases, 8 M. 821, quoted in "The Law in Relation to Women," *Westminster Review* 128 (1887): 705.
[28] "The Law in Relation to Women," *Westminster Review* 128 (1887): 705.

legal reforms affecting married women irresistible. Several commentators suggested that the passage of the Married Women's Property Act had established the principle that men and women should have equal rights within marriage, and that therefore other forms of married women's disabilities would crumble in its wake. With respect to custody, Mr. Arnold Morley, M.P., remarked that he thought "a measure for the co-equal rights and obligations of parents is a necessary consequence of the Married Women's Property Act."[29] Mr. Bryce remarked in 1884 that "the [Infant Custody] Bill might be regarded as a corollary to the Married Women's Property Act."[30] But as *Justice of the Peace* and the *Irish Law Times and Solicitors' Journal* cautioned their readers, "Notwithstanding the recent Married Women's Property Act, and the advancing claims of women, married and unmarried, there has been no change in the doctrines or practice of the court on the subject of custody of children," while the *Englishwoman's Review* issued a similar warning.[31]

The wisdom of their caution was well illustrated by a widely publicized case that was before the Court of Chancery just after the passage of the Married Women's Property Act of 1882. In 1878 Mr. and Mrs. Agar-Ellis had engaged in a bitter and well-known custody suit in Chancery, and now, five years later, their family disputes again erupted in litigation. Mr. Agar-Elis was a Protestant, Mrs. Agar-Ellis a Catholic. Before their marriage he had promised in the presence of her family that all of their children would be brought up as Catholics, but he later went back on his word and had the children raised as Protestants. Their mother secretly instructed them in her religion. The dispute became so severe that when the parents separated in 1878 the father had the children made wards of the Court of Chancery, which he asked to settle the question of their religious instruction. The Court would make no direct decision concerning the children's religion, but ordered that they must be raised as the father wished. They agreed with counsel to Mr. Agar-Ellis, who argued that the Custody Acts of 1839 and 1873 were "never intended to protect a wife in disobedience to her husband's lawful authority."[32]

The father then removed the children from their mother's care and sent them to boarding schools. He subjected all of their written communications with their mother to scrutiny, and mother and daughters

[29] Quoted in the *Englishwoman's Review* 14 (November 1883): 484.

[30] 3 Hansard 286 (26 March 1884), 814.

[31] *Justice of the Peace*, reprinted in *Irish Law Times and Solicitors' Journal* 18 (28 June 1884): 328; *Englishwoman's Review* 16 (June 1885): 247–48.

[32] *Annual Register* (1878), 210.

were forbidden to discuss religion together. In 1883, the seventeen-year-old daughter asked for permission to take her vacation with her mother, because the family to whom she had been boarded out was going abroad and could not take her with them. Her father refused permission. The daughter appealed as a ward of the court to Chancery, which ruled that Mr. Agar-Ellis had a right to refuse such a request, although Justices Cotton and Bowen observed that "if they were capable of being moved by feelings of favour or disfavour, they might have been tempted to comment with more or less severity upon the way in which it appeared . . . the father was exercising his paternal right."[33] But it was not the Court's place to interfere with or limit the scope of paternal authority; the law was very clear that unless the father threatened a child's safety, neither mother nor court could interfere with the exercise of his paternal prerogative. (Ironically, the daughter would have done better to have run away to her mother. Her father would not have been able to use a writ of habeas corpus to regain custody, because she was over sixteen.)

Public opinion, like the court, thought that Mr. Agar-Ellis had gone too far in keeping his wife and daughter apart, and sentiment grew for some modification in the law which would undercut such absolute paternal authority. Elizabeth Wolstenholme Elmy, fresh from the married women's property campaign, seized the moment and organized a drive to convince Parliament to give fathers and mothers equal rights to the custody of their children.

Parliamentary Rejection of Equal Parental Rights

Even before the end of the married women's property campaign, Wolstenholme Elmy began laying the groundwork for approaching Parliament with a child custody statute based on the principle of equal parental rights. At the 1880 annual meeting of the Social Science Association she attended a session devoted to married women's property law in Scotland. When John Boyd Kinnear concluded his formal presentation, Wolstenholme Elmy was the first to gain the floor. She rose ostensibly to object to a suggestion in the paper that when husband and wife both possessed their own property, both should contribute to the support of the household. Given Wolstenholme Elmy's commitment to spousal equality, this seemed an odd position for her to take, but she explained that she could not acknowledge the fairness of

[33] *Irish Law Times and Solicitors' Journal* 17 (25 August 1883): 446.

joint financial responsibility, because even if a wife was given legal control of her property, she would remain her husband's legal inferior with respect to the custody of their children.[34] Henceforth whenever Wolstenholme Elmy discussed married women's grievances with respect to property, she linked them to mothers' even more acute grievances with respect to custody of their children.

Three years later, freed from the duties of the married women's property campaign, and taking advantage of the publicity generated by the Agar-Ellis case, Wolstenholme Elmy prevailed upon James Bryce, M.P. to introduce a custody bill in Parliament. Bryce and Wolstenholme Elmy were long-time political associates, having worked together for passage of the Educational Endowments Act of 1870. When Bryce agreed to sponsor the measure, Wolstenholme Elmy and other colleagues prepared the ground for the introduction of Bryce's bill, giving lectures and publishing articles wherever they could find an audience.[35] By the spring of 1884, supporters had forwarded 180 petitions with 19,513 signatures to Parliament.[36] Wolstenholme Elmy wrote a leaflet, "To the Wives and Mothers of Every Class," protesting the injustice of the common law rules of custody. The *Englishwoman's Review*, which quoted the leaflet extensively, and the *Irish Law Times and Solicitors' Journal* published a series of articles calling for the reform of custody law.[37]

The bill that Bryce introduced in 1884 reflected the feminists' proposal that parents have equal rights to the custody of their offspring. In explaining the proposal, Wolstenholme Elmy abjured any sugges-

[34] NAPSS, *Transactions* (1880), 191.

[35] In January 1883, Mr. Herbert N. Mozley read a paper on custody law at the London meeting of the Social Science Association, and in October Mr. A. Baker, Her Majesty's consul at Khartoum, had a paper read at the annual meeting of the Association. The next month John Boyd Kinnear argued in the pages of the *Manchester Examiner* that when either spouse died the survivor should become sole guardian, but that when parents separated the court should decide who should be custodian with regard to the interests of the child. During the winter of 1883–1885 Dr. Frances Hoggan, Mrs. E. M. Lynch, and Mr. Arthur Nichols gave lectures on the necessity for reforming the law. In at least one instance, in Nottingham, a member of Parliament was questioned by his constituents on the proposed bill. See Elizabeth Wolstenholme Elmy, *The Infants' Act, 1886: The record of a three years' effort for Legislative Reform, with its results* (London: Women's Printing Society, n.d. [1888]), hereafter referred to as *Three Years' Effort*; A. Baker, *The Custody and Guardianship of Children*, 2d ed. (Hanley: Atkinson Brothers, 1883); *Englishwoman's Review* 14 (February 1883): 80–81 and 14 (November 1883): 481.

[36] *Englishwoman's Review* 15 (April 1884): 147.

[37] *Englishwoman's Review* 14 (September 1883): 395–98; *Irish Law Times and Solicitors' Journal* 17 (15 September 1883): 484.

tion of Caroline Norton's plea that married women needed "protection." Characteristically, Wolstenholme Elmy argued that as "a rational and accountable creature" a wife had as much right to the custody of her children as her husband. To her it was clear that "parental claims resting upon co-equal duties and obligations involve for the adequate fulfillment of these duties, rights co-equal and co-determinate." With custody law as with other facets of marriage law, Wolstenholme Elmy wanted "nothing less than the entire re-adjustment of the legal position of the mother in the family," and "the establishment of the family on the basis of justice, equality, and mutual duty and love."[38]

Even as these egalitarian ideas about family relations made headway, some prominent feminists argued that women's "natural" functions of childbearing, lactation, and the care of infants gave mothers *superior* claims to custody. One such widely-circulated argument was made by Dr. Frances Hoggan, a dentist and an advocate of women's rights. Hoggan's *The Position of the Mother in the Family in its Legal and Scientific Aspects* turned the practice of giving scientific validation to the separate-spheres ideology on its head. Social philosopher Herbert Spencer, biologists such as Patrick Geddes and J. Arthur Thomson, and others had tried to explain and justify the inferior position of women as a function of natural laws that could not be changed by human intervention.[39] Hoggan adapted the notion of men's and women's different natures and "separate spheres" to her own ends, arguing that women's predominant responsibility for the care of children should give mothers at least an equal and probably a superior claim to custody of their children.[40] Other feminists invoked the universality of "mother love" to argue that women were bound together in this cause and had to act politically on the basis of their common maternity. At a suffrage meeting in Manchester, Jessie Craigen reminded her listeners that "The mother's love . . . is one. The richest woman here to-night that is the mother of children loves them dearly; the poorest no less. And the laws which wrong the mother's love are an outrage on the common womanhood by the bond of which we have all been drawn together here."[41]

[38] Elizabeth Wolstenholme Elmy, *The Infants Bill* (Manchester: A. Ireland and Co., 1884), 3, 12.

[39] Susan Kent, *Sex and Suffrage in Britain, 1860–1914* (Princeton: Princeton University Press, 1987), 34–35.

[40] Frances Hoggan, *The Position of the Mother in the Family in its Legal and Scientific Aspects* (London, 1884).

[41] *Women's Suffrage Journal* 11 (14 February 1880): 46.

In spite of its popular appeal, however, talk about a mother's special relationship to her child seemed to Wolstenholme Elmy to be likely to do the cause of married women's rights more harm than good, for it reinforced the notion that women were essentially domestic creatures. Although Wolstenholme Elmy always mentioned Dr. Hoggan's essay with respect, she was quick to point out that it referred to the mother's preeminence in "the physical order," whereas in "the moral and social order" a child needed "the love, the tender nurture, the educating influence, moral and intellectual, of both parents."[42] Even though the mother normally "does more, suffers more, and most frequently loves more," the law must embody the principle that parents' responsibilities for their child "are, though diverse, co-equal."[43]

The difference between Wolstenholme Elmy's and Hoggan's approaches exemplified a perennial dispute among feminists over whether to emphasize or ignore men's and women's different roles in reproduction when trying to promote gender equality by means of the law. That question has been posed recently over the question of whether pregnancy should be treated as a "temporary disability" for purposes of granting workers' leaves, or whether pregnancy leave should be governed by unique stipulations.[44] It has also erupted in discussions of "surrogate" mothering. Many feminists have contended that regardless of a biological mother's agreement to relinquish custody to the biological father after birth, her unique relationship to the child must always give her a superior prima facie claim to custody. This position runs the risk of having the law define women by their reproductive capacity, and of deemphasizing men's responsibility for children. In egalitarian terms, one could argue that the woman, who "does more [and] suffers more" during pregnancy and childbirth than the man, has a superior claim to custody at the moment of birth, which diminishes as the father cares for the child. The dilemma of how to recognize reproductive differences while maintaining a commitment to gender equality is still unresolved.

Wolstenholme Elmy's commitment to spousal equality before the law was evident in the provisions of Bryce's original bill. Clause 2 stipulated that during their marriage parents were to be joint guardians of their children. Other clauses provided that on the death of either par-

[42] Wolstenholme Elmy, *Infants Bill*, 3.

[43] Elizabeth Wolstenholme Elmy, *The Custody and Guardianship of Children* (London: John Bale & Sons, n.d. [1884]), 11–12.

[44] For a discussion of various aspects of this dilemma, see Christine A. Littleton, "Reconstructing Sexual Equality," *California Law Review* 75 (1987): 1279–1337.

ent, the survivor would be the children's guardian, that the surviving parent could appoint a testamentary guardian for an unmarried child, and that if a dispute arose between parents living separately, the court had the power to make an order concerning the children's upbringing or religious education. The single exception to equal parental rights was the clause providing that if a child possessed property, a testamentary guardian appointed by the father would act jointly with the mother, whereas a surviving father would act as sole guardian. This was a concession to the widely held belief that matters affecting estate management should not be left solely in women's hands.

The debate on Bryce's bill revealed general agreement that the absolute presumption in favor of the father could work great injustice, and that the courts should have greater discretion in awarding custody. There was also agreement that after her husband's death a mother's place as guardian of her children should not be usurped by a testamentary appointee. The notion of equal custody rights for parents living together, however, came under strong attack. Mr. Fowler, sponsor of the Custody Act of 1873, rose to say that he "very reluctantly" might have to vote against the second reading: "The Bill started with the idea that the husband and wife were equal, a theory which was against scripture and reason. . . . The man and the woman could not be made equal by any Act of Parliament in the world." Mr. Balfour, Gladstone's advocate general, announced that the Government would not oppose the second reading but had strong reservations about the clause providing that parents be joint guardians during their lifetimes, and added that he would hope to see the bill amended in Committee.[45] Although the bill passed its first reading by the sizable margin of 208 in favor, 73 opposed, it was clear that there would be considerable difficulty in passing the measure into law. Wolstenholme Elmy repeatedly urged supporters of the measure to lobby their members to retain clause 2.[46] But in the early hours of the morning on July 22, the House in Committee voted to delete the provision for joint parental custody, thereby eliminating the central principle of the bill, the coequal rights of husbands and wives.

It was clearly evident that the feminists' parliamentary allies did not fully share their conviction that equal spousal rights had to be at the heart of meaningful marriage law reform. Once clause 2 was eliminated, even Mr. Bryce seemed to forget the original rationale for the bill. The debate over the court's power to make orders respecting a

[45] 3 Hansard 286 (26 March 1884), 824, 836–38.
[46] *Englishwoman's Review* 15 (April 1884): 148 and 15 (July 1884): 331.

child's upbringing and religion provoked strenuous protest from members who feared giving the courts too much discretion to override traditional rights of fathers, even those who had died; Irish members, for example, worried that Protestant judges would interfere in the upbringing of children of Catholic widows. In the face of strong opposition, which seemed to threaten the entire bill, Mr. Bryce remarked that "there was nothing in the construction of this new 5th clause to negative or extinguish the permanent Common Law right of the father . . . ; and, therefore, *prima facie* the child would be brought up in the religion of the father."[47] But the original purpose of the custody law reformers had been precisely to *overturn* the common law presumption, and Wolstenholme Elmy was furious. Unwilling to attack Bryce personally, she denounced the procedures of the House of Commons that made passage of private Members' bills so difficult that legislators were "often willing to buy off the obstructive forces by sacrifices of the most important details, or, what is still more fatal, by the surrender of some vital principle."[48] Once again her dream of spousal equality had been compromised, as Parliament ameliorated the legal situation of married women while leaving male dominance in place.[49]

The Lords made short shrift of the bill that session. No sooner had Lord Fitzgerald introduced the bill than Lord Cairns opposed the second reading on the grounds that it was too late in the session for adequate consideration of the measure. In the face of Lord Cairns's active opposition, Lord Fitzgerald was forced to withdraw the bill.[50] When he reintroduced the custody bill in November 1884, Lord Fitzgerald indicated in his remarks that the chance of gaining acceptance of the principle of joint custody was dead; he asserted that the main objective of the bill was "to constitute the wife, *if she survived her husband*, guardian of her children," not to recognize the principle that custody law should be based on the joint and coequal responsiblity of husband

[47] 3 Hansard 291 (25 July 1884), 606.

[48] Wolstenholme Elmy, *Three Years' Effort*, 22.

[49] The House of Commons did make relief under the bill available to women of modest means, as well as the rich, by extending the jurisdiction of the County Courts in England and Ireland and the Sheriff Courts in Scotland to custody cases. (Parliamentary distrust of the abilities of County Court judges produced an additional clause which enabled either party to have a case removed to the High Court.) See 3 Hansard 291 (31 July 1884), 1332.

[50] Mr. Bryce complained to the *Times* that one scarcely knew what to think of a "second Chamber which thus surrenders itself to the will of one man, and which refuses to extend its sitting over the dinner-hour for the sake of remedying grave and long-admitted evils" (*Times* (London), 7 August 1884, p. 7). See subsequent letters of 8, 13, and 16 August 1884.

and wife.[51] When a Select Committee appointed by the Lords to consider the bill met in March 1885, Lord Fitzgerald made one last attempt to restore clause 2 and thus allow parents to exercise joint custody of their minor children. His motion failed, and the issue of joint custody was not raised again.[52]

The measure that Parliament considered thereafter dealt essentially with widows' rights to custody. Even this was a problem for those Members who felt committed to a patriarchal model of the family. The Marquess of Salisbury saw the bill as "the greatest interference with the rights and privileges which men valued more than they did their own lives." For Earl Beauchamp it raised questions "not so much for the consideration of lawyers as for the consideration of fathers of families."[53] But this extreme hostility to women's claims was not shared by the majority of either Lords or Commons, who regarded a surviving mother as having rights to the custody of her children that should outweigh a deceased father's wishes embodied in a last will and testament. The only alteration made in the rights of the surviving parent replaced language stating that the mother's testamentary guardian would serve jointly with the father if the court was "satisfied that such appointment is necessary or desirable for the welfare of such infant" with language stating that the mother's testamentary guardian would serve "if it be shown to the satisfaction of the court that the father is for any reason unfitted to be the sole guardian of his children."[54] By requiring that the father be shown to be positively "unfitted" to be sole guardian, the amendment weakened the power of the court to install the mother's testamentary guardian to act with the father. On the face of it, this looked like a conservative reaffirmation of paternal rights at the expense of the welfare of the child and the mother's testamentary guardian. But advocates of women's rights welcomed the amendment, believing, as Wolstenholme Elmy put it, that "either surviving parent is the natural guardian of the child, whose authority ought not to be interfered with except in cases of the greatest necessity." Although this law allowed the father to impose a co-guardian on his wife, "it is yet better to accept this temporary inequality, in the hope of soon correcting it, . . . than to perpetuate the present injustice by extending this unjust power to the mother."[55] Wolstenholme Elmy might also have

[51] 3 Hansard 294 (24 November 1884), 224 (emphasis added).
[52] Wolstenholme Elmy, *Three Years' Effort*, 25–26.
[53] 3 Hansard 297 (24 April 1885), 623; (21 April 1855), 298.
[54] 3 Hansard 297 (30 April 1885), 1088.
[55] Wolstenholme Elmy, *Three Years' Effort*, 42. See also *Irish Law Times and Solicitors' Journal* 19 (16 May 1885): 252.

thought that it would be wise not to bestow too much discretionary power on the court, whose judgment as to the child's best interest was, after all, the judgment of an all-male tribunal.

The measure thus amended passed the Lords in 1885, but was blocked in the Commons and went no further before Parliament was dissolved.[56] The elections of February 1886 returned the Liberals to office, and Gladstone's third ministry was persuaded to introduce the custody bill as a government measure. Sponsored by the government, the bill passed both Commons and Lords easily and received the Royal Assent on June 25, 1886.[57]

At the same time that Parliament was considering the infant custody measures, it disposed of two other bills in ways which provide a gauge of how far government was willing to go in stepping between husband and wife, parent and child. In 1880 Charles Hopwood and John Thomasson introduced a "Bill to Provide a Remedy by Law for Married Women against their Husbands Neglecting or Refusing to Maintain and Educate their Children," which Hopwood resubmitted in 1881 and 1883. The bill, which would have permitted a woman to obtain from her husband "a sum of money proportionate to his means" for the support of their children under age sixteen, never reached a second reading. It seemed to one M.P. a "meddling interference with . . . the domestic concerns of life," and to another a threat "to those whom God had joined together."[58] In 1886 Parliament did enact the "Married Women (Maintenance in Case of Desertion) Act," which allowed deserted wives to sue for maintenance for themselves and their children without first going to the workhouse. Parliament would keep a deserted wife from destitution (and off the parish rolls), but it would not order a man to support his wife and children if he was living with them. It was a pattern consistent with other reforms in domestic relations law: Parliament was ready to help women, but a pater

---

[56] 3 Hansard 300 (4 August 1885), 1025–26.

[57] The Commons made the Act applicable to mothers widowed prior to the passage of the Act. They also added a clause providing that the Divorce Court, in pronouncing a separation or divorce, might declare the guilty party unfit to have custody of any children of the marriage; in such a case if the guilty spouse survived the other parent, he or she would not have the right to custody under the Act. Members of the government may have allowed the new clause because they shared this punitive attitude, but it is more likely that they calculated that the clause was of little consequence since the Divorce Court would have discretion to decide whether to bar custody to the guilty party. See 3 Hansard 304 (16 April 1886), 1874–75.

[58] George K. Behlmer, *Child Abuse and Moral Reform in England, 1870–1908* (Stanford: Stanford University Press, 1982), 91.

familias residing with his wife and children was not to suffer interference from either his wife or the state.

Children's Rights and Contractual
Models of the Family

Reform of custody law involved not only the rights of mothers and fathers, but the rights and welfare of children as well. Arguments about women's rights were often jarring to the ears of M.P.s, but the solicitude of custody law reformers for children and their needs struck a resonant chord in legislative and judicial circles. By the 1880s various traditional parental (particularly paternal) rights were increasingly subject to limitation by what Parliament and the courts regarded as the needs and rights of the child. Officials believed that they had a particular obligation to protect the young, even if this meant allowing the state to step between parent and child.

Feminists shared the attitude that children deserved legal protection, and in advocating custody law reform they invariably appealed first and foremost to the needs of children. Wolstenholme Elmy believed deeply that the true basis of custodial authority was neither the mother's nor the father's rights, but "the needs of the human child itself."[59] Mr. A. Baker agreed that it could never be right to think that parents "own" their children; in cases of separation the courts should decide custody with regard to the best interests of the child.[60] Mr. Bryce argued that custody law should be based on the principle of joint custody "to guard the interests of children in the first place, and, in the next, the interests of the parents as persons on a footing of equality."[61]

The persuasiveness of such an appeal to children's welfare was a relatively recent development in parliamentary circles. Parliament had rejected the crowded dwellings prevention bill of 1857 (which would have allowed housing inspections) on the grounds that it was contrary to the spirit of liberty and violated the sanctity of the English home.[62] So strong was the reluctance to allow the state to intervene in parent-child relations at mid-century that John Stuart Mill took pains in 1859 to point out that the arguments of his *On Liberty* should not be used to safeguard parents from the scrutiny of the state: "It is in the case of

[59] Wolstenholme Elmy, *Infants Bill*, 3.

[60] Baker, *Custody and Guardianship of Children*, 8.

[61] James Bryce and Horace Davey, *Speeches . . . on the Second Reading of the Infants Bill* (London: Cornelius Buck, 1884), 7.

[62] Anthony Wohl, *The Eternal Slum: Housing and Social Policy in Victorian London* (London: E. Arnold, 1977), 75.

children, that misapplied notions of liberty are a real obstacle to the fulfillment by the State of its duties. One would almost think that a man's children were supposed to be literally, and not metaphorically, a part of himself, so jealous is opinion of the smallest interference of law with his absolute and exclusive control over them."[63]

The debates on the Education Act of 1870 showed that the ground was shifting, however. Opponents of the Act unsuccessfully argued that compulsory education unjustifiably restricted the liberty of parents to raise their children as they saw fit. Nonetheless, in 1881 Lord Shaftesbury still contended that child abuse was "of so private, internal, and domestic a character as to be beyond the reach of legislation."[64] Samuel Smith countered in 1883 that "we have far too long considered that children were the property of their parents, who were free to abuse, starve, or corrupt them as they thought proper." Now, said Smith, England required measures "to make it obligatory on a parent to feed, clothe, and bring up his child in a decent manner."[65]

Consonant with this concern for children, Parliament passed the Criminal Law Amendment Act of 1885 [48 & 49 Vict., c. 69], which was intended to protect children from exploitation by raising the age of consent (that is, the age at which a young person is held to be legally capable of consenting to sexual intercourse). Although final passage occurred in the wake of the furor generated by W. T. Stead's publication of "The Maiden Tribute of Modern Babylon" in the *Pall Mall Gazette* in July 1885, reformers had been proposing such legislation for several years. Deborah Gorham has observed that the significance of any age of consent legislation "can only be understood in the context of other legal definitions that relate to the boundaries that a society draws between childhood, youth, and maturity."[66] The Criminal Law Amendment Act reflected an expanded definition of childhood as well as a new impulse to use state authority to control sexual behavior.

In 1889 Parliament accepted what many contemporaries called the "Children's Charter," the Act for the Better Prevention of Cruelty to Children, which represented "England's first attempt to deal comprehensively with the domestic relationship between parent and child." The extent of, and limitations on, parental power were now "made explicit in a single statute." If a parent was convicted of cruelty, the

[63] J. S. Mill, *On Liberty*, quoted in Behlmer, *Child Abuse*, 2.

[64] Lord Shaftesbury to George Staite, n.d., quoted in Behlmer, *Child Abuse*,, 52.

[65] Samuel Smith, "Social Reform," *Nineteenth Century* 13 (May 1883): 902.

[66] Deborah Gorham, "The 'Maiden Tribute of Modern Babylon' Reexamined: Child Prostitution and the Idea of Childhood in Late-Victorian England," *Victorian Studies* 21 (Spring 1978): 362–63.

court could remove the child from the home, either to the custody of a relative or other "fit person" (which could mean an industrial school or charitable organization). The parent was liable to contribute up to five shillings per week for the child's maintenance, showing that, in theory at least, parental responsibility did not end with the departure of the child.[67]

Taken together, these pieces of legislation of the 1880s revealed that solicitude for the child was becoming increasingly capable of overriding the traditional deference to familial privacy. Parents were the natural protectors of their offspring, but if they violated that trust, it was legitimate for the state to step in on the child's behalf. This view regarded parent-child relations as "voluntaristic" as well as natural. Rather than treating fathers as enjoying a near-proprietary right in their children stemming from procreation, the legislation of the 1880s suggested that by the act of procreation parents had entered into implicit agreements with one another, their children, and the state to nurture and care for their offspring. Parents who fulfilled their obligations would not suffer state interference, but those who violated the terms of their "contract" could be forced to fulfill it—for example, by paying maintenance or sending their child to school. If the violation was so gross as to sever the contract, parents might forfeit custody altogether, and if the covenant between parent and child was broken by the natural parent, it might later "be renewed by another willing to accept the responsibilities of parenthood."[68] The severing of legal relations based on biological ties (and, later, the voluntary assumption of parental responsibilities through legal adoption) was possible only if parenthood was regarded as a voluntary or contractual role as well as a biological or natural one. The development of custody law thus depended upon changing attitudes not only about women's rights and the relationship between husband and wife, but also about children's needs and the nature of the tie between parent and child.

In their challenge of the common law rules regulating custody decisions, just as in their challenge of the common law doctrine of coverture, Victorian feminists counterpoised a model of voluntaristic, contractual family relations to traditional models of family life based upon "nature." Patriarchal authority in the family was based on the assump-

[67] Behlmer, *Child Abuse*, 109.

[68] Zainaldin, "Emergence," 1083. Robert E. Goodin criticizes the voluntaristic view of the origin of parental obligations, arguing instead that they derive from the vulnerability of children. See *Protecting the Vulnerable: A Reanalysis of Our Social Responsibilities* (Chicago: University of Chicago Press, 1985).

tion that a father had "natural" authority over the children he had sired and "natural" authority over his wife, for as "the abler and the stronger" of the matrimonial pair it was proper that he rule the household.[69] These dual assumptions of paternal and marital authority placed the husband clearly at the head of the family.

The liberal values of individual freedom and equality, and the notion that all legitimate authority derives from consent, seemed the most promising means by which to challenge the notion of natural male authority. When feminists attacked traditional custody law, they argued first that mothers had just as much a part in procreation as fathers, and therefore "by nature" they should have equal rights to custody of their children. Second, they asserted, no woman could be presumed to have consented to relinquish all hold on any children she might bear when she agreed to marry. The common law assumption that custodial authority lay with the father deeply offended liberal principles of consent as well as equality.

Arguments based on liberal notions of individual rights had a strong attraction for English lawmakers. The relative ease with which Parliament accepted all of Mr. Bryce's custody bill except the clause declaring parents to be joint guardians of their children showed that Parliament was prepared both to give courts more discretion to interfere with fathers' traditional control over their children and to recognize many of women's claims to equal treatment under the law. But Members of Parliament balked at the feminists' persistent demand that Parliament put husband and wife in an *ongoing* marriage on a *completely equal* legal footing with respect to custody, just as it had refused to do with married women's property law. The deference accorded to the custodial rights of fathers gave men enormous indirect power over women. Wives were dependent upon their husbands to keep their children near them, for wifely insubordination might be punished by a child's being dispatched to live with relatives, apprenticed out to work, or sent away to a school abhorrent to the mother. In leaving custody exclusively in a father's hands, Parliament gave men a potent weapon for bending their wives' wills to their own.

Despite the reforms in married women's property and custody law in the 1880s, Parliament clung tenaciously to the remnants of patriar-

[69] The phrase "the abler and the stronger" is John Locke's, and constituted the only justification he could think of for a husband's authority over his wife. See the introduction to this volume, and John Locke, *Two Treatises of Government*, ed. Peter Laslett, rev. ed. (New York: Mentor Books, 1963), second treatise, sec. 55, p. 347. On patriarchal thought, see Gordon Schochet, *Patriarchalism in Political Theory* (New York: Basic Books, 1975).

chal authority ensconced in family law, and was as yet unwilling to consider the possibility of legislating on the basis of spousal equality. Unlike such feminists as Josephine Butler, Emmeline and Richard Pankhurst, or Ben Elmy and Elizabeth Wolstenholme Elmy, Parliament would not concede that in a family where mother and father both lived with their children, equality between husband and wife would lead to moral and spiritual elevation rather than to confusion, insubordination, and social disintegration. Parliament's intransigence increased the activists' conviction that their goal of spousal equality would never be achieved until women, including married women, had the power to vote in parliamentary elections.

· 6 ·

A HUSBAND'S RIGHT TO HIS WIFE'S BODY: WIFE ABUSE, THE RESTITUTION OF CONJUGAL RIGHTS, AND MARITAL RAPE

A spaniel, a woman, and a walnut tree,
The more they're beaten, the better they be.

—Old English Proverb

It is the fear of men that women will cease to be any longer their sexual slaves either in or out of marriage that is the root of the whole opposition to our just claim [women's suffrage]. No doubt their fear is justified, for that is precisely what we do mean.

—Elizabeth Wolstenholme Elmy to
Harriet M'Ilquham, 21 May 1897

In 1888 Elizabeth Wolstenholme Elmy published a four-page pamphlet, *The Emancipation of Women*, which had been intended, she explained, to form "the concluding portion of the Report of the agitation which secured the passing of the Infants Act, 1886." She had eliminated these pages from that report out of deference to friends and fellow-workers "who do not yet feel prepared for the acceptance of the full programme" of the feminist movement. Her more reticent colleagues were not ready to assert publicly that "foremost of all the wrongs from which women suffer, and in itself creative of many of them, is the inequality and injustice of their position in the marriage relation, and the legal denial to wives of that personal freedom, which is the most sacred right of humanity." Married women were unable to prosecute husbands who forced them to have sexual intercourse; sexual access was taken to be part of the marriage contract, and marital rape was not legally cognizable. A woman who left her husband because he forced her to have sexual relations with him was guilty of desertion and could lose all rights to maintenance and custody.

As Wolstenholme Elmy recognized, not many Victorians were prepared to discuss marital rape, but hers was not an isolated voice. Nearly twenty years before, John Stuart Mill had contended that with respect to rape a wife was worse off than a slave.

156

[A] female slave has (in Christian countries) an admitted right, and is considered under a moral obligation, to refuse her master the last familiarity. Not so the wife: however brutal a tyrant she may unfortunately be chained to—though she may know that he hates her, though it may be his daily pleasure to torment her, and though she may feel it impossible not to loathe him—he can claim from her and enforce the lowest degradation of a human being, that of being made the instrument of an animal function contrary to her inclinations.[1]

Mill clearly presented an idealized image of the lives of slave women here.[2] But his rhetoric emphasized that even people who expressed outrage at the breeding of slaves or at a master's making a slave his mistress regarded it as a married woman's duty never to reject her husband's sexual demands.

During the debates on divorce and married women's property during the 1850s, a pamphleteer protesting a wife's inability to control her own property denounced as well her inability to refuse her husband's sexual advances. A "very industrious and decent woman," whose husband was convicted of sexually assaulting their ten-year-old daughter, moved to a distant part of the country under an assumed name. For several years she maintained herself and her children, and even accumulated some savings. Her precaution was for naught. "One fatal evening . . . a well known diabolical countenance is seen at the window of her peaceful cottage inflamed with drink, and lust, and cruelty. The monster comes to claim his marital rights over her earnings and her person—he comes in the name of the English law, and who shall resist or gainsay him?"[3] The connection made here between a wife's inability to control either her own property or her sexual activity against her husband's wishes underscored the relationship between economic, sexual, and legal autonomy. In the eyes of the law, neither a married woman's money nor her body were her own—both were the "property" of her husband.

In the 1870s Victorian feminists set out to reclaim married women's control over their bodies, just as they asserted their rights to own prop-

[1] John Stuart Mill, *The Subjection of Women*, in *Essays on Sex Equality*, ed. Alice Rossi (Chicago: University of Chicago Press, 1970), chap. 2, 160.

[2] For a sound historical assessment of black slave women and rape, see Jacqueline Jones, *Labor of Love, Labor of Sorrow: Black Women, Work, and the Family from Slavery to the Present* (New York: Basic Books, 1985).

[3] *Remarks on the Law of Marriage and Divorce; suggested by the Honourable Mrs. Norton's Letter to the Queen* (London: James Ridgway, 1855), 22–23.

erty and to obtain custody of their children. The feminists' main effort in this respect was directed toward changing the laws dealing with wife abuse in order to make it possible for a battered woman to leave her husband and live as a feme sole, even if she could not divorce him. As a result of their agitation, Parliament passed the Matrimonial Causes Act of 1878, which allowed a wife beaten by her husband to apply for a separation order from a local magistrates' court. By the Summary Jurisdiction (Married Women's) Act of 1895, Parliament extended this relief to women who had already left their husbands because of assault, desertion, cruelty, or neglect.

Feminists could do less about other ways in which a husband might assert his jurisdiction over his wife's body. If a wife who was *not* a victim of wife abuse left her husband, she risked the possibility that he would obtain a court order for the "restitution of conjugal rights." This writ ordered an errant spouse to return to the marital bed and board, and disobedience of it was punishable by imprisonment until the guilty spouse promised to comply with the writ. A woman thus had the choice of returning to a husband she loathed or serving an indeterminate jail sentence. In his Palliser novels Anthony Trollope grippingly portrayed the tragedy of Lady Laura Kennedy, who, unable to bear living with her inflexible and moralistic husband, went back to her father's house. But Mr. Kennedy obtained a writ for restitution of conjugal rights, and Lady Laura and her father fled to rented rooms in Belgium, where their exile was itself a kind of imprisonment, cutting them off from home, work, family and friends.

In 1884 Parliament abolished the penalty for noncompliance with the writ for restitution of conjugal rights, although the action itself was not abolished. (Noncompliance thereafter was taken as evidence of willful desertion.) In 1891, in *Regina* v. *Jackson*, the Court of Appeal held that a writ for the restitution of conjugal rights did not entitle a husband to detain his wife against her will. Feminists had long insisted that while in a good marriage husband and wife might well be "one in spirit," to claim ownership or control of another's body was not only abhorrent but violated the liberal principle of individual freedom. By the century's end Parliament and the courts had come partially to agree.

Hovering in the background of these changes was the question of whether the "marital exemption" in rape law should be abolished in order to give married women the right to prosecute sexual assault by their husbands. With very few exceptions, however, that issue was not explicitly raised, and indeed to this day the "marital exemption" exists in many English-speaking jurisdictions.[4] Obtaining the right to leave an abusive husband with a court's protection, and the right to leave any husband without being subject to jail or a writ of habeas corpus, nonetheless constituted significant victories for Victorian feminists, and were integrally linked to the reconceptualization of the marriage tie that lay at the heart of late nineteenth-century feminism.

WIFE BEATING, THE MATRIMONIAL CAUSES ACT OF 1878, AND THE SUMMARY JURISDICTION (MARRIED WOMEN) ACT OF 1895

Defining the Problem: Punishing Men or Liberating Women?

The resurgence of organized political feminism after 1867 increased public attention to wife beating. In his speech introducing the women's suffrage amendment to the Reform Bill of 1867 John Stuart Mill asserted that the records of police courts clearly showed not only that women could not rely on men for protection, but that often the men closest to them posed the greatest threat to their welfare. In a dramatic challenge that became a staple of subsequent arguments, Mill stated:

> I should like to have a Return laid before this House of the number of women who are annually beaten to death, kicked to death, or trampled to death by their male protectors; and, in an opposite column, the amount of the sentences passed in those cases in which the dastardly criminals did not get off altogether. I should also like to have, in a third column, the amount of property, the unlawful taking of which was, at the same sessions or assizes, by the same judge, thought worthy of the same amount of punishment. We should then have an arithmetical estimate of the value set by a male legislature and male tribunals on the murder of a woman . . . which . . . would make us hang our heads.[5]

This was not the first time Mill had spoken out against wife beating. In 1850 and 1851 he and Harriet Taylor Mill had written a series of letters to the *Morning Chronicle* decrying the light sentences meted out

---

[4] See, for England, Carole Smart, *The Ties That Bind: Law, Marriage and the Reproduction of Patriarchal Relations* (London: Routledge & Kegan Paul, 1984); for the United States, Lenore Weitzman, *The Marriage Contract: Spouses, Lovers and the Law* (New York: The Free Press, 1981); and for Australia, Carole Pateman, *The Sexual Contract* (Stanford: Stanford University Press, 1988).

[5] 3 Hansard 187 (20 May 1867), 826.

to wife-beaters and parliamentary indifference to drafting legislation to deter domestic violence, both of which they saw as reflections of the low regard in which women were held. With respect to a case dismissed by a magistrates' court, they contended that there was no offense "in the whole criminal code of which a prisoner would have been acquited, in the face of such evidence, except that of an attempt at wife-murder."[6] In "The Enfranchisement of Women," Harriet Taylor Mill again denounced wife beating. She did not attribute the high incidence of assaults to the reluctance of the legal system to punish wife-beaters, but rather to the low legal status of wives, particularly to the lack of married women's property rights:

> The truly horrible effects of the law among the lowest of the working population, is exhibited in those cases of hideous maltreatment of their wives by working men, with which every newspaper, every police report, teems. Wretches unfit to have the smallest authority over any living thing, have a helpless woman for their household slave. These excesses could not exist if women both earned, and had the right to possess, a part of the income of the family.[7]

Harriet Taylor Mill's linking of married women's property rights with wife beating suggested that if married women possessed property their husbands would show them greater respect, and also that if they earned money they could more easily leave brutal husbands. This position was more advanced and more realistic than the notion of John Stuart Mill and others that married women simply needed the *right* to possess property. Harriet Mill believed that material independence might deter some violence. For his part, in *The Subjection of Women*, John Stuart Mill reiterated his condemnation of the legal sanctioning of "the right of the strong to power over the weak." Eradicating the false sense of superiority that made judges excuse men who regarded their wives as "fair game" for mistreatment would require the transformation of marriage into a relationship of equality. In the meantime, said Mill, as long as women were unable to separate from abusive hus-

---

[6] A few months later they vowed they would report in letters to the editor the names of "those wretches who forget their duties as men and Christians," until the legislature adopted measures to halt domestic violence. See *Morning Chronicle*, 28 April 1851, p. 4; 24 August 1851, p. 2; and 28 August 1851, quoted in Jan Lambertz, *Male-Female Violence in Late Victorian and Edwardian England* (B.A. honors thesis, Harvard University, 1980), 84 and ch. 4, n. 33.

[7] "The Enfranchisement of Women," *Westminster Review* 55, Am. ed. (July 1851): 154n.

bands, they would not prosecute their tormentors; not much was likely to be achieved by way of relief to the victim until aggravated assault entitled the woman "*ipso facto* to a divorce, or at least to a judicial separation."[8]

Comparisons of punishments meted out to wife-beaters and to other criminals became regular features in the columns of the *Women's Suffrage Journal*, which began publication in 1870, and in some nonfeminist newspapers as well. The editors of the *Women's Suffrage Journal* emphasized the discrepancies among sentences as a way of demonstrating that the divorce law had to be amended so that battered women could divorce their husbands. They also insisted that women were not protected by an all-male legislature and therefore needed the vote.

Partly in response to the agitation over domestic violence, some Members of Parliament took up the issue of wife beating, not with the aim of altering divorce law or granting women suffrage, but because they hoped that Parliament would reinstitute flogging as a punishment for personal assaults.[9] In 1872 Mr. Douglas Straight and Mr. Eykyn (the former a supporter of women's suffrage, the latter an opponent) introduced a bill "To Authorize the Punishment of Whipping for Certain Offenses against Women and Children"—although it appears that, due to the press of other business, the bill never reached the floor for discussion.[10] But proponents of flogging were persistent. In 1874 Col. Egerton Leigh rose in the House of Commons to ask the government to impose increased punishment for crimes of violence against women: "Garotting had been stopped by means of the 'cat' in gaols,

---

[8] Mill, *Subjection of Women*, chap. 4, 220; chap. 2, 164.

[9] A similar proposal had also been submitted to Parliament in 1853 and 1856. In 1853, as part of their deliberations on the Act for the Better Punishment of Aggravated Assaults on Women and Children of 1853 [16 & 17 Vict., c. 30], Parliament had considered and rejected a proposal for flogging wife-beaters (3 Hansard 124 [10 March 1853], 1414–22, and 125 [6 April 1853], 669–85). In 1856 Mr. Dillwyn had brought forward a bill proposing that violent assaults against women and children be punished by flogging (3 Hansard 141 [12 March 1856], 24–28, and 3 Hansard 142 [7 May 1856], 165–77). Dillwyn's bill sparked some interesting commentary on domestic violence, including J. W. Kaye's "Outrages on Women" in the *North British Review* 25 (May 1856). Kaye, a military historian, succeeded J. S. Mill at the India Office, and one could conjecture that Kaye was inspired to write his essay by conversations with Mill. In "Outrages on Women," Kaye tried to shift the ground of discussion from Dillwyn's proposal to use flogging as a deterrent and punishment to other ways of ameliorating violence against women.

[10] *PP*, 1872, III, bill 131. The bill would have empowered any court imposing a sentence for assaults on women and children under the Offences against the Person Act of 1861 to add the penalty of flogging to the sentence (3 Hansard 211 [6 May 1872], 285).

and he did not see why it might not be used against men who were in the habit of beating their wives." Mr. Disraeli responded that he hoped Colonel Leigh would allow the home secretary, "whose mind is now occupied with this and similar subjects," time to reflect on the practical mode in which "the feeling of the country upon this subject can be carried into effect." Colonel Leigh expressed his satisfaction, and then in one of those jocular and condescending remarks which seemed inevitable in all parliamentary discussions of women's issues, and which Frances Power Cobbe found "inexpressibly sickening," he said as he sat down that he was merely seeking "fair play for the fairer sex."[11]

True to Disraeli's word that the government was concerned with the ability of the criminal law to deter violence, the home secretary issued a circular on October 15, 1874, to the Judges, Chairmen of Quarter Sessions, Recorders of Boroughs having Quarter Sessions, Stipendiary Magistrates of Metropolitan Police Courts, and Sheriffs of Scotch Counties asking if the penal law against brutal assaults was sufficiently stringent, and if not, in what way it should be amended, and second, whether flogging should be authorized for cases of assaults on women and children. The *Report . . . on the State of the Law relating to Brutal Assaults, &c.*, which was published in 1875, provides useful information both on the extent of wife beating and on law officers' perceptions of that crime.[12] The total number of convictions for brutal assaults for the five years from 1870 to 1874 was 6,029, or about 1,205 each year. Many of the counties, such as Cardiganshire, reported *no* brutal assaults (an immunity which Frances Power Cobbe remarked was "little short of miraculous").[13] Using the *Report*, Cobbe estimated that the number of brutal assaults committed on women in England and Wales and brought before the courts was some 1,500 per year during the 1870s. These statistics encompassed only aggravated assaults, those involving gross physical injury or use of a dangerous or deadly weapon. Common assaults involving black eyes, bruises, and teeth knocked out would have been very much more prevalent.

Based on London police court records, Nancy Tomes has provided other estimates of violence against women in working-class neighborhoods. She found that on the average there was "one conviction for aggravated assault on a woman for every two to four hundred houses." Although no consistent statistics were kept on common assaults on women, "the available figures suggest that the number ranged from 9

[11] 3 Hansard 219 (18 May 1874), 396–99; Frances Power Cobbe, "Wife-torture in England," *Contemporary Review* 32 (April 1878): 78.

[12] *PP*, 1875, LXI.

[13] Cobbe, "Wife-torture in England," 72.

to 25 times the number of aggravated assaults." Tomes concluded that in any given neighborhood ten to twenty men would be convicted of common assaults on women each year, and that other assaults went unreported and unpunished. "Based on a neighborhood perspective, it is safe to conclude that whatever his or her personal experience, no working-class individual could escape exposure to acts of violence between the sexes," most of them between husbands and wives.[14] It was certainly the perception of all commentators in Victorian England that physical harm to women occurred overwhelmingly in the lower classes, while upper-class men tortured their wives with adultery, irony, and indifference. Although recent research shows that spousal abuse occurs in all social classes—and there is no reason to think this was different in the Victorian period—what middle-class observers believed to be true became the basis on which officials formulated public policy.[15]

The response to the questionnaire circulated by the Home Office indicated that most law officers thought that the present law was insufficient to deter brutal assaults. Thirteen of Her Majesty's Judges favored—under various conditions and safeguards—flogging for brutal assaults, as did sixty-four of sixty-eight chairmen of Quarter Sessions and magistrates in Sessions. By mid-century, however, the majority of Members of Parliament regarded flogging as a "barbaric" form of punishment, unsuitable for a civilized nation, and proposals to flog convicted wife-beaters were defeated repeatedly. Given the political opposition to flogging, it is not surprising that after publishing the answers to its circulars, the Home Office did nothing more about wife beating.[16]

The government could not easily cut off the debate it had helped to stimulate. In the following year Mr. Serjeant Pulling suggested at the annual meeting of the Social Science Association that some steps short of flogging might help to curtail wife beating. He proposed the creation of an office of Public Prosecutor which could bring suit on behalf of beaten women, and suggested that the rules of criminal procedure be

---

[14] Nancy Tomes, "A 'Torrent of Abuse': Crimes of Violence between Working-class Men and Women in London, 1840–1875," *Journal of Social History* 11, no. 3 (Spring 1978): 328–45.

[15] For a discussion of contemporary literature on wife beating, child abuse, and incest, see Wini Breines and Linda Gordon, "The New Scholarship on Family Violence," *Signs: Journal of Women in Culture and Society* 8, no. 3 (Spring 1983): 490–531.

[16] On efforts in the United States (some successful) to institute flogging as a punishment for wife beating, see Elizabeth Pleck, *Domestic Tyranny: The Making of Social Policy Against Family Violence from Colonial Times to the Present* (New York: Oxford University Press, 1987), chap. 6.

altered to allow taking a woman's testimony on the spot, rather than requiring her to appear in court.[17] Pulling's proposals rejected flogging but continued to focus attention on the prosecution of wife-beaters.

Pulling's listeners, however, shifted attention to the larger dynamics of family life and family law. The Reverend C. Geldart of London thought that any man convicted of brutal assault on his wife should be prevented by law "from ever living with that wife again." Mrs. Louisa Lowe agreed, but pointed out that under the current law the father would retain custody of any children of the marriage. No woman "would risk having her children taken away from her" as the cost of leaving her husband, and separation orders should stipulate that the husband "should lose all his parental rights over his children, and the woman should succeed to those rights." Mr. Groom Napier felt that a battered wife should be able to divorce her husband, but "ought to be able to avoid the necessity of [appearing before] the Divorce Court," which was very expensive. Others feared that if battered wives were allowed to divorce their husbands, the number of assaults would in fact increase, "because many a man would be only too glad to get rid of his wife."[18] The debate at the Social Science Association meeting reflected the division between those reformers who hoped to deter brutality by creating a fear of punishment in the perpetrator, and feminists who wanted to empower women by giving them the right to leave abusive men. It was a tribute to Victorian feminists, and to Frances Power Cobbe in particular, that the legislation Parliament passed in 1878 adopted their definition of the problem.

The Matrimonial Causes Act of 1878

In her autobiography, Frances Power Cobbe recounted that "one day in 1878 I was by chance reading a newspaper in which a whole series of frightful cases of this kind [brutal beatings] were recorded, here and there, among the ordinary news of the time. I got up out of my armchair, half dazed, and said to myself: 'I will never rest till I have tried what I can do to stop this.'" She then told how she read the statistics on brutal assaults contained in the home secretary's *Report* of 1875 and a compilation of cases of wife beating drawn up for her by Arabella Shore, and concluded that battered women must be given the ability to obtain separation orders in Courts of Summary Jurisdic-

[17] NAPSS, *Transactions* (1876), 345–61.
[18] Ibid., 349–61.

tion.[19] Cobbe was a frequent contributor to the *Women's Suffrage Journal*, which for several years had been printing accounts of wife beatings and of the low sentences meted out to wife-beaters as a way of showing that women needed the vote in order to enact measures to protect themselves. In a widely-circulated essay, "Wife-torture in England," which was published in the *Contemporary Review* of April 1878, Cobbe brought the feminist interpretation before the general public rather than simply the small circles of feminist activists. "Wife-torture in England" electrified public opinion and was widely recognized as the inspiration for the Matrimonial Causes Act of 1878.[20]

The essay's title was deliberately chosen, Cobbe explained, because "wife-beating in process of time and in numberless cases, advances to wife-torture and the wife-torture usually ends in wife-maiming, wife-blinding or wife-murder." The list of examples she gave was drawn from the press and included the following cases:

James Mills cut his wife's throat as she lay in bed. He was quite sober at the time. On a previous occasion he had nearly torn away her left breast.

J. Coleman returned home early in the morning, and, finding his wife asleep, took up a heavy piece of wood and struck her on the head and arm, bruising her arm. On a previous occasion he had fractured her ribs.

Frederick Knight jumped on the face of his wife (who had only been confined a month) with a pair of boots studded with hobnails.

Alfred Roberts felled his wife to the floor, with a child in her arms; knelt on her, and grasped her throat. She had previously taken out three summonses against him, but had never attended.

Richard Scully knocked in the frontal bone of his wife's forehead.

George Ralph Smith, oilman, cut his wife, as the doctor expressed it, "to pieces," with a hatchet, in their back parlour. She died af-

[19] Frances Power Cobbe, *The Life of Frances Power Cobbe*, 2 vols. (Boston: Houghton Mifflin & Co., 1895), 2:235.

[20] Testimony to Cobbe's influence appeared almost immediately in the *Englishwoman's Review* 66 (15 October 1878): 433–34. Carol Bauer and Lawrence Ritt conclude that Cobbe's efforts to "rouse Parliament to action cannot be over-estimated" (Carol Bauer and Lawrence Ritt, " 'A Husband Is a Beating Animal': Frances Power Cobbe Confronts the Wife-Abuse Problem in Victorian England," *International Journal of Women's Studies* 6, no. 2 [March/April 1983]: 114).

terwards, but he was found Not Guilty, as it was not certain that her death had resulted from the wounds.

Fletcher Bisley, a clerk, struck his wife violently on the head with a poker, after having tried to throw a saucepan of boiling soup at her son. Both had just returned home and found Bisley in bed.[21]

Cobbe believed that although wife beating existed in the upper and middle classes "rather more ... than is generally recognized," the "dangerous wife-beater belongs almost exclusively to the artisan and labouring classes," which were brutalized by their surroundings both at work and in urban tenements.[22]

The brutalizing effect of their surroundings was greatly exacerbated by drink, particularly the adulterated drink so often sold to working-class men. Cobbe insisted that wife-beaters were drawn from "the drunken, idle, ruffianly fellows who lounge about the public-houses instead of working for their families," not "that ideal wife-beater of whom we hear so much, the sober, industrious man goaded to frenzy by his wife's temper or drunkenness." Some of their victims "drink whenever they can procure drink," are "bad and cruel mothers," are "hopelessly depraved, and lead as loose lives as their male companions," but "there are among them at least as many good women as bad ... sober, honest, chaste, and industrious."[23] Cobbe's picture of the brutal male drunkard abusing his wife was appallingly stereotypical and devoid of analysis (statistical or otherwise) of actual cases, although Cobbe had worked for a time in Mary Carpenter's ragged school and as a home visitor in Bristol.

Cobbe linked the brutality of working-class men to a much broader system of social, economic, and political tyranny which implicated men of all classes, including those of the middle and upper classes who controlled access to the professions and political life. Her analysis has been echoed recently by Linda Gordon in her historical study of family violence in nineteenth- and twentieth-century America. Gordon concludes that "the basis of wife-beating is male dominance—not superior physical strength or violent temperament (both of which may well have been the effects rather than causes of male dominance), but social, economic, political, and psychological power.... [I]t is male dominance that makes wife-beating a social rather than a personal problem."[24]

[21] Cobbe, "Wife-torture in England," 74–75.

[22] Ibid., 72 and 58.

[23] Ibid., 66, 67–68, 70.

[24] Linda Gordon, *Heroes of Their Own Lives: The Politics and History of Family Violence* (New York: Viking Penguin, 1988), 251, reference omitted.

The men who wrote the laws and presided over the courts that administered them also perpetuated wife beating. Woman's position in law as "wife, mother, and citizen" remained so far below that of a man that it was a "matter of course that she must be regarded by him as an inferior." More particularly, "the special depreciation of *wives* is more directly responsible for the outrages they endure." The fact that men found guilty of wife beating frequently received very light sentences reinforced notions of women's inferiority: "In this as in many other things the educating influence of law immeasurably outstrips its direct action; and such is the spirit of our laws, such will inevitably be the spirit of our people."[25]

Despite her biting analysis of male domination in law and society, Cobbe, when approaching Parliament, cast the problem of wife beating into terms with which that body could deal. Although members of Parliament were not about to acknowledge the existence of systematic male sex-privilege, they would enact measures to discipline working-class males and save decent working-class women from brutal husbands.

At Cobbe's insistence, Alfred D. Hill, Esq., Justice of the Peace of Birmingham, drafted a bill that shifted the grounds of discussion from the punishment due the wife-beater to the remedy to be offered to the woman.[26] Unlike Mr. Straight, Col. Egerton Leigh, Alexander Pulling, and many of the respondents to the home secretary, Cobbe focused her proposal on providing relief to the *victim* rather than on punishing the *offender*. Specifically, Cobbe suggested that wives whose husbands were convicted of assault

> be enabled to obtain from the Court which sentences their husbands a Protection Order, which should in their case have the same validity as a judicial separation. In addition to this, the *Custody of the Children should be given to the wife*, and an order should be made for *the husband to pay the wife such weekly sum for her own and her children's maintenance as the Court may see fit.*[27]

This in effect amended the Divorce Act of 1857, which allowed magistrates to grant protection orders only in cases of desertion, thus requiring victims of cruelty to apply to the Divorce Court, a recourse

[25] Cobbe, "Wife-torture in England," 62, 72, 61.

[26] Alfred D. Hill was the son of Matthew Davenport Hill, who had drafted the married women's property bill of 1856 at the request of Barbara Leigh Smith, and the nephew of Frederick Hill, who had written the report of the Social Science Association on married women's property.

[27] Cobbe, "Wife-torture in England," 82, emphasis in the original.

totally out of reach of the poor. Cobbe also struck a blow at the custody laws by insisting that a magistrate have the discretionary authority to award the mother custody of her children (this was eight years before the Infant Custody Act of 1886). The maintenance order was to insure that no man would be led to think that his brutality could wipe away "his natural obligation" to support his wife and children. Cobbe would not free a battered wife to the extent of permitting her to remarry; in her eyes this seemed "too dangerous a recourse, [which] might act as an incentive to commit the assault in the case of the husband, and an incentive to provoke one in the case of the wife."[28] Cobbe's bill rested on the premise that no husband had a right to abuse his wife, and that even though she remained married, a woman had a right to take herself and her children out of reach of her husband.

Taking Alfred Hill's draft bill in hand, Cobbe went to call on Russell Gurney (the original sponsor of the Married Women's Property Act of 1870) to ask him to sponsor the measure. Due to failing health Gurney declined. But Lord Penzance had apparently seen either the draft bill or Cobbe's article in the *Contemporary Review*. In the course of a debate on a measure to remedy certain technical defects of the Divorce Act and its amendments, he proposed that an entirely new clause be inserted in the bill, to provide that if a husband was convicted of aggravated assault on his wife, the court that convicted him could issue the wife an order having "the force and effect . . . of a decree of judicial separation."[29] Further, the husband could be obligated to pay "such weekly sum as the court or magistrate may consider to be in accordance with his means," which the board of guardians would then pay to the wife, while "the legal custody of any children of the marriage under the age of ten years shall be given to the wife." Neither maintenance nor custody were to be awarded to any wife—no matter how badly she had been abused—who had been guilty of adultery. Any rulings made by the magistrate could be appealed to the High Court of Justice. Lord Penzance's new clause was readily accepted.[30]

[28] Ibid., 85, 87. Cobbe sent a copy of her article and bill to the American feminist Lucy Stone, who submitted a bill based on Cobbe's to the Massachusetts legislature in 1879, 1883, and 1891; it failed all three times. Stone, who was also an opponent of divorce, saw the measure as a means of protecting abused wives short of divorce. See Elizabeth Pleck, "Feminist Responses to 'Crimes against Women,' 1868–1896," *Signs: Journal of Women in Culture and Society* 8, no. 3 (Spring 1983): 460–61, and her *Domestic Tyranny*, chap. 5.

[29] *PP*, 1878, bill 117.

[30] 3 Hansard 239 (29 March 1878), 191. Several aspects of Cobbe's account in her autobiography of the bill's legislative history are questionable. Cobbe reported in her autobiography that her bill was taken up in the Commons by Mr. Herschell and Sir

There was one significant difference between the bill drafted by Frances Power Cobbe and Alfred Hill and the measure Lord Penzance submitted to Parliament. The draft bill had proposed that "in any case where a husband has been convicted summarily or otherwise of an assault on his wife," the court could issue a wife a protection order "upon her request."[31] Lord Penzance's amendment, however, empowered the court to issue such an order "if satisfied that the *future safety* of the wife is in peril" (sec. 4, emphasis added). In the final bill, then, the conviction for assault did not itself justify the issuance of the protection order, but only the judge's estimate of the wife's "future safety." Since all magistrates were male, the suggestion that a male "sex class" was protecting its ability to control women does not seem farfetched. As we shall see, some magistrates used this broader discretionary authority to send the wives of even habitual wife-beaters back to their husbands. Where judges had hopes for reconciliation, a wife was out of luck no matter what her *own* desire and judgment concerning her welfare might be.

Even though it made a woman's ability to claim her right to physical autonomy dependent upon the discretionary judgment of a male magistrate, the Matrimonial Causes Act of 1878 helped lay to rest the notion that a husband's authority over his wife's body gave him the right to chastise her physically. But while Parliament was prepared to free

---

Henry Holland, and "[e]very arrangement was made for the second Reading," but much opposition was feared from those opposed to the weakening of the marriage bond. She continued, "Just at this crisis, Lord Penzance, who was bringing a Bill into the House of Lords to remedy some defects concerning the costs of the intervention of the Queen's Proctor in Matrimonial causes, introduced into it a clause dealing with the case of assaulted wives, and giving them precisely the benefit contemplated in our Bill and in my article. . . . That Lord Penzance had seen our Bill, then before the Lower House (it was ordered to be printed February 14th) and had had his attention called to the subject, either by it, or by my article in the *Contemporary Review*, I have taken to be probable, but have not exact knowledge" (Frances Power Cobbe, *Life of Frances Power Cobbe*, 2:535 and 538–39). But the Matrimonial Causes Acts Amendment Act brought in by Mr. Herschell and Sir Henry Holland on February 14 was not Alfred Hill's draft bill, but a measure to remedy technical defects in the Divorce Act and its amendments, and it passed through the Commons without debate (3 Hansard 238 [27 February 1878], 440). This bill was then introduced into the Lords by Lord Sudeley (not Lord Penzance as Cobbe reported). Here it passed the second reading with the support of Lord Cairns, the lord chancellor, before Lord Penzance's amendments were added (3 Hansard 238 [12 March 1878], 1138). During the debate on Lord Coleridge's married women's property bill in 1877, Lord Cairns indicated that he was firmly opposed to any further loosening of the marriage tie. Lord Cairns's support for Lord Sudeley's bill indicates the degree to which that bill was perceived as simply a set of technical amendments to Divorce Court procedures.

[31] Cobbe, "Wife-torture in England," 83.

women from the obligation to live with violent husbands, it was not about to permit them to divorce and remarry. A husband's repeated abuse of his wife, no matter how severe, was not considered as serious an offense against marriage as a single instance of a wife's infidelity.

Enforcement of the Matrimonial Causes Act

Evidence concerning the practical effects of the Matrimonial Causes Act of 1878 is ambiguous. Statistical evidence indicates that wife beating declined, at least in London working-class neighborhoods, between 1850 and 1890. Nancy Tomes summarizes data indicating that "aggravated assaults recorded in the London police courts dropped from approximately 800 cases in 1853 to 200 cases in 1889. A parallel decline occurs in the national figures for all serious 'offenses against the person' "; furthermore, this decline was also true of aggravated assaults against women, and "seems to reflect a real change in behavior, rather than a change in the recording of crime." Tomes regards the change in behavior as a reflection of an attitudinal change: the Matrimonial Causes Act contributed to what Tomes refers to as "middle-class values regarding family life," which gradually influenced working-class behavior and led working-class men to disdain wife beating and assaults on women as "the acts of the 'ruffian' class."[32] It is likely, however, that factors such as a rising standard of living and more dispersed housing were more important in lowering the assault rate than was the provision for judicial separations contained in the Matrimonial Causes Act of 1878. Nonetheless, that provision did give public voice to the notion that to beat one's wife was so unacceptable as to justify a court's placing a protection order in a wife's pocket as she left home.

There was apparently more change in the behavior of married men—who appeared less frequently before the courts for wife beating—than there was in the attitudes of those administering the law. I say "apparently" because to the best of my knowledge no one has studied magistrates' court records to determine the number of requests for protection orders, the percentage of these granted, and the circumstances which in each magistrate's eyes justified a legal separation. Such an analysis would provide important information on late Victorian attitudes towards domestic violence, but in its absence there is no way to resolve the rather inconsistent accounts found in the available sources on the actual operation of the Matrimonial Causes Act.

[32] Tomes, "A 'Torrent of Abuse,' " 330, 341.

J. L. Barton, in an essay on financial provisions for wives, concluded that the Matrimonial Causes Act of 1878 was "more generally useful" than it might appear to have been. There were "some indications" that the justices "were apt to interpret the term 'aggravated assaults' very generously where disputes between husband and wife were concerned."[33] Certainly one "indication" of the law's usefulness was the grateful testimony of a woman whose niece had obtained a separation order and custody of her children after suffering her husband's brutal treatment: when told of Frances Power Cobbe's role in passing the Matrimonial Causes Act, she "kept saying, 'She's a lady—she's a lady. Bring her to O——, Misses! and we'll *percession* her down t' street!' "[34]

Unfortunately, Barton's assertion is not documented, and this one woman's testimony is contradicted by many other nineteenth-century writers. In 1879 *Punch* commented acerbically on the case of John Whelan, who was sentenced to death at the Manchester Assizes in 1879 for kicking his wife to death. At the same time *Punch* got in a jibe at the light sentences handed down in Liverpool's notorious "Kicking District." Whelan, according to the *Times*, had been strongly recommended to mercy "on account of his wife's irregular habits and the provocation he received," and he was respited. *Punch* observed, "Of course he has been, poor fellow! Sentenced to death for kicking his wife to death—and an aggravating wife too! Hard lines, indeed! They manage these things better at Liverpool. There, the sentence in such a case is six months' imprisonment."[35] During the same year the *Women's Suffrage Journal* vehemently protested that in the wake of the Matrimonial Causes Act "a very dangerous doctrine is coming to be recognized by the judicial bench, . . . namely, that bad conduct or provoking language on the part of the wife extenuates the guilt of slaying her," citing a case where a man was sentenced to only three months' hard labor for kicking his foul-mouthed wife to death.[36]

Edward Cox, a serjeant-at-law, the recorder of Portsmouth, and author of a leading textbook of the day, *Principles of Punishment*, helped disseminate the view that wife beating was often provoked by a shrill and shrewish wife, and that a blow to such a woman was almost in the nature of self-defense. That was why "the exhaustive inquiry made by

[33] J. L. Barton, "The Enforcement of Financial Provisions," in *A Century of Family Law*, ed. R. H. Graveson and F. R. Crane (London: Sweet & Maxwell, 1957), 364.

[34] Cobbe, *Life of Frances Power Cobbe*, 2:541.

[35] *Punch*, 29 November 1879, 251.

[36] *Women's Suffrage Journal* 10 (October 1879): 166.

Mr. Cross . . . revealed so many doubts" about flogging wife-beaters.[37] Furthermore, husband and wife must continue to live together, and to punish the husband might make the couple's life thereafter intolerable. (Cox did not seem to consider that living with an abusive husband might also be intolerable, so intolerable as to justify the court in awarding a separation.) The difficulty of reconciling "punishment for the past with the fact of future cohabitation" led Cox, in his own practice, to appeal "to the good feelings of both husband and wife . . . asking both if they would endeavour to live more happily together for the future," and to bind the husband in recognizances. Cox hoped that "the opportunity given for repentance and reconciliation had not been altogether thrown away." Cox's book, written a year prior to the passage of the Matrimonial Causes Act of 1878, reveals attitudes that were utterly subversive of the ends of the Act.[38]

In 1893 Mabel Sharman Crawford looked back over the fourteen years in which the Matrimonial Causes Act of 1878 had been in operation and claimed that it was "a rare event" for magistrates' courts to issue a separation order. She cited as typical a case in which a husband who had been repeatedly convicted of brutally beating his crippled wife was sentenced to only twenty-one days in prison, while his wife's request for a separation order was not granted. She then gave accounts of literally dozens of cases that were disposed of during a six-week period in 1892. In one a man deliberately set fire to his wife, and in another a pregnant wife was "kicked, and dragged upstairs by the hair, thrown down and jumped upon with both feet, well nigh strangled by a cord tied round her throat," and was found "by a policeman lying saturated in blood." In this case the husband was sentenced to two months' imprisonment, and no separation order was granted.[39]

The *Women's Suffrage Journal* also continued to print regular reports of the light sentences doled out to wife-beaters and documented many instances in which magistrates denied a wife's request for a pro-

---

[37] Edward W. Cox, *Principles of Punishment* (London: Law Times Office, 1877), 99–102.

[38] Ibid., 103–5.

[39] Mabel Sharman Crawford, "Maltreatment of Wives," *Westminster Review* 139 (1893): 293–96. Crawford's research established clearly that light sentencing remained the practice in cases of wife beating. Yet although she described case after case of brutal assault where no separation order was granted, she did not specify whether the wife *requested* a separation, making it difficult to evaluate that part of her claim. Other essays that decried the lenient sentences given to wife-beaters included "The Law in Relation to Women," *Westminster Review* 128 (1887): 708; Lee Meriweather, "Is Divorce a Remedy?" *Westminster Review* 131 (1889): 676–85; and Matilda M. Blake, "Are Women Protected?" *Westminster Review* 137 (1892): 43–48.

tection order. In 1879 it complained that a man convicted in the Lambeth Police Court of a brutal assault received only a one-month sentence; in 1880 it reprinted an article from the *Manchester Guardian* which reported that the sentence for a rabbit poacher was £5 plus costs or a month in prison, while that for a wife-beater was 10s. plus costs, or fourteen days in prison. An 1880 decision rendered by the magistrates at Croydon was particularly striking. One Alfred Long was in the habit of beating his wife, and in two-and-a-half years she had left home fifteen times. The magistrates who heard the case bound the husband to keep the peace, but would not issue a protection order, saying it was their "invariable rule" not to grant such decrees. If husband and wife could not bear to live together, they could live apart, but the magistrates would be no party to splitting up the home. As the *Women's Suffrage Journal* commented, this kind of attitude rendered the Act a "dead letter."[40]

The Croyden magistrates do not seem to have been alone in their reluctance to grant separation orders. Indeed, the goals of the Act seemed to be so jeopardized by judicial attitudes that on February 15, 1881, Jacob Bright on behalf of Charles McLaren (like Bright a strong parliamentary supporter of feminism) asked Sir William Harcourt, Gladstone's home secretary, if he was aware of "the strong sentiment of educated Englishwomen against the leniency with which crimes of violence against a person were habitually viewed by judges and magistrates," and if the government planned to submit legislation to remedy the problem of light sentencing for wife-murder. He referred specifically to the case of Thomas Beckett, recently tried at the Leeds Assizes for the willful murder of his wife by cutting her throat. " 'I meant to do it—I had made up my mind to do it,' " Beckett had confessed. He was found guilty of manslaughter, and sentenced to four days' imprisonment from the beginning of the Assizes, which, as the Assizes were well-advanced, he did not have to serve. The home secretary's response to Bright's query was an appalling example of official indifference to punishing spousal violence and of hostility to organized feminism. He pointed out that Beckett's wife was an adulteress, and had stabbed him when he tried to prevent her from returning to her paramour. He, the home secretary, did not think "such conduct as that calls for much sympathy from the educated women of England." Having thus dismissed the feminists' concerns as unworthy of respectable ladies, the home secretary concluded that "as far as I am aware there is no defect in the law which requires amendment. . . . I know no

[40] *Women's Suffrage Journal* 11 (July 1880): 123.

means by which juries can be compelled to deliver verdicts, or Judges to pass sentences, other than those that the dictates of their own judgments prescribe."[41]

The Matrimonial Causes Act of 1878 did not give a wife the *right* to leave a brutal husband, but to *appeal* to a court to be allowed to do so. The distinction is a significant one, as the reports of magistrates refusing to issue protection orders show. Without such a decree, a battered wife might leave her husband, but in doing so she would be guilty of desertion. Her property would not be protected (prior to 1882), she would forfeit custody of her children, she would have no claim to maintenance, and her husband might at any time take out a writ for restitution of conjugal rights and force her (prior to 1884) to choose between returning home and going to jail. Even with a separation order, most women had so little in the way of economic resources that the inability to support themselves and their children must have kept innumerable women from applying to the courts for protection. Many women saw their choice as remaining at home and continuing to be beaten, or forfeiting home, children, and support. Although the Matrimonial Causes Act recognized that there were some limits to a husband's control over his wife's body, it gave male judges, not women themselves, the power to define those limits, and did not address the lack of social and economic resources which made it so difficult for any woman to live without a male "protector" and provider.

The Summary Jurisdiction (Married Women) Act of 1895

The Summary Jurisdiction (Married Women) Act of 1895 [58 & 59 Vict., c. 39] expanded the provisions of the Matrimonial Causes Act of 1878 by stipulating that a wife who *left her husband* because of his "persistent cruelty" or "wilful neglect to provide reasonable maintenance" for her and their children could apply to a court of summary jurisdiction for a separation decree, custody of their children, maintenance, and court costs. As with previous statutes, a woman was not eligible for such relief if she was guilty of adultery, but this time the statute added "provided that the husband has not . . . by his wilful neglect or misconduct conduced to such act of adultery," giving the magistrates the discretion to make the award even if the wife had been adulterous. Significantly, a wife could first leave her husband and then appeal to a court for a separation order, which greatly increased her

---

[41] 3 Hansard 258 (15 February 1881), 882–84.

autonomy over that provided by the Matrimonial Causes Act. Prior to 1895, such a woman was guilty of desertion; after 1895, if she could present a court with evidence that her husband had been cruel or had failed to maintain the family, the court could sanction her leaving and award her custody and maintenance.

While the Summary Jurisdiction (Married Women) Act of 1895 reflected a growing respect for individual autonomy within marriage, an equally strong impetus for passsage of the Act was Parliament's desire to keep indigent women off the public rolls. Nine years earlier Parliament had enacted the Married Women (Maintenance in Case of Desertion) Act of 1886 [49 & 50 Vict., c. 52] to remedy defects in the way the Divorce Act of 1857 dealt with desertion. The Divorce Act provided that stipendiary magistrates could issue a protection order to a deserted wife, which meant that with respect to her earnings and property and ability to contract she would be treated as a feme sole. But a protection order was of limited use to a working-class woman with children to support, for her wages would almost never be enough to maintain a family. The Married Women (Maintenance in Case of Desertion) Act helped meet this problem by doing away with the expensive and cumbersome procedure of requiring women to apply to the parish before the parish could sue their husbands for support, and by giving magistrates the authority to order a husband to pay maintenance directly to the wife he had deserted. Only if the husband stayed away two years could the wife apply for a separation order ending her obligation to resume cohabitation should her husband return, and allowing the court to award her custody of her children.

Significant numbers of women took advantage of the Summary Jurisdiction (Married Women) Act. Courts of summary jurisdiction granted more than eighty-seven thousand separation and maintenance orders during the ten years from 1897 to 1906.[42] During the same period the well-to-do obtained some six thousand divorces and eight hundred judicial separations from the Divorce Court. The magistrates' courts thus granted more than ten times the number of separation orders as the Divorce Court issued divorce and separation decrees. The ability to leave one's husband legally clearly mattered a great deal to women, despite the fact that it often imposed severe economic hardship.

Prior to the Matrimonial Causes Act of 1878 and the Summary Ju-

---

[42] O. R. McGregor, *Divorce in England* (London: Heinemann, 1957), 24. McGregor says that the 1886 Act applied to husbands who failed to maintain their wives, as well as to those guilty of desertion, but this seems to be an error.

risdiction (Married Women) Act of 1895, the law tacitly assumed that when she married a woman lost some of the right to bodily autonomy she had enjoyed while single. The notion of coverture did not obliterate the legal personality of the wife to such an extent that wives could not prosecute their husbands for assault, but convictions were rare and sentences were scandalously light. Furthermore, a married woman remained legally obligated to cohabit with her abusive husband unless she could afford to apply for a judicial separation from the Divorce Court. This, combined with the provision of the Divorce Act that a wife but not a husband could be divorced for adultery alone, constituted virtually a proprietary right by husbands in their wives' bodies.

Victorian feminists strongly denounced the presumption that a husband had the right to control his wife's body. They appealed to the respect for individual autonomy upon which British law presumably rested when they insisted that while marriage created obligations which restricted the freedom of both husbands and wives, those obligations had to be mutual and reciprocal and could not be taken to include the right to physically control, chastise, or coerce one's spouse. The provisions for issuing separation orders to married women contained in the Matrimonial Causes Act of 1878 and the Summary Jurisdiction (Married Women) Act of 1895 reflected Parliament's partial acceptance of these arguments.

Obtaining the right to leave an abusive or grossly negligent husband, however, was hardly the door to freedom for a woman without property. Enforcement of maintenance orders must have been extremely difficult, and the legislation did not touch the main sources of the grinding poverty of many widows and separated wives, their low wages and the paucity of jobs available to them. Children, as well as the prospect of poverty, must have tightly bound many women even to miserable marriages, for to appeal to a court for custody ran the risk of losing one's children altogether. Since a separation order did not allow remarriage, women who wanted to live with men for emotional or economic reasons had to do so outside of marriage. Moreover, the right to *leave* an abusive or negligent husband did not secure the physical autonomy of married women living with their husbands. The "marital exemption" in rape law retained the notion of a husband's ownership of his wife's body, as did the sexual double standard in divorce law. The difficulty in our own day of prosecuting cases of wife battering and marital rape shows how arduous it has been to purge the law of the assumption that upon marriage women relinquish authority over their bodies to their husbands.

A Husband's Custody of his Wife's Body

Conjugal Rights and the Clitheroe Decision

The most intense and dramatic discussion of the extent of a husband's control of his wife's body occurred in 1891, when the Court of Appeal handed down its decision in *Regina* v. *Jackson*, a case involving a husband's suit against his wife for the "restitution of conjugal rights." The "Clitheroe case," as it became known from the name of the town where the drama began, was the sensation of the day.[43] The case involved the marriage of Emily and Edmund Jackson. On November 5, 1887, Emily, then forty-two years old, left her home in Clitheroe, where she had been living with her sister for the past nine years, and without informing any member of her family, married Edmund Haughton Jackson at Blackburn. On the evening of the marriage Mr. Jackson brought his wife back to her sister's house, and returned to Blackburn. The next day he went to London, and on November 10 he sailed to New Zealand, intending to have his wife follow him shortly. While he was away they corresponded, and she asked him to return to England. Her sister alleged that husband and wife had quarrelled in subsequent correspondence, and that Mrs. Jackson asserted she would not live with him. Eight months after the wedding, in July 1888, Mr. Jackson returned to England, but Mrs. Jackson refused to have anything to do with him. Mr. Jackson began proceedings for the restitution of conjugal rights.

The action for restitution of conjugal rights, which had been part of canon law, was transferred from the ecclesiastical courts to the Divorce Court by the Divorce Act of 1857. The suit was intended to enforce compliance with the marital duty of cohabitation. If one spouse left home, the other could ask the court for a writ for restitution of conjugal rights, and if the wayward spouse could not show cause for his or her absence, the court would order the spouse to return home. When the action was under the jurisdiction of the Ecclesiastical Court, the sanction for noncompliance was "admonition," a mild form of ecclesiastical censure; under the Divorce Court, the penalty for noncompliance was "attachment," that is, imprisonment until the guilty party agreed to obey the court order.

The meaning of the term *conjugal rights* was not well-defined. A letter published in the *Times* suggested that "previous to 1733 legal

[43] The *Times* (London) published twenty-two articles on the Clitheroe case during March and April, 1891, including accounts of their relationship by both Mrs. Jackson and Mr. Jackson.

proceedings were recorded in Latin, and the word then used where we now speak of 'rights' was *obsequies.*" *Obsequies* was originally translated as "rites," and "conjugal rites" meant observances. In time, "conjugal rites" was transcribed as "conjugal rights." Whether rendering conjugal rights also meant engaging in sexual intercourse was uncertain. On the one hand, a suit for restitution of conjugal rights could not be instituted on the ground that a wife, although residing in the same house with her husband, was denied access to his person and bed.[44] "For, 'the duty of matrimonial intercourse cannot be compelled by the Court, though matrimonial cohabitation may be.' "[45] On the other hand, a husband could not be charged with rape of his wife under the criminal law, so ordering her to live with him for all intents and purposes compelled intercourse if *he* wanted it. The physiological differences between men and women often made it possible for a husband to force sexual relations on his wife while neither she nor the court could force them upon him: gender-neutral language marked very real differences in power between men and women.

Legal authorities of the late nineteenth century claimed that the main use of the suit for restitution of conjugal rights in their day was to affix blame for marital breakdown and to force a monetary settlement on the aggrieved spouse. Lord Hannen, president of the Divorce Court, remarked that "so far are suits for restitution of conjugal rights from being . . . what they purport to be, . . . [that] I have never known an instance in which it appeared that the suit was instituted for any other purpose than to enforce a money demand."[46] Feminists, however, saw in the suit implications for the question of whether a husband might control and "own" his wife's body as he had once controlled and owned her property.

In 1884 Parliament changed the penalty for refusing to comply with a writ for restitution of conjugal rights from "attachment" to a judgment of desertion against the offending spouse, in response to a decision in the Divorce Court in 1883 in the case of *Weldon* v. *Weldon.* The *Weldon* case was unusual because a woman, not a man, sued for restitution of conjugal rights. Captain Weldon had found living with his wife unbearable. He took every step to provide for her: he rented a

[44] *Orme* v. *Orme* (1824), 2 Add., 383, quoted in Nevill Geary, *The Law of Marriage and Family Relations: A Manual of Practical Law* (London: Adam & Charles Black, 1892), 372.

[45] *Forster* v. *Forster* (1790), 1 Hag. Con. 144, p. 154, quoted in Geary, *Law of Marriage*, 372.

[46] *Marshall* v. *Marshall* (1879), 5 P.D., 19, p. 23, quoted in Geary, *Law of Marriage*, 376.

furnished house for her at Acton, engaged two servants, offered to pay the rent as long as she lived there, and paid her an allowance of £500 a year on a monthly basis. He also offered to move Mrs. Weldon to a similar dwelling in any place she might find more convenient and continue his other payments. But he would not live with her. She sued for restitution of conjugal rights, and the court granted her plea. In such cases, the court pointed out, it had no discretion to impose the penalty or not.[47]

The image of Captain Weldon languishing in jail because he could not tolerate living with his wife was more than Parliament could bear, although earlier in the century a Suffolk woman had been allowed to die in prison when she refused to return to her husband.[48] The Matrimonial Causes Act of 1884 [47 & 48 Vict., c. 68] provided that noncompliance with a writ for restitution of conjugal rights was to be taken as an act of desertion. If a spouse could obtain a writ for restitution of conjugal rights and the other spouse did not return home, the deserted spouse could immediately apply to the court for a separation order rather than waiting for two years as the Divorce Act required. The court could order the respondent to pay alimony or maintenance to the plaintiff, and could make orders as to the custody of any children of the marriage.

Had events in Clitheroe unfolded according to this pattern, Mr. Jackson would have sued for a judicial separation from Mrs. Jackson when she failed to comply with the writ for restitution of conjugal rights. Perhaps the court, in addition to granting the separation, would have ordered Mrs. Jackson to make some kind of monetary award to Mr. Jackson (it appeared that she had considerably more money than he). But Mr. Jackson pursued another course. One Sunday morning in the spring of 1891, as Mrs. Jackson was leaving church with her sister, Mr. Jackson came up to his wife and forced her into a waiting carriage. She was taken to Mr. Jackson's house, which he did not allow her to leave. Mr. Jackson placed his sister in charge of Mrs. Jackson, hired a nurse to attend her, and had a physician check her periodically to insure that she remained in good health. Mrs. Jackson's relatives went to the house and in effect "picketed" it, establishing a watch across the street and calling up to Mrs. Jackson whenever she appeared in an upper-story window. In response, Mr. Jackson brought in men to guard the house from any attempt at forcible entry.

[47] *Weldon* v. *Weldon* (1883), 9 P.D., 52, quoted in Geary, *Law of Marriage*, 377.
[48] Elizabeth Wolstenholme Elmy, *The Decision in the Clitheroe Case, and Its Consequences: A Series of Five Letters* (Manchester, 1891), 9n.

Despite this drama in the street, Mrs. Jackson's relatives did not succeed in persuading Mr. Jackson to release his wife, and they attempted to procure a writ of habeas corpus in order to force him to let her go. A writ of habeas corpus, a very powerful instrument for the defense of personal liberties, orders whoever is detaining another person to bring that person into the presence of the court. Mrs. Jackson's relatives first applied to the Court of Queen's Bench. In support of their petition, one of Mrs. Jackson's sisters submitted an affidavit stating that Mrs. Jackson "repeatedly told me she wanted to get out, and said she was locked in, and wished me to get her solicitor, Mr. Weeks, to take proceedings to have her set at liberty." Mr. Weeks's affidavit asserted that "if Mrs. Jackson makes up her mind to remain where she is, it will be perfectly right to her relatives. . . . [But] she ought to come to a decision of her own free will," which she could hardly do "when she is forcibly imprisoned under lock and key."[49] The court did not agree that she was unlawfully restrained, and on March 16 refused to issue the writ of habeas corpus. Their reasoning was a concise restatement of the traditional view that marriage created a unique relationship giving a husband authority over his wife.

A husband, the justices of Queen's Bench declared, had "a right to the custody of his wife unless he uses it for some improper purpose or is guilty of some excess or misconduct." One justice remarked that "though generally the forcible detention of a subject by another is *prima facie* illegal, yet *where the relation is that of husband and wife the detention is not illegal*." The court noted that "this is not a case in which charges are made against the husband"—had there been charges of cruelty or misconduct they should have been lodged at the time he applied for the writ for restitution of conjugal rights, months ago. The fact that he had been issued that writ showed that he had been judged to be blameless. Or, in the present case, had Mr. Jackson used undue force against his wife, he could have been charged with assault, but "*prima facie* he had a right to regain possession of her from those who were endeavouring by force to prevent him from having the custody of her." As Mr. Jackson was guilty of no misconduct towards his wife, her relatives had engaged in "injudicious and unwarranted proceedings" to try to remove her from his house. The court refused to issue a writ which would "tend to unsettle the lady's mind, and make her believe that the court was going to do what the court will not do—remove her from her husband's custody—upon no ground whatever, ex-

[49] Quoted in *Justice of the Peace* 55 (28 March 1891): 199–200.

cept that she does not like to be with him."[50] A wife belonged in her husband's presence if he desired her to be there, although the court made no attempt to square this ruling with the fact that no other adults except the mentally incompetent or criminals were placed in anyone's legal custody.

Mrs. Jackson's relatives appealed this decision, and three days later the Court of Appeal reversed the decision of the Court of Queen's Bench and issued the writ of habeas corpus ordering Mr. Jackson to release his wife. Lord Halsbury, the lord chancellor, insisted that no such right as Mr. Jackson claimed "exists or ever did exist," for it was the settled law of England that "no English subject has such a right of his own motion to imprison another English subject, whether his wife or any one else."[51]

Many legal scholars took issue with the lord chancellor's assertion that the law of England had never recognized a husband's right to imprison or restrain his wife. The lord chancellor's "reluctan[ce] to suppose [that such authority] had ever been the law of England," they said, did not alter the fact that previous decisions had recognized that authority. Lord Mansfield, for example, had once stated that "the husband has, in consequence of his marriage, a right to the custody of his wife; and who ever detains her from him violates that right; and he has a right to seize her wherever he finds her."[52] In the case of *In re Cochrane* (1840), Justice Coleridge had declared that "there can be no doubt of the general dominion which the law of England attributes to the husband over the wife." He therefore found nothing unlawful in the fact that Mr. Cochrane sought to "confine [his wife] in his own dwelling house, and restrain her from her liberty, for an indefinite time, using no cruelty, nor imposing any hardship or unnecessary restraint on his part."[53] But Lord Chancellor Halsbury treated *In re Cochrane* as an abberation, and a fellow justice, Lord Fry, distinguished it from the *Jackson* case because it did not involve "the right to capture." Whether or not *Regina* v. *Jackson* technically overruled

---

[50] *In re Jackson,* Queen's Bench Division, 16 March 1891, as reported in *Justice of the Peace* 55 (28 March 1891): 199–201.

[51] *Regina* v. *Jackson,* 1 Q.B. 671 at 681.

[52] *Mrs. Wilkes' case* (1780), 20 St. Tr. 1, quoted in *Justice of the Peace* 55 (28 March 1891): 196.

[53] *In re Cochrane* (1840), 8 Dowling 633. In *Regina* v. *Leggatt,* 18 Q.B. 781 (1852), the Court of Queen's Bench had refused to issue a writ of habeas corpus to a husband who sought to bring his wife, then residing with her son, back home. This showed that the court would not force a reluctant spouse back home by means of a habeas corpus proceeding, but it did not address the issue of a wife already detained or "imprisoned" by her husband.

Cochrane, the different conclusions of the Court of Queen's Bench and the Court of Appeal dramatically juxtaposed two paradigms of the extent of a husband's authority over his wife, and the nature of the marriage relationship itself.

Scarcely was the ink dry on the law reports than Eliza Lynn Linton was protesting indignantly that "Marriage, as hitherto understood in England, was suddenly abolished one fine morning last month!" The "wild women," remarked Linton, "are elate at the decision, but they like the Court have forgotten the fundamental truth that 'When two people ride on one horse one must sit behind.' " She energetically depicted how a wife (in her view it was always a wife who erred) might "break her vows and play at ninepins with her duties, and so long as she keeps clear of the seventh commandment [against adultery], . . . she may make mince-meat of the rest." Marriage had become "a voluntary union during pleasure!" Women would now leave marriage on a mere caprice—an aversion to tobacco smoke or differing taste in dress or music. Even these trifles, said Linton, would be more substantial than "the famous Clitheroe paradigm, which seems to have been founded on nothing more solid than the froth of caprice and 'I have changed my mind.' " The Court of Appeal had unwittingly promoted "the prancing desire of the free lovers" and "the grimmer designs of the women's rights women." The agenda of the free-lovers would lead "to the destruction of the family by the virtual abolition of marriage," that of the women's rights women "to the absolute supremacy of women over men and justice alike."[54]

One "wild woman," Elizabeth Wolstenholme Elmy, embraced the Clitheroe decision as wholeheartedly as Linton denounced it. Writing to her friend Harriet M'Ilquham, she declared: " 'Coverture' is dead and buried . . . It [*Regina* v. *Jackson*] is the grandest victory the women's cause has ever yet gained, greater even than the passing of the Married Women's Property Acts."[55] In a pamphlet originally published as letters in the Manchester *Guardian*, Wolstenholme Elmy wrote:

> Of the momentous character of this judgment there can be no question whatever. It is a declaration of law which is epoch-making in its immediate consequences, and its ultimate results reach far into the future, involving indeed the establishment of a higher

[54] Eliza Lynn Linton, "The Judicial Shock to Marriage," *Nineteenth Century* 29 (May 1891): 691–700.

[55] Elizabeth Wolstenholme Elmy to Harriet M'Ilquham, 21 March 1891, Elmy Collection, British Library.

morality of marriage, and the substitution in the relation of husband and wife, of the ethics of justice and equality for the old and worn-out code of master and slave.

The decision declared unequivocally the "legal right of a wife to her personal freedom," overturning the common law assumption that a husband was to command, a woman to obey. Henceforth, she said, "the relative claims of the parties to the conjugal relation will have to be considered and established in accordance with the rule of personal freedom."[56]

Diametrically opposed as they were in their judgments about the value of the decision, Linton and Wolstenholme Elmy both saw in *Regina* v. *Jackson* a watershed in the law governing marriage. In each woman's eyes the Court of Appeal had endorsed an understanding of a husband's marital rights that was fundamentally different from that which had prevailed when she had begun to comment on women's position in England some thirty years earlier. The Divorce Act had recognized some, albeit very limited, grounds that would free a woman from the previously indissoluble bonds of marriage; the Married Women's Property Acts had severely undercut the notion that all of a wife's possessions, and therefore she herself, "belonged" to her husband; during the decade between the two property acts the Matrimonial Causes Act of 1878 had opened the door a crack for an abused wife to leave her husband; the Infant Custody Act of 1886 had curtailed a father's nearly exclusive right to the children of a marriage; and now the Court of Appeal refused to let a husband have custody of his wife against her will. Sixty years earlier the young Caroline Norton had been subjected to a trial for criminal conversation with no chance for a legal action herself. In 1895 she might have obtained a separation order from her abusive husband, been awarded custody of their children, and retained the earnings from her writing. Despite the very real shortcomings left in marriage law, Norton might well have agreed with Wolstenholme Elmy's statement that "step by step [beginning with the Infant Custody Act of 1839, which Norton initiated] progress has been made and the law has gradually become the expression and embodiment of a higher morality, until now we dare to hope that at no distant date justice will rule in every home, and, smiling upon childhood, teach the highest and holiest of the lessons yet to be learned by our growing humanity."[57]

[56] Wolstenholme Elmy, *Clitheroe Case*, 4, 10–12.
[57] Ibid., 7.

The Effort to Define Marital Rape

Wolstenholme Elmy's enthusiasm for the decision in *Regina* v. *Jackson* may at first glance seem misdirected or excessive. The decision simply held that a writ of habeas corpus could not be issued against a wife who had of her own free will left her husband. It did not touch the action for the restitution of conjugal rights itself (which was not abolished until 1970). Since noncompliance with a writ for restitution of conjugal rights constituted desertion, any woman following Mrs. Jackson's example would automatically have been the guilty party in a divorce proceeding, and therefore likely to suffer pecuniary loss, the possible forfeit of custody, and the inability to remarry. *Regina* v. *Jackson* thus scarcely marked the full liberation of the married woman from her husband's custody, as Wolstenholme Elmy well knew. But by providing her with the opportunity to speak out publicly against the "sexual slavery" of married women, a bondage inseparable from coverture and women's disenfranchisement, the Clitheroe decision opened a new phase of Wolstenholme Elmy's work, and it encouraged other feminists to speak and write more openly about sexuality.

Most of Wolstenholme Elmy's energy during the 1890s was devoted to taking whatever steps she could to rectify the injustice of married women's sexual subordination to their husbands. In 1880 Wolstenholme Elmy had written a paper presented to the Social Science Association in which she lambasted the section of the proposed Criminal Code which defined rape as "the act of a man, not under the age of 14 years, having carnal knowledge of a woman, *who is not his wife*, without her consent." The effect of such a provision was to "degrade every English wife to the legal position of the purchased slave of the harem, and to reduce her to a bodily slavery for which earth offers no other parallel."[58] That particular bill did not become law, but the marital exemption was already a well-established rule of law.

In 1888 the Court of Crown Cases Reserved held in *Regina* v. *Clarence* that a husband who had infected his wife with venereal disease from which he, but not she, knew he was suffering, could not be convicted of assault. The wife's only recourse was to apply for a judicial separation on the ground of cruelty (the courts having previously decided that the communication of venereal disease to an unsuspecting spouse constituted legal cruelty). In the course of delivering their opinions, several justices pointed out that husbands could not be guilty of

[58] Elizabeth Wolstenholme Elmy, *The Criminal Law in Relation to Women* (Manchester, 1880), 10.

raping their wives. In the words of Justice Pollock, "The husband's connection with his wife is not only lawful, but it is in accordance with the ordinary condition of married life. It is done in pursuance of the marital contract, and of the status which was created by marriage, and the wife, as to the connection itself, is in a different position from any other woman, *for she has no right or power to refuse her consent.*" Or, as Justice Hawkins put it, "The wife submits to her husband's embraces, because at the time of marriage she gave him an irrevocable right to her person. . . . Consent is immaterial."[59]

Wolstenholme Elmy hoped to use the Court of Appeal's decision in *Regina* v. *Jackson* to convince Parliament that by the liberal principle of individual autonomy no one, not even a wife, could give "irrevocable consent" to sexual access to her body. The principle enunciated in *Regina* v. *Jackson*—that a wife's right to bodily autonomy had to include the right to leave a husband—implied the right to refuse him sexual intercourse. Indeed, she wrote to Harriet M'Ilquham in 1896: "The only absolute right I should claim for a woman as against a man is that she should never be made a mother against her will."[60]

Wolstenholme Elmy apparently tried, without success, to get Parliament to enact a measure removing the marital exemption. She could not even get such a bill introduced. In 1897 she complained that "it is within the personal knowledge of the present writer that one woman, deeply indignant at the iniquity of the existing marriage law of England . . . has, during the last fourteen years, in vain asked some forty to fifty different Members of Parliament to introduce a Bill . . . for the abolition of this infamy." Although each member professed great sympathy with the bill's object, none would sponsor the measure. "The plain truth," she declared, "is that that [*sic*] no one of them dared face the ridicule and opposition of his male colleagues in the sex-privileged House of Commons."[61] A male "sex class" here wielded legislative and judicial power to perpetuate the notion that wives could not ever justifiably refuse sexual relations with their husbands, and that their bodies in that sense "belonged" to their husbands.

One way to free women from what Wolstenholme Elmy called "enforced maternity" (that is, the sanctioning of marital rape) was to give them greater knowledge about sexuality itself, another was by women's "political enfranchisement." After passage of the Infant Custody

[59] *The Law Times*, 59 n.s. (26 January 1889): 791.

[60] Elizabeth Wolstenholme Elmy to Harriet M'Ilquham, 13 December 1896, Elmy Collection, British Library.

[61] Elizabeth Wolstenholme Elmy, "Women's Suffrage," *Westminster Review* 148 (October 1897): 365.

Act of 1886, suffrage became Wolstenholme Elmy's main legislative goal, because the vote would enable women "to compel attention to their most just claims and needs." But most of Wolstenholme Elmy's time and energy during the 1890s was devoted to writing pamphlets about sexuality with her husband, Ben Elmy, under the pen name "Ellis Ethelmer." *Woman Free* (1893), a thirty-page poem, replete with 187 pages of notes, explained the progress of the race that would ensue when women were freed from their political and sexual bondage and became true companions of men. The Elmys then published two sex-education books: *The Human Flower* (1894), which was intended to teach the facts of human reproduction to adolescents, and *Baby Buds* (1895), addressed to younger children. *Life to Woman* (1896), a book for adults, was an exposition of the Elmys' understanding of menstruation as a physiological manifestation of centuries of women's sexual exploitation at the hands of men. They had first set forth this theory in *Woman Free*:

> Action repeated tends to rhythmic course,
> And thus the mischief, due at first to force,
> Brought cumulative sequence to the race,
> Til habit bred hereditary trace;
> On woman falls that heritage of woe,
> And e'en the virgin feels its dastard blow.[62]

Bred into women over thousands of years of "persistent and inconsiderate excess and wrong usage by the male portion of the race," menstruation kept women "still in bondage, in varying degrees, to a physical infirmity or incommodity which is, we assert, abnormal,—both needless and useless in the economy of Nature."[63] When the movement for women's rights finally triumphed, menstruation (but not ovulation) would gradually cease. Various changes would help bring about this emancipation from women's physical "infirmity." As women entered the medical profession, they would do the research necessary to shatter the myth that menstruation was inevitable, and when women had the vote, they would see to it that Parliament ended the marital exemption in rape law, thus curbing men's sexual licentiousness. Scientific discovery and law would both work to ameliorate women's situation.

Phases of Love: as it Was, as it Is, as it May Be (1897), a companion piece to *Life to Woman*, was a rhapsodic evocation of the more com-

---

[62] Ellis Ethelmer, *Woman Free* (Manchester: Women's Emancipation Union, 1898), stanza 23.
[63] Ellis Ethelmer, *Life to Woman* (n.p., 1896), 8–9.

plete spiritual, psychic, and sexual union that men and women of the future would experience when the "bodily subjection" of women and consequently the enervation that accompanied menstruation had ended. Only the emancipation of women would enable all men and women to know the "ever wider scope of love" possible in that new social order. A "newer, truer generation, born and bred to the realization of justice, equality, and sympathy between the sexes" would, before long, enter "the nobler paradise that shall yet be the estate of man [sic] upon this our earth."[64]

Unscientific as the Elmys' views seem today, it would be wrong, as Susan Kent has pointed out, to dismiss them as absurd or laughable. Doctors themselves did not understand the process of menstruation or the cycle of women's fertility (as many of the medical authorities quoted by the Elmys show). What is important is not the accuracy of the Elmys' views but the meaning attached to them. The Elmys' analysis of menstruation once again showed the link that they and some other feminists made between the most personal aspects of daily life and politics. Their mistakes about physiology are less significant in this light than is the boldness of their assault on the separation between what is private (menstruation) and what is public (politics and law). Menstruation was a consequence of male sexual excess, which was sanctioned by public law, most obviously by the women's inability to prosecute marital rape, but also by the sexual double standard in legislation concerning the age of consent and in divorce law. Moreover, public policy which allowed universities to exclude women from medical schools meant that men monopolized, and perhaps distorted or supressed, knowledge that might free women from menstruation. And if women were spared the discomfort and inconvenience of menstruation, they would be in a better position to end men's monopoly of the professions and public offices. The road to sexual liberation for women, therefore, was *the same* as that to political emancipation; knowledge about human sexuality and the exercise of political power were both necessary to set women free.

THE feminists' campaigns to free married women from the physical control of their husbands, like their campaigns for married women's property and child custody rights, drew heavily on liberal principles of individual liberty and bodily autonomy. The right to liberty was meaningless, they argued, if it did not encompass the fundamental right of control over one's body, self-ownership of one's own person. For most

[64] Ibid., 8–9, 64; Ellis Ethelmer, *Phases of Love: as it Was, as it Is, as it May Be* (n.p., 1897), 7–9, 58.

Victorian feminists the main component of women's sexual liberation consisted in curbing men's "licentiousness"; most were silent about or hostile to contraception. They did not propose severing women's sexual activity from the possibility of pregnancy and childbirth. Their conception of sexual "freedom" was therefore essentially freedom from male domination.[65] A battered woman had to be able to separate from her husband, a wife had to be able to walk out on her husband without being forced back home by a court order, and a married woman had to be able to refuse sexual intercourse with her husband. Parliament and the Court of Appeal each partially accepted the feminists' arguments, although neither would strike down a husband's right to sexual access to his wife at will.

As useful as liberal principles of equality and autonomy were to Victorian feminists, their vision of reformed marriage went beyond simply the destruction of male privilege. The abolition of a husband's control over his wife's body, like the end of coverture, was a precondition for the creation of a far deeper and more complete emotional and spiritual union between husband and wife than had ever before existed. The Elmys expressed their belief in the radical transformation that would follow from women's emancipation in *Woman Free*:

> For but a slave himself must ever be,
> Till she to shape her own career be free;—
> Free from all uninvited touch of man,
> Free mistress of her person's sacred plan;
> Free human soul; the brood that she shall bear,
> The first—the truly free, to breathe our air;
> From woman slave can come but menial race,
> The mother free confers her freedom and her grace.
>
> . . . .
>
> Man's destiny with woman's blended be
> In one sublime progression,—full, and strong, and free.[66]

The ideal of a marriage of true equals could only be dimly envisioned in a world infused with sexual inequality. The dream of a transformed marriage, a truer meeting of minds, souls, and bodies than any yet known, was one of the legacies of nineteenth-century feminists to our own day.

[65] See J. A. and Olive Banks, *Feminism and Family Planning in Victorian England* (New York: Schocken Books, 1964); and Angus McLaren, *Birth Control in Nineteenth Century England* (New York: Holmes & Meier, 1978).

[66] Ethelmer, *Woman Free*, stanzas 40, 62.

EPILOGUE
THE SEARCH FOR SPOUSAL EQUALITY:
A LEGACY FOR FEMINISTS

> Sir, we believe and know that the time is fast coming
> when, men having learnt purity and women courage,
> the sexes shall live together in harmony, each other's
> helpers towards all things high and holy; no longer
> tyrant and victim, oppressor and oppressed, but,
> hand in hand, eye to eye, heart in heart, building up
> that nobler world which yet shall be. In this faith we
> have lived and worked; in this faith we shall conquer.
>
> —Elizabeth Wolstenholme Elmy,
> *Women and the Law*, 1896

The vision of a transformation of the marriage relationship from one
of "tyrant and victim" to one where husband and wife would walk
"hand in hand, eye to eye, heart in heart" underlay the Victorian feminists' repeated campaigns to rid British law of the myriad injustices of
the common law doctrine of coverture. The spousal friendship they
desired could not be achieved unless family law embodied the principle
of the strict legal equality of husband and wife. At the heart of the
marriage law reform campaigns and the struggle for women's suffrage
was the principle that sex alone should make no difference in the as-
cription of either public or private rights. The insistence on individual
rights and equality before the law for men and women, whether married or single, constituted a frontal assault on the notion that by nature
men and women occupied separate spheres and that women, and in
particular married women, should be confined to the domestic sphere,
while husbands moved in the public world. Feminists undermined the
sharp distinction liberal theory had traditionally drawn between what
was "public" and political, and what was "private" and shielded from
political discussion and decision making. In contrast, the Victorian
feminists attacking coverture contended that the criteria of justice had
to underpin domestic as well as public law. Both their practical and
their theoretical accomplishments were of enormous consequence for
subsequent feminist theorists and activists.

Still, even though these feminists made brilliant and radical use of
the liberal principle of equality as a tool to challenge inequitable marriage laws, their emphasis on equal rights kept them from seeing other

189

prerequisites for the realization of justice in the family. They paid a great deal of attention to married women's lack of economic and contractual rights, but devoted less time to analyzing those disabilities which stemmed from the economic dependency of most wives on their husbands. Feminists hoped that their efforts for a married women's property law, combined with greater employment opportunities, would keep women from entering marriages out of economic necessity and would enable them to support themselves so that they could leave bad marriages. But these changes by themselves could not substantially affect the actual balance of economic power between husband and wife. The Married Women's Property Act of 1882 gave a woman control over any money she brought to a marriage, but the number of middle-class women with substantial premarital property was not large, and even feminists did not envision middle-class wives going out to work.

John Stuart Mill expressed the views of many when he wrote that it is not in general "a desirable custom, that the wife should contribute by her labour to the income of the family."[1] Yet as Harriet Taylor Mill had noted in "The Enfranchisement of Women," a woman who contributes to the family income is "raised from the position of a servant to that of a partner. . . . [A] woman who contributes materially to the support of the family cannot be treated in the same contemptuously tyrannical manner as one who, however she may toil as a domestic drudge, is dependent on the man for subsistence."[2] The awareness that she might work and keep her earnings if she left her husband did not liberate a married woman from the subordination within marriage that stems from economic dependency.

In principle, the common law made provision for married women and recognized the economic contribution wives made through household management and the care of children by obligating husbands to support their wives. But the husband's obligation was (and still is) unenforceable in an ongoing marriage unless the woman became destitute. In cases of separation and divorce, alimony and maintenance orders never recognized that a woman had a claim to half of her husband's earnings. Furthermore, without training, work experience, or job opportunities, women had little economic power in the marketplace. As a result, the economic consequences of leaving their hubands were for most wives bad enough to deter all but the most desperate

---

[1] John Stuart Mill, *The Subjection of Women*, in *Essays on Sex Equality*, ed. Alice Rossi (Chicago: University of Chicago Press, 1970), chap. 2, 179.

[2] Harriet Taylor Mill, "The Enfranchisement of Women," in *Essays on Sex Equality*, ed. Rossi, 104–5.

from walking away from a marriage. Their economic vulnerability not only kept many women from leaving bad marriages, but also affected the relationship between husband and wife in an ongoing marriage, for without the possibility of leaving, a wife had little power other than that of supplication and persuasion to decide issues or even to raise them. In short, inequality of economic resources could not (and still cannot) help but skew the ability of spouses to engage one another as equals and to experience the reciprocity of friendship in marriage, regardless of the equal legal rights the Victorian feminists achieved.[3]

The early feminists also paid little attention to the absence of men from the private world of domestic life, yet this absence also provides grounds for serious injustice in marriage relations. At the most obvious level, some domestic work is unattractive and undesirable and should not, in a fair division of responsiblity, fall wholly on either spouse.[4] Further, as a practical matter, if spouses do not share domestic work, the person doing it either does not enter the outside workplace, or does so with serious burdens and restrictions. Effective equality between husbands and wives thus necessarily requires that men share responsibility with women for domestic and child-rearing chores.

The contention that justice requires the greater involvement of men in the home goes considerably deeper than questions of a fair division of labor. It rests too on the assumption that there is positive value in performing many of the tasks traditionally assigned to women, and that men themselves and human society as a whole would be better off if men as well as women did them. Victorian feminists certainly believed in the value of "women's work." In 1869 Josephine Butler wrote that "home is the nursery of all virtue, the fountain-head of all true affection, and the main source of the strength of our nation."[5] In 1883 Sarah Norton cautioned that the women's movement ran the danger

[3] The necessity for rough economic equality between husband and wife does not mean that for marriage to be a just institution both husband and wife must work at equal-paying jobs outside the home; it does mean that the low wages women earn are a source of domestic as well as marketplace injustice. To rectify the injustice, upon separation or divorce the law needs to guarantee that the division of property recognizes both spouses' contributions to the marriage (this is done in theory but often breached in practice). Furthermore, public policy measures must facilitate the raising of children. See Barbara Bergmann, *The Economic Emergence of Women* (New York: Basic Books, 1986).

[4] Contemporary studies show that in households where both husband and wife work full-time outside the home, a woman spends an average of 28.1 hours on unpaid "family" work to a man's 9.2 hours of such work each week (Bergmann, *Economic Emergence of Women*, 263).

[5] Josephine Butler, Introduction to *Woman's Work and Woman's Culture: A Series of Essays*, ed. Josephine Butler (London: Macmillan, 1869), xxv.

of denigrating women's work in the home because of its public emphasis on women's employment and enfranchisement; women's entry into
the public realm was important, but "we [also] want a healthier public
opinion about *these* . . . toilers in the home. . . . [W]e want . . . a sort
of general admission that bringing up the next generation and keeping
the home morally and physically pure and healthy" is challenging and
important work.[6] It was indeed part of the feminists' brief for women's
suffrage that women would bring particular moral sensibilities and
distinct ethical insights to discussions of public affairs, what Butler
called the "diffusion of the home influence and character among the
masses."[7]

Victorian feminists spoke of bringing women's distinct viewpoint
into the public realm, but not of developing those same sensibilities in
men by having men engage in traditionally female activities. Frances
Power Cobbe jealously defended the unique quality of women's domestic skills: "The making of a true home is really our peculiar and
inalienable right,—a right which no man can take from us. . . . It is a
woman, and only a woman,—a woman all by herself, if she likes, and
without any man to help her,—who can turn a house into a home."[8]
The *Englishwomen's Review* agreed: "[W]omen are the natural guardians of the morals of the nation; they should be the educators of its
youth, the upholders of the highest standards of family honour, social
purity, individual self-respect, and moral responsibility."[9] Even Elizabeth Wolstenholme Elmy, who in most cases insisted upon the identical nature of women's and men's capabilities and duties, acknowledged that "the father can offer no equivalent in kind" for the mother's
care of children during their early years. (It should be noted, though,
that Wolstenholme Elmy nonetheless insisted on identical parental
rights for mother and father.)[10] The *Journal of Jurisprudence* summed
up the prevalent view when it remarked that "it seems natural to a
woman to take care of children; it does not seem so natural to a
man."[11] While some Victorian feminists, Cobbe and Butler among
them, refuted the common notion that *every* woman was intended by
nature to care for children, virtually no one suggested that when a cou-

---

[6] Sarah Norton, "*Blackwoods* and the *Westminster Review* on Women," *Englishwoman's Review* 14 (April 1883): 152–57.

[7] Butler, Introduction to *Woman's Work*, xxxi.

[8] Frances Power Cobbe, *The Duties of Women: A Course of Lectures* (Boston: Geo.
H. Ellis, 1881), 139.

[9] *Englishwomen's Review* 14 (May 1883): 193–98.

[10] *Englishwomen's Review* 14 (November 1883): 483.

[11] *Journal of Jurisprudence* 28 (1884): 259.

ple had children the man should involve himself with either their daily care or other household tasks.

This is not the place to reconstruct in detail various theories suggesting that men and women develop different moral perspectives and modes of ethical reasoning due to the social reality that most men and women perform different activities. Nancy Chodorow and others have argued that the predominant role of women in raising children creates a different process of psychological maturation for boys and girls, one which makes it difficult for men to treat women nonaggressively and as equals.[12] Others, including Carol Gilligan, have argued that men and women develop different modes of moral reasoning. Men tend to be concerned with rights, hierarchical relationships, and the application of abstract principles to ethical problems, while women tend to think more contextually and to give greater emphasis to the relational aspects of moral questions.[13] The recent upsurge of attention by moral philosophers to the "ethics of care" is clearly inspired by—although not limited to—feminist efforts to articulate the philosophical bases of a moral system based on notions of relationship rather than of rights.[14]

The kinds of changes in understanding and intellectual life that might occur if women were more deeply involved in public discourse and activity, and men were more integrally involved in the nurturing activities associated with the home and the upbringing of children, would not affect only the relationships among adults. More important, perhaps, children would grow up with very different perceptions and experiences of gender relationships than they have now. As John Stuart Mill insisted, the family is a school of justice, the place where we initially develop our sense of fairness and our capacity for self-control. But, he noted, the "tradition of domestic existence" is in fact "contradictory to the first principles of social justice," for the subordination of women in the family "pervert[s] the whole manner of existence of

[12] Nancy Chodorow, *The Reproduction of Mothering* (Berkeley and Los Angeles: University of California Press, 1978); Dorothy Dinnerstein, *The Mermaid and the Minotaur: Sexual Arrangements and Human Malaise* (New York: Harper Colophon, 1977).

[13] Carol Gilligan, *In A Different Voice* (Cambridge: Harvard University Press, 1982). For a critique of Chodorow and Gilligan on the grounds that they do not adequately distinguish among women, see Elizabeth V. Spelman, *Inessential Woman* (Boston: Beacon Press, 1989).

[14] See, for example, Joan Tronto, "Beyond Gender Difference to a Theory of Care," *Signs: Journal of Women in Culture and Society* 12 (Summer 1987): 644–63; Virginia Held, *Rights and Goods: Justifying Social Action* (New York: Free Press, 1984), chap. 11, "Family and Society," 191–214, and her "Non-contractual Society: A Feminist View," in *Science, Morality and Feminist Theory*, ed. Marsha Hanen and Kai Nielsen (Calgary: University of Calgary Press, 1987), 111–37.

the man, both as an individual and as a social being."[15] Susan Okin has similarly argued that the moral development of children is dependent upon the loving attention and care they receive from whoever raises them—that is, upon activities which throughout history have overwhelmingly been women's responsibility.

> Unless the households in which children are first nurtured, and see their first interaction, are based on equality and reciprocity rather than on dependence and domination, as is so often the case, whatever love they receive from their parents may not make up for the injustice they see before their eyes. Unless they are parented equally by adults of both sexes, how will children of both sexes come to develop a sufficiently similar and well-rounded moral psychology as to enable them to engage in [an adequate] deliberation about justice?[16]

The gender-structured environment of both family and public life has inhibited *both* sexes' development not only of a sense of justice, but also of the capacity to carry just principles into practice. Until people live out better, more just marriages, and until children see their parents act in ways which break free from present practices, our conceptions of what constitutes—and how to achieve—both marital and political justice will remain incomplete.

The Victorian marriage law reformers studied here did not advocate the radical restructurings of economic and family life that I suggest are necessary prerequisites for achieving justice in marriage. They simply asked that married women be given equal legal status with men in both the family and the state. As Wolstenholme Elmy put it, "the full equality and responsibility of women with men" might be achieved by "a Bill of two clauses," the first stating that husband and wife were to be "two distinct persons in law," the second that women were to exercise the electoral franchise "equally with men."[17] Victorian feminists' belief in the emancipatory power of the law has led some commentators to downplay the importance of their efforts, pointing out that liberal feminism's demand for "equal rights" essentially seeks entry for women into male-structured offices and privileges, but does not suggest alternatives to present economic and social structures. I have argued, however, that the insistence that any bill to liberate women would have to have "two clauses," one concerning marriage, the other suffrage, sub-

---

[15] J. S. Mill, *The Subjection of Women*, in Rossi, chap. 4, 172–74.

[16] Susan M. Okin, *Justice, Gender, and the Family* (New York: Basic Books, 1989).

[17] Elizabeth Wolstenholme Elmy, *The Emancipation of Women* (London: Women's Printing Society, 1888), 4.

verted liberalism's traditional understanding of the distinction between private and public life and in so doing pointed beyond the legal
reforms that Victorian feminists advocated. The reflections here on the
changes needed to achieve spousal equality build unmistakably upon
the nineteenth-century feminists' understandings of spousal equality
and political justice.

The fact that Victorian feminists did not understand the complexity
of the economic, social, and political forces obstructing the realization
of spousal equality, nor push liberal theory towards a new and more
adequate understanding of equality between husbands and wives, in
no way diminishes their accomplishment. The campaigns for marriage
law reform, along with those for women's suffrage, won acceptance of
the proposition that principles of justice must govern relations in the
family as well as in the public realm. As Virginia Held has argued,
"Harmony, love, and cooperation cannot be broken down into individual benefits and burdens. . . . To focus only on contractual relations
and the gains and losses of individuals obscures these often more important relational aspects of societies."[18] To formulate an adequate
theory of familial justice we must develop an understanding of what
equality means for mutually dependent or interdependent persons living not only their individual lives but a shared life as well. Such an
understanding will encompass both relations within the family and the
distribution of political and economic resources in our society. Only
when we as individuals and as a polity act in the light of these insights
will the family become what Mill hoped it would be, a school of true
justice for future generations.

[18] Held, "Non-contractual Society," 129.

BIBLIOGRAPHY

ARCHIVES

Josephine Butler Collection, Fawcett Library, London.
John Stuart Mill–Harriet Taylor Mill Collection, British Library of Political and Economic Science (BLPES), London.
Elizabeth Wolstenholme Elmy Collection, British Library, London.
Manchester Society for Women's Suffrage Collection, Manchester Central Library, Manchester.

PUBLIC DOCUMENTS

Great Britain, Hansard, *Parliamentary Debates*, 3rd series.
First Report of the Commissioners Appointed by her Majesty to Enquire into the Law of Divorce. Parliamentary Papers 1852–1853 (1604), vol. XL.
Report from the Select Committee of the House of Lords on the Divorce and Matrimonial Causes Bill . . . together with the Proceedings of the Committee. Sessional Papers (Lords), 1856 (H.L. 181), vol. XXIV.
Report to the Local Government Board on Proposed Changes in Hours and Ages of Employment in Textile Factories. Parliamentary Papers, 1873, vol. LV.
Report . . . on the State of the Law relating to Brutal Assualts, &c. Parliamentary Papers, 1875, vol. LXI.
Report of the Commissioners appointed to inquire into the working of the Factory and Workshops Acts, with a view to their consolidation and amendment; together with The Minutes of Evidence. Parliamentary Papers, 1876 [c. 1443], vols. XXIX and XXX.

REPORTS AND PROCEEDINGS

Law Amendment Society (LAS), *Report of the Personal Laws Committee . . . on the Laws Relating to the Property of Married Women*. London, 1856.
Married Women's Property Committee (MWPC), *Reports*: 1870, 1871, 1872, 1873, 1877, 1879, 1880, 1882.
Married Women's Property Committee (MWPC), *Annual Reports*: 1868, 1869, 1870, 1871, 1872, 1873, 1876, 1879, 1880, 1882.
National Association for the Promotion of Social Science (NAPSS), *Transactions*: 1867, 1868, 1869, 1870, 1875, 1876, 1877, 1879, 1880, 1883.
North of England Council for Promoting the Higher Education of Women, *Reports*: 1868, 1869, 1871.
Women's Franchise League, *Report of the Proceeding at the Inaugural Meeting*, 1889.

197

Trades' Union Congress (TUC), *Report of the Annual Trades' Union Congress*: 1875, 1877.
Vigilance Association for the defence of personal rights, *Annual Report*, 1876.

NEWPAPERS AND PERIODICALS

All the Year Round: 1868.
Annual Register: 1878.
British and Foreign Review: 1838.
Congleton Chronicle: 1984.
Contemporary Review: 1878.
English Woman's Journal.
Englishwoman's Review of Social and Industrial Questions: 1867, 1868, 1873, 1877, 1878, 1883, 1884, 1885.
Irish Law Times and Solicitors' Journal: 1883, 1884, 1885.
Journal of Jurisprudence: 1884.
Juridical Review: 1900.
Justice of the Peace: 1891.
Law Journal: 1871.
Law Review: 1844–1845, 1848, 1854, 1855–1856.
Law Times: 1873, 1889.
North British Review: 1856.
Punch: 1879.
Times (London): 1857, 1870, 1878, 1881, 1884, 1891.
Victoria Magazine: 1868.
Westminster Review: 1856, 1872, 1887, 1889, 1892, 1893, 1897; 1851 (Am. ed.).
Woman: 1872.
Women's Penny Paper: 1889.
Women's Suffrage Journal: 1871, 1872, 1873, 1874, 1876, 1878, 1879, 1880, 1882.

INTERVIEW

Stockton, Frank. Interview in Congleton, Cheshire, August 1984.

BOOKS, ARTICLES, AND PAMPHLETS PUBLISHED BEFORE 1900

Baker, A. *The Custody and Guardianship of Children.* 2d ed. Hanley: Atkinson Brothers, 1883.
Barrett-Lennard, Sir Thomas. *The Position in Law of Women.* London: Waterlow & Sons, 1833.
Becker, Lydia. "The Political Disabilities of Women." *Westminster Review* 41 n.s. (January 1872): 50–70.

Blackburn, Helen. "Law and Women-Earners." *Englishwoman's Review* 50 (June 1877): 251–56.

———. "The Night Cometh When No 'Woman' Can Work." *Englishwoman's Review* 58 (February 1878): 97–102.

Blackstone, William. *Commentaries on the Laws of England*, 4 vols. Oxford: Clarendon Press, 1765–1769.

Blake, Matilda M. "Are Women Protected?" *Westminster Review* 137 (1892): 43–48.

Bryce, James, and Horace Davey. *Speeches . . . on the Second Reading of the Infants Bill*. London: Cornelius Buck, 1884.

Butler, Josephine, ed. *Woman's Work and Woman's Culture: A Series of Essays*. London: Macmillan, 1869.

Butler, Josephine, et al. *Legislative Restrictions on the Industry of Women, Considered from the Women's Point of View*. n.p., [1874].

Cobbe, Frances Power. "Criminals, Idiots, Women and Minors: Is the Classification Sound?" Manchester: A. Ireland, 1869. (First published in *Fraser's Magazine*, December 1868.)

———. *The Duties of Women: A Course of Lectures*. Boston: Geo. H. Ellis, 1881.

———. *The Life of Frances Power Cobbe*, 2 vols. Boston: Houghton Mifflin, 1895.

———. "What Shall We Do with Our Old Maids?" in *Essays on the Pursuits of Women*, edited by Frances Power Cobbe. London: Emily Faithfull, 1863.

———. "Wife-torture in England." *Contemporary Review* 32 (April 1878): 55–87.

———, ed. *Essays on the Pursuits of Women*. London: Emily Faithfull, 1863.

Committee to Amend the Law in Points wherein it is Injurious to Women (CALPIW). *Infant Mortality: Its Causes and Remedies*. Manchester, 1871.

Cornwallis, Caroline. "The Property of Married Women." *Westminster Review* 66 (1856): 331–60.

Cox, Edward W. *Principles of Punishment*. London: Law Times Office, 1877.

Crawford, Mabel Sharman. "Maltreatment of Wives." *Westminster Review* 139 (1893): 292–303.

Curgenven, J. Brandon. *On Baby-Farming and the Registration of Nurses*. London, 1869.

Dictionary of National Biography.

"Divorce." *Law Review* 1 (1844–1845): 353–81.

Elmy, Elizabeth Wolstenholme. *See* Wolstenholme Elmy, Elizabeth.

Ethelmer, Ellis [Ben Elmy and Elizabeth Wolstenholme Elmy]. *Baby Buds*. n.p., 1895.

———. *The Human Flower*. n.p., 1894.

———. *Life to Woman*. n.p., 1896.

———. *Phases of Love: as it Was, as it Is, as it May Be*. n.p., 1897.

———. *Woman Free*. Manchester: Women's Emancipation Union, 1898.

Geary, Nevill. *The Law of Marriage and Family Relations: A Manual of Practical Law*. London: Adam & Charles Black, 1892.

[Handley, Edwin Hill]. "Custody of Infants Bill." *British and Foreign Review* 7 (July 1838): 269–411.

Hoggan, Frances. *The Position of the Mother in the Family in its Legal and Scientific Aspects*. London, 1884.

Jameson, Anna Murphy. *Sisters of Charity and The Communion of Labour*. London, 1859.

Kaye, J. W. "Outrages on Women." *North British Review* 25 (May 1856): 233–56.

"Law in Relation to Women, The." *Westminster Review* 128 (1887): 698–710.

"Laws Relating to Women, The." *The Law Review* 20 (1854): 1–34.

Leigh Smith, Barbara, *A Brief Summary in Plain English of the Most Important Laws of England Concerning Women*. London, 1854.

Linton, Eliza Lynn. "The Judicial Shock to Marriage." *Nineteenth Century* 29 (May 1891): 691–700.

———. "Womanly Dependence." In *Ourselves: A Series of Essays on Women*. 2d. ed. London: G. Routledge & Sons, 1870.

Locke, John. *Two Treatises of Government*. Edited by Peter Laslett. Rev. ed. New York: Mentor Books, 1963. (Orig. published 1690.)

Lynn, Eliza. "One of Our Legal Fictions." *Household Words* 9 (April 1854): 257–60. *See also* Linton, Eliza Lynn.

Meriweather, Lee. "Is Divorce a Remedy?" *Westminster Review* 131 (1889): 676–85.

Mill, Harriet Taylor. "The Enfranchisement of Women." *Westminster Review* (July 1851). Reprinted in *Essays on Sex Equality*, edited by Alice Rossi, 91–121. Chicago: University of Chicago Press, 1970.

Mill, John Stuart. *The Collected Works of J. S. Mill*. Vols. 12–13, *The Earlier Letters of John Stuart Mill*. Edited by Francis E. Mineka. Toronto: University of Toronto Press, 1963; Vols. 4–5, *Essays on Economics and Society*. Edited by John M. Robson. Toronto: University of Toronto Press, 1975.

———. "Evidence of John Stuart Mill, taken before the Royal Commission of 1870 on . . . the Contagious Diseases Acts of 1866 and 1869." London: National Association for the Repeal of the Contagious Diseases Acts, 1871.

———. *The Subjection of Women*. Reprinted in *Essays on Sex Equality*, edited by Alice Rossi. Chicago: University of Chicago Press, 1970.

Norton, Caroline. *English Laws for Women in the Nineteenth Century*. Privately printed, 1854.

———. *A Letter to the Queen on Lord Chancellor Cranworth's Marriage and Divorce Bill*. London: Longman, Brown, Green & Longmans, 1855.

———. [Pearce Stevenson, pseud.]. *A Plain Letter to the Lord Chancellor on the Infant Custody Bill* . . . London: James Ridgway, 1839.

———. *Selected Writings of Caroline Norton*. Edited by James O. Hoge and Jane Marcus. Delmar, N.Y.: Scholars' Facsimiles and Reprints, 1978.

———. *Separation of Mother and Child by the 'Law of Custody of Infants' Considered*. Privately printed, 1837.

Norton, Sarah. "*Blackwoods* and the *Westminster Review* on Women." *Englishwoman's Review* 14 (April 1883): 152–57.

Parkes, Bessie Rayner. "Barbara Leigh Smith Bodichon." *Englishwoman's Review* 210 (July 1891): 145–49.

Remarks on the Law of Marriage and Divorce; suggested by the Honourable Mrs. Norton's Letter to the Queen. London: James Ridgway, 1855.

"Report of the Society for Promoting the Amendment of the Law. Ecclesiastical Committee." *Law Review* 13 (1848): 347–52.

Ruskin, John. *Works*. Edited by E. T. Cook and A.D.C. Wedderburn. 39 vols. London: G. Allen, 1902–1912.

"Slaves of the Ring." *All the Year Round* (4 July 1868): 86–88.

Smith, Samuel. "Social Reform." *Nineteenth Century* 13 (May 1883): 896–912.

Wharton, J.J.S. *An Exposition of the Laws Relating to the Women of England*. London: Longman, Brown, Green & Longmans, 1853.

Wolstenholme Elmy, Elizabeth. *The Criminal Law in Relation to Women*. Manchester, 1880.

———. *The Custody and Guardianship of Children*. London: John Bale & Sons, [1884].

———. *The Decision in the Clitheroe Case, and Its Consequences: A Series of Five Letters*. Manchester, 1891.

———. *The Emancipation of Women*. London: Women's Printing Society, 1888.

———. *The Infants' Act, 1886: The record of a three years' effort for Legislative Reform, with its results*. London: Women's Printing Society, n.d. [1888].

———. *The Infants Bill*. Manchester: A. Ireland and Co., 1884.

———. *Women and the Law, a series of four letters by Mrs. Wolstenholme Elmy*. London, 1896.

———. "Women's Suffrage." *Westminster Review* 148 (October 1897): 357–72.

"Women's Law: Mrs. Norton's Letter to the Queen." *Law Review* 23 (1855–1856): 334–45.

BOOKS, ARTICLES, DISSERTATIONS, AND THESES
PUBLISHED AFTER 1900

Annas, Julia. "Mill and the Subjection of Women." *Philosophy* 52 (1977): 179–94.

Banks, Olive. *Becoming a Feminist: The Social Origins of 'First Wave' Feminism*. Athens: University of Georgia Press, 1986.

Banks, Olive. *The Biographical Dictionary of British Feminists*. New York: New York University Press, 1985.

Banks, Olive, and J. A. Banks. *Feminism and Family Planning in Victorian England*. New York: Schocken Books, 1964.

Basch, Norma. *In the Eyes of the Law: Women, Marriage and Property in Nineteenth-Century New York*. Ithaca, N.Y.: Cornell University Press, 1982.

Bauer, Carol, and Lawrence Ritt. " 'A Husband Is a Beating Animal': Frances Power Cobbe Confronts the Wife-Abuse Problem in Victorian England." *International Journal of Women's Studies* 6, no. 2 (March/April 1983): 99–118.

Behlmer, George K. *Child Abuse and Moral Reform in England, 1870–1908*. Stanford: Stanford University Press, 1982.

Bergmann, Barbara. *The Economic Emergence of Women*. New York: Basic Books, 1986.

Blackburn, Helen. *Women's Suffrage: A Record of the Women's Suffrage Movement in the British Isles with Biographic Sketches of Miss Becker*. London: Williams & Norgate, 1902.

Blewett, Neil. "The Franchise in the United Kingdom, 1885–1918." *Past and Present* 32 (1965): 27–56.

Breines, Wini, and Linda Gordon. "The New Scholarship on Family Violence." *Signs: Journal of Women in Culture and Society* 8, no. 3 (Spring 1983): 490–531.

Bristow, Edward. *Vice and Vigilance: Purity Movements in Britain since 1700*. Totowa, N.J.: Rowman & Littlefield, 1977.

Chodorow, Nancy. *The Reproduction of Mothering*. Berkeley and Los Angeles: University of California Press, 1978.

Daniels, Elizabeth Adams. *Jesse White Mario: Resorgimento Revolutionary*. Athens: Ohio University Press, 1971.

Degler, Carl. *At Odds: Women and the Family in America from the Revolution to the Present*. New York: Oxford University Press, 1980.

Dicey, A. V. *Lectures on the Relation between Law and Public Opinion in England during the Nineteenth Century*. 1905. Reprint. London: Macmillan, 1930.

Dinnerstein, Dorothy. *The Mermaid and the Minotaur: Sexual Arrangements and Human Malaise*. New York: Harper Colophon, 1977.

Eisenstein, Zillah. *The Radical Future of Liberal Feminism*. New York: Longman, 1981.

Elshtain, Jean Bethke. *Public Man, Private Woman: Women in Social and Political Thought*. Princeton: Princeton University Press, 1981.

Finley, Lucinda M. "Transcending Equality Theory: A Way Out of the Maternity and the Workplace Debate." *Columbia University Law Review* 86 (October 1986): 1118–82.

Forster, Margaret. *Significant Sisters: The Grassroots of Active Feminism 1839–1939*. London: Secker & Warburg, 1984.

Gilligan, Carol. *In a Different Voice*. Cambridge: Harvard University Press, 1982.

Gillis, John. *For Better, For Worse: British Marriages, 1600 to the Present.* New York: Oxford University Press, 1985.

Goldman, Harold. *Emma Paterson: She Led Women into a Man's World.* London: Lawrence & Wishart, 1974.

Goldstein, Leslie F. "Mill, Marx, and Women's Liberation." *Journal of the History of Philosophy* 18 (1980): 319–34.

Goodin, Robert E. *Protecting the Vulnerable: A Reanalysis of Our Social Responsibilities.* Chicago: University of Chicago Press, 1985.

Gordon, Linda. *Heroes of Their Own Lives: The Politics and History of Family Violence.* New York: Viking Penguin, 1988.

Gorham, Deborah. "The 'Maiden Tribute of Modern Babylon' Reexamined: Child Prostitution and the Idea of Childhood in Late-Victorian England." *Victorian Studies* 21 (Spring 1978): 353–79.

Graveson, R. H., and F. R. Crane *A Century of Family Law 1857–1957.* London: Sweet & Maxwell, 1957.

Griswold, Robert. *Family and Divorce in California, 1850–1890: Victorian Illusions and Everyday Realities.* Albany: State University of New York Press, 1982.

Grossberg, Michael. *Governing the Hearth: Law and the Family in Nineteenth-Century America.* Chapel Hill: University of North Carolina Press, 1985.

Harrison, Brian. *Separate Spheres: The Opposition to Women's Suffrage in Britain.* New York: Holmes & Meier, 1978.

Hayek, F. A. *John Stuart Mill and Harriet Taylor: Their Friendship and Subsequent Marriage.* London: Routledge & Kegan Paul, 1951.

Held, Virginia. "Non-contractual Society: A Feminist View," In *Science, Morality and Feminist Theory,* edited by Marsha Hanen and Kai Nielsen, 111–37. Calgary: University of Calgary Press, 1987.

———. *Rights and Goods: Justifying Social Action.* New York: Free Press, 1984.

Herstein, Sheila R. *A Mid-Victorian Feminist: Barbara Leigh Smith Bodichon.* New Haven: Yale University Press, 1985.

Holcombe, Lee. *Victorian Ladies at Work: Middle-class Working Women in England and Wales 1850–1914.* New York: Archon Books, 1973.

———. *Wives and Property: Reform of the Married Women's Property Law in Nineteenth-Century England.* Toronto: University of Toronto Press, 1983.

Hollis, Patricia. *Ladies Elect: Women in English Local Government 1865–1914.* Oxford: Oxford University Press, 1987.

———, ed. *Women in Public: The Women's Movement 1850–1900.* London: George Allen & Unwin, 1972.

Holton, Sandra Stanley. *Feminism and Democracy: Women's Suffrage and Reform Politics in Britain, 1900–1918.* New York: Cambridge University Press, 1986.

Horstman, Allen. *Victorian Divorce.* New York: St. Martin's, 1985.

Huddleston, Joan, ed. *Caroline Norton's Defense.* Chicago: Academy Chicago, 1982.

Humphries, Jane. "Protective Legislation, the Capitalist State, and Working Class Men: The Case of the 1842 Mines Regulation Act." *Feminist Review* 7 (Spring 1981): 1–33.

Hutchins, B. L., and A. Harrison. *A History of Factory Legislation*. 1903. Reprint. New York: Burt Franklin, 1970.

Jones, Jacqueline. *Labor of Love, Labor of Sorrow: Black Women, Work, and the Family from Slavery to the Present*. New York: Basic Books, 1985.

Kanowitz, Leo. *Women and the Law: The Unfinished Revolution*. Albuquerque: University of New Mexico Press, 1969.

Kent, Susan. *Sex and Suffrage in Britain, 1860–1914*. Princeton: Princeton University Press, 1987.

Krouse, Richard W. "Patriarchal Liberalism and Beyond: From John Stuart Mill to Harriet Taylor." In *The Family in Political Thought*, edited by Jean Bethke Elshtain, 145–72. Amherst: University of Massachusetts Press, 1982.

Lambertz, Jan. "Male-Female Violence in Late Victorian and Edwardian England." B.A. honors thesis, Harvard University, 1980.

Lasch, Christopher. *Haven in a Heartless World: The Family Besieged*. New York: Basic Books, 1977.

Lebsock, Suzanne. *The Free Woman of Petersburg: Status and Culture in a Southern Town*. New York: W. W. Norton, 1984.

Lewis, Jane. *Women in England 1870–1950*. Bloomington, Ind.: Wheatsheaf, 1984.

Lewis, Judith Schneid. "The Price of a Woman's Chastity: The Criminal Conversation Procedure in England." Paper presented at the annual meeting of the Southern Historical Association, November 1984.

Liddington, Jill. *The Life and Times of a Respectable Rebel: Selina Cooper 1864–1946*. London: Virago, 1984.

Liddington, Jill, and Jill Norris. *One Hand Tied Behind Us*. London: Virago, 1978.

Littleton, Christine. "Equality and Feminist Legal Theory." *University of Pittsburgh Law Review* 48 (Summer 1987): 1043–59.

McGregor, O. R. *Divorce in England: A Centenary Study*. London: Heinemann, 1957.

McHugh, Paul. *Prostitution and Victorian Social Reform*. New York: St. Martin's, 1980.

McLaren, Angus. *Birth Control in Nineteenth Century England*. New York: Holmes & Meier, 1978.

Morrell, Caroline. *"Black Friday": Violence against Women in the Suffrage Movement*. London: Women's Research & Resource Centre, 1981.

Okin, Susan M. *Justice, Gender, and the Family*. New York: Basic Books, 1989.

———. "Patriarchy and Married Women's Property in England: Questions on Some Current Views." *Eighteenth-Century Studies* 17 (1984): 121–38.

———. "Women and the Making of the Sentimental Family." *Philosophy and Public Affairs* 11 (1982): 65–88.

Pankhurst, E. Sylvia. *The Suffragette Movement*. London: Longmans, Green, 1931.

Pateman, Carole. " 'The Disorder of Women': Women, Love, and the Sense of Justice." *Ethics* 91 (October 1980): 20–34.

———. *The Sexual Contract*. Stanford: Stanford University Press, 1988.

Pateman, Carole, and Teresa Brennan. " 'Mere Auxiliaries to the Commonwealth': Women and the Origins of Liberalism." *Political Studies* 27 (1979): 183–200.

Pleck, Elizabeth. *Domestic Tyranny: The Making of Social Policy against Family Violence from Colonial Times to the Present*. New York: Oxford University Press, 1987.

———. "Feminist Responses to 'Crimes against Women,' 1868–1896." *Signs: Journal of Women in Culture and Society* 8, no. 3 (Spring 1983): 451–70.

Poovey, Mary. *Uneven Developments: The Ideological Work of Gender in Mid-Victorian England*. Chicago: University of Chicago Press, 1988.

Powell, L. Chilton. *English Domestic Relations 1487–1653*. New York: Columbia University Press, 1917.

Reiss, Erna. *The Rights and Duties of Englishwomen*. Manchester: Sheratt & Hughes, 1934.

Rhode, Deborah. "Feminist Perspectives on Legal Ideology." In *What Is Feminism?*, edited by Juliet Mitchell and Ann Oakley, 151–60. New York: Pantheon, 1986.

Ritt, Lawrence. "The Victorian Conscience in Action: The National Association for the Promotion of Social Science 1857–1886." Ph.D. diss., Columbia University, 1959.

Rosen, Andrew. *Rise Up, Women!* London: Routledge & Kegan Paul, 1974.

Rover, Constance. *Love, Morals and the Feminists*. London: Routledge & Kegan Paul, 1970.

———. *Women's Suffrage and Party Politics in Britain 1866–1914*. London: Routledge & Kegan Paul, 1962.

Schochet, Gordon. *Patriarchalism in Political Thought*. New York: Basic Books, 1975.

Shanley, Mary Lyndon. "Marital Slavery and Friendship: John Stuart Mill's *Subjection of Women*." *Political Theory* 9 (May 1981): 229–47.

———. "Marriage Contract and Social Contract in Seventeenth-Century English Political Thought." *Western Political Quarterly* 32 (March 1979): 79–91.

———. " 'One Must Ride Behind': Married Women's Rights and the Divorce Act of 1857." *Victorian Studies* 25 (Spring 1982): 255–76.

Shorter, Edward. *The Making of the Modern Family*. New York: Basic Books, 1975.

Smart, Carol. *The Ties That Bind: Law, Marriage and the Reproduction of Patriarchal Relations*. London: Routledge & Kegan Paul, 1984.

Smith, F. B. *The People's Health: 1830–1910*. London: Croom Helm, 1979.

Stetson, Dorothy. *A Woman's Issue: The Politics of Family Law Reform in England*. Westport, Conn.: Greenwood Press, 1982.

Stone, Lawrence. *The Family, Sex and Marriage in England 1500–1800*. New York: Harper & Row, 1977.

Strachey, Ray. *The Cause: A Short History of the Women's Movement in Great Britain*. 1928. Reprint. London: Virago, 1978.

Taylor, Barbara. *Eve and the New Jerusalem: Socialism and Feminism in the Nineteenth Century*. New York: Pantheon, 1983.

Thomas, Keith. "The Double Standard." *Journal of the History of Ideas* 20 (April 1959): 195–216.

Tilly, Louise, and Joan Scott. *Women, Work, and Family*. New York: Holt, Rinehart & Winston, 1978.

Tomes, Nancy. "A 'Torrent of Abuse': Crimes of Violence between Working-class Men and Women in London, 1840–1875." *Journal of Social History* 11, no. 3 (Spring 1978): 328–45.

Tronto, Joan. "Beyond Gender Difference to a Theory of Care." *Signs: Journal of Women in Culture and Society* 12 (Summer 1987): 644–63.

———. "Women and Caring: What Can Feminists Learn about Morality from Caring?" In *Body, Gender and Knowledge*, edited by Alison Jaggar and S. Bordo, forthcoming.

Trumbach, Randolph. *The Rise of the Egalitarian Family: Aristocratic Relations in Eighteenth-Century England*. New York: Academic Press, 1978.

Vicinus, Martha. *Independent Women: Work and Community for Single Women, 1850–1920*. Chicago: University of Chicago Press, 1985.

Walkowitz, Judith. *Prostitution and Victorian Society*. Cambridge: Cambridge University Press, 1980.

Weitzman, Lenore. *The Divorce Revolution: Unexpected Social and Economic Consequences for Women and Children in America*. New York: Free Press, 1985.

———. *The Marriage Contract: Spouses, Lovers and the Law*. New York: Free Press, 1981.

Williams, Wendy. "The Equality Crisis: Some Reflections on Culture, Courts, and Feminism." *Women's Rights Law Reporter* 7 (Spring 1982): 175–200.

Wohl, Anthony. *Endangered Lives: Public Health in Victorian Britain*. Cambridge: Harvard University Press, 1983.

———. *The Eternal Slum: Housing and Social Policy in Victorian London*. London: E. Arnold, 1977.

———, ed. *The Victorian Family*. New York: St. Martin's, 1978.

Woodhouse, Margaret K. "The Marriage and Divorce Bill of 1857." *American Journal of Legal History* 3 (1959): 260ff.

Worzala, Diane Mary Chase. "The Langham Place Circle: The Beginnings of the Organized Women's Movement in England, 1854–1870." Ph.D. diss., University of Wisconsin, 1982.

Zainaldin, Jamil S. "The Emergence of a Modern American Family Law: Child Custody, Adoption, and the Courts, 1796–1851." *Northwestern University Law Review* 73 (1979): 1038–89.

INDEX